Principles and Techniques of Silkworm Seed Production

PRINCIPLES AND TECHNIQUES OF SILKWORM SEED PRODUCTION

By

Dr. Tribhuwan Singh

Senior Research Officer
Central Silk Board
Madivala, Bangalore—560 068

Dr. Berra Saratchandra

Director
Central Silk Board
Ministry of Textiles
Government of India
Bangalore

DISCOVERY PUBLISHING HOUSE
NEW DELHI

Published by:
Namit Wasan

DISCOVERY PUBLISHING HOUSE PVT. LTD.
4383/4B, Ansari Road, Darya Ganj
New Delhi-110 002 (India)
Phone : +91-11-23279245; 23253475; 43596065
E-mail : discoverybooksindia@gmail.com
discoverypublishinghouse@gmail.com
namitwasan9@gmail.com
web : www.discoverypublishinggroup.com

Edition: **2020**

ISBN: 978-81-7141-750-6

Principles and Techniques of Silkworm Seed Production

Printed at:
Infinity Imaging Systems
Delhi

FOREWORD

Sericulture in India has been a powerful tool for rural employment and poverty alleviation as every acre of irrigated mulberry garden can provide full time employment to as many as 13 persons. Silk being an exclusive fibre and popular as the queen of textiles, the money moves from the rich and urban markets to the poor and rural producers. As the developed countries have been retreating from silk production in view of increased cost of human power, silk production provides hope and new opportunities to developing countries in the coming days. Currently India is the second largest producer of raw silk next only to China and has been recording consistent growth in production.

Productivity and quality of silk would no doubt depend on the quality and productivity of mulberry, silkworm breeds, healthy seed, scientific rearing and modern reeling technologies. Of these, the silkworm seed gains prominence as any disease or defect in the health of seed can lead to heavy crop losses while healthy seed could give a bumper crop. Seed production requires special attention since many defects are not visible to human eye and one largely depends on breeds selected, history of the crop and examination of the mother moth. At present, mulberry sericulture is practiced in 15 states of India with an approximate silkworm seed requirement of 350 million disease-free layings. For healthy and reliable silkworm seed production, it is necessary to follow scientific techniques and practices.

This book, 'Principles and Techniques of Silkworm Seed Production,' provides information on seed production technologies generated over the years by sericulture scientists. It provides an exhaustive information on various aspects of silkworm seed production techniques including embryology, physiology, diapause, seed multiplication, artificial hatching, preservation and handling, seed crop rearing, disease control, etc. and serves as a guide or reference book to all those involved in seed production activity as well as researchers and students.

P. Joy Oommen
Member Secretary
Central Silk Board
Bangalore

PREFACE

In the history of Indian sericulture, the R & D contributions towards introduction of improved mulberry varieties and silkworm hybrids, mulberry cultivation practices and silkworm rearing techniques have helped in spreading sericulture in varied agro-climatic areas of the country. It is the establishment of network of silkworm seed production, which has stabilized the quality cocoon production. As a result, the country has experienced a quantum jump in silk production and India has emerged as the second largest producer of silk in the world. Sericulture techniques covering various aspects have also advanced greatly. In recent times, cocoon production has emerged as an important cash crop from the status of a very traditional and small subsidiary crop of marginal returns. Thanks due to pioneering efforts of Indian sericulture scientists to improve productivity per unit area, in fact, sericulture industry in India has been making steady and sustained progress. The current improvement in productivity and quality has made Indian sericulture highly attractive to the farmers.

Silkworm seed, which forms the basic foundation and backbone of sericulture industry, plays a decisive role in the production of silk. The two most cherished objectives of seed productions are – production of quality seed and attainment of self-sufficiency. The quality seed is often defined as entirely free from diseases, having more number of viable eggs and assuring stable cocoon crop. The performance and success of the cocoon crop depend on the use of mulberry variety, quality of the feed and silkworm seed besides adoption of various technologies of seed production including seed preservation, physiology and incubation. Production of high-grade quality cocoons and timely supply of required quantity of disease-free silkworm eggs prepared on systematic and scientific lines to the sericulture farmers is one of the prerequisites of egg production. To achieve these objectives, technical packages need to be adopted.

Among the various aspects of sericulture science, the one on 'silkworm egg production' deals with the information required for planning the egg production and preservation on scientific lines by adopting technological advancements achieved on the subject. Besides, various aspects of seed crop rearing also involves selection of eggs suited for the purpose and period of rearing to produce eggs of excellent quality for supply to the sericulturists in order to produce and harvest stable cocoon crop.

The production of seed cocoon is entirely different from producing cocoons for commercial reeling. In view of spreading sericulture in larger areas, large-scale production of quality seed, based on the appropriate technology is absolutely essential which in turn enhance the production and quality of commercial cocoons and raw silk. Production of silkworm seed, which is not only free from all kinds of diseases but also ensures the purity and vigour of the breeds to exploit heterosis, involves various technologies at various levels of egg production. Further, adoption of techniques for egg production on a mass scale, to meet the huge demand of silkworm seed, differs from those of small scale in laboratories.

Sericulture in India is mostly practised in sub-tropical and tropical regions. The information available in Japanese or Chinese literature relates basically to temperate and sub-temperate climates. However, the trends in silkworm egg production, knowledge relating to silkworm varieties and their improvement as also the physiology of silkworm eggs are effectively utilized in the production and preservation of eggs. Since, silkworm rearing is closely related to the silkworm health (hygiene), sericulturists should have a thorough knowledge on this aspect also. Rearing of pure races differs from commercial hybrids. There is no up-dated compendium of information in sericulture on these aspects, which relates to various strategies of seed production particularly for tropical regions. Therefore, it was thought desirable to publish a book on the subject.

This book is designed specially for use by university teachers, students, researchers, technologists, licensed seed producers, grainures, NGOs and all those engaged in sericulture in general and seed production in particular. It will serve as a very useful guide to them and will motivate to find solutions to the existing problems in order to increase productivity. The book has many unique features. It comprises mulberry varieties cultivated/evolved over the years in India and its productivity and suitability in different regions, soil and fertilizer application and its reclamation to make it suitable for mulberry cultivation, raising of mulberry garden for seed crop rearing, disinfections and hygiene, silkworm hybrids authorized in India for commercial rearing, seed organization in India and seed multiplication, egg production technologies, oviposition, preservation of eggs, embryogenesis, metabolic changes during embryogenesis, artificial hatching of eggs for rearing at appropriate time and season, methods of incubation, rearing of young and late age silkworm for seed crop besides sex separation, heterosis, impact of correlation of characters on egg production and prevention of silkworm diseases and pests to achieve sustained and quality silkworm eggs. The information furnished in this book will be of immense importance not only to Indian sericulture but also to South Asian and African countries enjoying tropical and sub-tropical climate and will find an application at all levels of sericulture.

To present the comprehensive and up to date information in this book *Principles and Techniques of Silkworm Seed Production,* we have drawn necessary information and scores from the published books, documents, periodicals and help taken from all of them is gratefully acknowledged. We profoundly and sincerely are deeply privileged and honoured by Sri P. Joy Oommen, IAS, Member Secretary, Central Silk Board, Bangalore, for encouragement to publish the book and for his blessings and encouraging Foreword. We deeply express our gratitude to Dr. B. R. Dayakar Yadav and Sri B. Rama Rao, Deputy Director, Central Silk Board, Bangalore, whose cooperation and involvement enabled us to prepare this book.

Our heartfelt thanks are also due to Dr. S. R. Ramesh, Dr. Geetha N. Murthy, Sri H. S. Phaniraj, Dr. R. N. Singh and Mrs. M. Maheswari, Senior Research Officers, Central Silk Board, Bangalore, for their valuable discussions and suggestions from time to time for the improvement of the contents of the book. We sincerely acknowledge the help rendered by Sri H. P. Panduranga, Assistant Director (Computer), Sri R. Punniyamurthy and Sri V. Narayanan, Central Silk Board, Bangalore, in the preparation of the manuscript. Our thanks are also due to all those who have directly or indirectly helped in one way or the other in bringing out this publication.

We profoundly thank Sri Tilak Wasan, Publisher, Discovery Publishing House, New Delhi, whose interest and enthusiasm have brought out this book with an excellent presentation within a short period.

Though all-out efforts have been made to incorporate correct and authentic information, some errors might have crept inadvertently. Please bring out such errors to the notice of the authors and the publishers. Views and suggestions from users of this book are welcome to improve upon future editions.

Dr. Tribhuwan Singh
Dr. Berra Saratchandra

CONTENTS

1

INTRODUCTION

India has made a phenomenal progress in silk production. Prior to independence, silk production was only 800 MT per year and sericulture was considered as a subsidiary occupation of the poor farmers. In fact, popularization of agronomical practices, release of improved mulberry varieties, evolution of productive silkworm hybrids coupled with crop protection and appropriate rearing technologies change the whole sericulture scenario in 1980. Total shift from the use of pure multivoltine eggs to multi × Bi or Bi × Bi eggs and replacement of local mulberry varieties by improved variety took place within a short period of time. The contribution of R&D resulted in increase in cocoon production/ha from 294 kg/ha/year in 1975-76 to about 601 kg/ha/yr in 2001-02. Raw silk productivity/ ha increased from 20.34 kg/ha in 1975-76 to 68.30 kg/ ha in 2001-02. The renditta, which is the most important parameter to judge the quality of silk, has come down from 14.5 kg in 1975-76 to 8.8 kg in 2001-02. The raw silk production has now reached to 15848 MT from 2500 MT in 1975-76 (Table 1.1). All these economic benefit has been generated through R&D in sericulture, thanks to the pioneering efforts of Indian sericulture scientists to improve productivity per unit area. As a result, the country has experienced a quantum jump in silk production and India has emerged as the second largest producer of silk in the world only after China.

There have been incessant endeavors to improve the silk both in terms of quality and quantity. One of the inputs that play a decisive role in the success of silkworm crop is

Table 1.1: Mulberry sericulture in India

Year	Area under mulberry (ha)	Dfls production (Lakh Nos)	Reeling cocoon production	Raw silk production (MT)	Renditta	Raw silk productivity /ha (Kg)	Cocoon productivity /ha (Kg)	Cocoon production /100Dfls (Kg)
1975-76	124913	1706.90	36739	2541	14.5	20.34	294.12	21.52
1980-81	170000	2189.51	58208	4593	12.7	27.02	342.40	26.58
1985-86	217839	2628.79	76717	7029	10.9	32.27	352.17	29.18
1990-91	316610	3171.88	116663	11486	10.2	36.28	368.48	36.78
1991-92	331237	3183.43	107153	10658	10.1	32.18	323.49	33.66
1992-93	342764	3402.44	129685	13000	10.0	37.93	378.35	38.12
1993-94	319215	3034.32	117268	12550	9.3	39.32	367.36	38.65
1994-95	283093	3189.70	123115	13450	9.2	47.51	434.89	38.60
1995-96	286496	2856.20	116362	12884	9.0	44.97	406.16	40.74
1996-97	280651	3199.49	115655	12954	8.9	46.16	412.10	36.15
1997-98	282244	3355.20	127495	14048	9.1	49.77	451.72	38.00
1998-99	270069	3318.62	126565	14260	8.9	52.80	468.64	38.14
1999-00	227151	3309.80	124531	13944	8.9	61.39	548.23	37.63
2000-01	215921	3182.86	124663	14432	8.6	66.84	577.35	39.20
2001-02 (P)	232076	3337.00	139616	15848	8.8	68.30	601.60	41.80

P: Provisional
MT: Metric Tonnes

the silkworm seed. If the quality of egg is good, one can harvest a successful crop and if it is inferior, the crop could be lost at any stage of the silkworm rearing depending on the magnitude of the defects or inadequacies of the seed. Quality is the product of technology and inputs. Input refers to inter alia breed, standard of seed cocoons, survival rate, pupation rate, disease freeness, seed cocoon quality, maintenance of temperature, humidity and light, examination for disease detection, infrastructure facilities etc. Quality seed is also true to its breed, rich in fecundity with high fertility rate, uniform hatching and above all ensures successful stable cocoon crop.

Production of seed is a production activity. How much seed the country needs of course depends on how efficient the rest of sericulture is. Naturally, if per hectare productivity or per 100 Dfls productivity of cocoons is better, the country can do with less seed. Because after all, the limiting factor is the leaf or the mulberry acreage. However, given a particular quantity of leaf or acreage under mulberry, it is not possible to increase productivity by using more seed. Consumpsion of more seed per unit area is due to low productivity per 100 Dfls. The average productivity/100 Dfls in China is approximately 70 kg but the productivity is only 42 kg/100 Dfls in India. This indicates that the country is consuming more layings compared to China to produce the same quantity of cocoons. If we had higher productivity, we could reduce the egg production. In other words, we are taking probably more of a burden than required by producing more layings and making farmers to consume more laying per unit area to produce cocoons at the lower yield level.

In sericulturally advanced countries like China and Japan, the seed production techniques have been perfected to its highest level. Though silkworm seed production is practised since decades, it is yet to be standardized to its perfection in India.

To meet the requirement of sericulture farmers to produce 15,848 MT of raw silk or 1,39,616 MT of reeling cocoons, the country requires about 35 crore disease-free commercial silkworm seed. Karnataka is the major silk producing state in the country, which needs about 21 crores of disease-free laying (Dfls) per year. The major production of seed (about 72.5%) comes from Licensed Seed Producers (LSPs), while Centre contributes about 7.3% of the total seed requirement in the country and remaining 20.2% is contributed from Directorate of Sericulture (DOS) of respective states. Silkworm seed plays a decisive role in the success of commercial cocoon crop. Timely supply of required quantity of silkworm seed to the sericulturists is one of the prerequisites for achieving stable cocoon production. Scientific/systematic seed multiplication and generation of genetically pure seed cocoons could achieve this. Despite technological developments and transfer of technologies to the field, the desired level of improvement is not observed in the field. The main reasons are inadequacies associated with the extension activities, poor infrastructure and socioeconomic conditions of the sericulturists. As a result, the seed cocoons produced by the seed farmers are not in conformity with the characters of pure breeds. Besides, due to climatic vagaries, coupled with field problems, the generation of seed cocoon is more often not commensurating with the requirements, resulting in diversion of large quantum of seed cocoons to the reeling sector and non-availability of seed cocoons during the season.

The factors responsible for deterioration of quality of seed cocoons are poor leaf quality, unhygienic conditions during rearing, non-maintenance of optimum micro-climatic conditions and lack of knowledge and low-level technology adoption. To overcome all these problems, efforts should be focused for the improvement of seed quality by:

- Adoption of better management strategies for seed cocoon procurement.
- Adoption of effective seed cocoon transportation technology.
- Adoption of sex separation technology at cocoon stage and or introduction of sex limited breeds at commercial level.

- Adoption of low temperature preservation technology for seed cocoons and moths for synchronization.
- Adoptions of standardized silkworm seed production practices.
- Introduction and popularization of loose egg production technology.
- Adoptions of new bivoltine seed preservation schedules.
- Introduction of custom designed equipments.
- Introduction of high productive breeds.
- Adoption of exclusive package of practices for mulberry and silkworm for seed crop rearing.
- Adoption of price fixation strategy for seed cocoons based on pupation rate/live pupa percentage.

The seed production scenario in Indian sericulture presents dichotomy. Seed organization can be categorized into reproductive seed maintenance and management and its multiplication up to quality hybrid seed production and its distribution for heterosis exploitation. Under Indian conditions, the organization of seed coupled with area development has to be addressed to domestic requirements and quality orientation. Maintenance and multiplication of stocks are built up into tiers with or without selection pressures at different levels, primarily not to allow variations in characters of authorized breeds, hence for true to mother multiplication up to mass production of industrial seed for determined goals.

In India, a systematic three-tier seed multiplication system is lacking in most of the states. In Karnataka, which is the major silk and seed producing state in the country, has well-established three-tier system of seed organization and seed production. Mostly, the supply of silkworm seeds in India is taken by the following agencies:

(a) Grainages run by State Department of Sericulture.

(b) Grainages run by Central Silk Board.

Table 1.2: Silkworm seed production in different states in India (Unit: Lakh numbers)

Year	*Karnataka*	*Andhra Pradesh*	*Tamil Nadu*	*West Bengal*	*J&K*	*Others*	*Total*
1980-81	1603.4	89.0	64.1	390.0	27.7	15.2	2189.5
1985-86	1703.9	158.2	146.1	676.0	42.6	40.8	2767.7
1990-91	2112.1	249.2	195.0	490.0	35.8	89.7	3171.9
1991-92	1912.4	378.8	162.3	598.5	41.5	89.9	3183.4
1992-93	2012.6	416.6	213.6	621.7	37.7	100.2	3402.4
1993-94	1962.1	236.3	152.6	572.6	19.4	91.3	3034.3
1994-95	2178.0	154.7	130.7	621.8	26.2	78.2	3189.7
1995-96	1768.2	206.9	212.6	532.6	33.2	102.7	2856.1
1996-97	1845.0	516.5	175.4	548.2	36.9	77.5	3199.5
1997-98	1886.3	627.4	139.7	600.2	31.6	69.9	3355.2
1998-99	1859.6	722.3	139.5	487.7	35.6	73.9	3318.6
1999-00	1726.4	810.8	153.0	507.2	36.2	76.3	3309.8
2000-01	1602.2	854.0	153.0	458.2	33.5	81.9	3182.9
2001-02 (P)	1690.0	879.0	131.5	529.0	33.0	74.5	3337.0

P: Provisional

(c) Other institutes recognized by Government like Karnataka State Sericulture Research & Development Institute (KSSRDI), Asian Institute of Rural Development etc.

(d) Private seed producers who are licensed for the preparation of commercial silkworm eggs.

Of the total silkworm seed produced in the country (3337 lakh Dfls) about 50% is produced in the state of Karnataka (1690 lakh Dfls) (Table 1.2). Though the silkworm seed produced in the country is almost constant from the last five years but cocoon productivity and raw silk productivity/ha is increasing significantly reveal the fact of adoption of new technologies of both silkworm rearing and mulberry cultivation, great awareness among farmers, adoption of hygienic conditions, incubation procedure, seed production and preservation technologies, prevention and control of diseases etc.

2

CULTIVATION OF MULBERRY FOR SEED CROP

CLASSIFICATION AND VARIETIES OF MULBERRY

India encompasses wide geographical and agroclimatic variation. Accordingly, mulberry sericulture is distributed in temperate, sub-tropical and tropical regions. However, the major cultivated area under mulberry is from tropical regions. The mulberry is a fast growing deciduous plant belonging to the family Moraceae and genus *Morus,* the primary food plant of the silkworm, *Bombyx mori* (L.). There are 35 species of *Morus,* which are broadly classified into Dolichostylae with long style, and Macromorus without style.

Phylum	:	Phenerogamme
Sub-phylum	:	Angiosperme
Class	:	Dicotyledoneae
Sub-class	:	Apetalae
Order	:	Urticales
Family	:	Moraceae
Genus	:	*Morus*

The classification of mulberry is mostly based on morphological characters of leaves, flowers, fruits and length of stigma or style of female flowers. There are 35 species of *Morus*, which are broadly classified into Dolichostylae with long style, and Macromorus without style. Geographical distribution and classification of some of the important mulberry species is as follows:

A. Dolochostylae Koidzumi

(a)	Pubescentes	*Morus arabica* Koidz.	Arabia, Oman
		Morus mizuno Hotta	Arabia, Oman
(b)	Papillosae		
		M. mongolica Schn.	Korea, China
		M. nigriformis Koidz.	China
		M. notabalis Schn.	China
		M. yunnanensis Koidz	China
		M. bombycis Koidz.	Japan, Korea, China
		M. rotundifolia Koidz.	Thailand
		M. mallotifolia Koidz.	Thailand
		M. australis Poiret	Taiwan, Japan, China, Himalayas
		M. acidosa Griff.	Taiwan, Japan, China, Himalayas
		M. kagayamae Koidz.	China

B. Macromorus Koidzumi

(a)	Pubescentes	*M. serrata* Roxb.	India
		M. nigra L.	Armenia, Persia, Iran
		M. tiliaefolia Makino	Japan, Korea
		M. cathayana Hemsi	China
(b)	Papillosae	*M. mesozygia* Staff.	Africa
		M. rubra L.	America
		M. mollis Rusby.	Maxico
		M. celtidifolia Kunth	America
		M. microphylla Buckl.	America
		M. peruviana Planchon	Peru
		M. insigyis Bur.	America
		M. boniensis Koidz.	China
		M. ihou Koidz.	China
		M. alba L.	Korea, China, India
		M. atropurpurea Roxb.	China

(c) Longispica

M. laevigata Wall.	India, China
M. macroura Mio.	Malaya
M. rinidis Hamilton	India
M. wittorum Handel	China
M. wallichiana Koidz.	India, Nepal, China
M. indica L.	China, India
M. latifolia Poilet.	China, India
M. multicaulis	China

Geographical distribution of genus *Morus* is summarized in Table 2.1. It is observed that more number of species of *Morus* is distributed in China (24 Nos.), Japan (19 Nos) and United States of America (14 Nos) and these countries have also more number of endemic species. In India only four species of mulberry is reported with only one endemic species.

Table 2.1: Geographical distribution of the genus *Morus*

Name of the country	*Total number of species*	*Number of endemic species*
China	24	17
India	4	1
Indonesia	3	2
Japan	19	14
Korea	6	1
Taiwan	4	1
Thailand	2	2
Argentina	1	1
Columbia	3	1
Mexico	3	2
Peru	1	1
U.S.A.	14	9

Mulberry plants usually grow from 50 latitude North to 10 latitude South and are mostly distributed in Northern hemisphere. It is distributed both in temperate and tropical regions of the world predominantly in eastern, southern and southeastern Asia, South Europe, Southern North America, North western South America and part of Africa. The general characteristics of mulberry plants are: deciduous, perennial, shrub, leaves alternate, leaf margin entire or serrate, stipule at base of the pedicel of the leaf, leaf drop off easily, leaf lanceolate, inflorescence amentaceous, diocious or monocious, fleshy, thick multiple fruit etc. Most of the *Morus* species are diploid having 28 chromosomes but few species like *M. tiliaefolia* (2n = 84); *M. cathayana* (2n = 56, 84 or 112) and *M. nigra* (2n = 308) are polyploids. All the mulberry varieties distributed in different regions of India can be grouped into four species:

(i) ***Morus alba:*** This species is cultivated in Punjab, north-west Himalayas ascending to 3500 m. The species mostly grow as a tree to a height of 10-15 m. It is wild in nature and cultivated for their fruit and timber.

(ii) ***Morus serrata:*** This species grows as tree up to a height of 20-25 m. It is distributed in Himalayas from Kumaon hills westward, up to an altitude of 3000 m.

(iii) ***Morus laevigata:*** This species is distributed in tropical and subtropical regions from Indus Valley to Assam. It is wild and distributed ascending to 1500 m.

(iv) ***Morus indica:*** Most of the Indian mulberry varieties belong to this species. They are moderate size deciduous trees distributed and cultivated throughout the country. This species is mostly cultivated as bushes.

Selection of mulberry varieties: Mulberry plants are perennial. One generation of plant can survive for more than 10-15 years and at times for even 30-40 years. Though selection is the oldest method of crop improvement, success depends on the amount of variability in given species or population and method of selection. The significant characters considered for selection of mulberry varieties are high yield, excellent quality of leaves and healthy conditions of plants. When fresh plants are planted, it is very essential to carefully study the features of the varieties for cultivation in accordance with the requirement and silkworm-rearing plan. The conditions for selecting the mulberry varieties include:

(a) **Varieties excellent in silkworm rearing**

- Leaf quality should be good.
- Leaf conditions should be congenial.
- Leaf should be suitable for different silkworm instars, rearing period and method of rearing.

(b) **Varieties excellent for cultivation**

- Varieties should be healthy, resistance to diseases, pests and natural calamities.
- Yield must be excellent.
- Management should be easy.
- Suitable for cultivation to varied climatic

Mulberry varieties cultivated/evolved over the years in India and their distribution are presented in Table 2.2 and the varieties released and authorized by Central Silk Board for commercial exploitation in Table 2.3.

Mulberry breeding programmes implemented have been able to develop varieties with high biomass and yield potential. The average leaf yield under rainfed conditions, which was approximately 4 MT only annually in 1950s, has increased to 18 MT in 1995s. Similarly, under irrigated conditions, the leaf yield has shown tremendous increase from merely 15 MT to 45 MT. Recently evolved mulberry variety V1 (Victory-1) is producing approximately 60-65 MT leaf yield annually under irrigated conditions. Mulberry varieties being recommended for cultivation in different regions of the country and popular varieties of China, Japan and some of the leading silk producing countries are presented in Table 2.4. Most of the varieties cultivated in India, a major silk producing country in the tropical

Table 2.2: Mulberry varieties cultivated/evolved over the years in India

Period	*Regions of cultivation and mulberry varieties*		
	South India	*North East India*	*Jammu & Kashmir*
1950s	Mysore Local, Japanese grafts	Kajjale	Goshoerami, Shatut, Tsukasaguwa
1960s	Mysore Local, Japanese grafts	Kajjale, Matigara Black	Goshoerami, Shatut, Sujanpuri
1970s	Kanava-2, Mysore Local	Kajjale, Matigara Black, Mandalaya	Goshoerami, Shatut, Sujanpuri, Chak Majra, Tsukasaguwa
1980s	Kanava-2, Mysore Local, S54, S36, MR2, S30	S1, TR-4, TR-10, BC259, Kosen	S-146, Chinese White
1990s	Kanava-2, S34, S36, S54, S13	TR-10, BC-259, S766, S779, Kosen, TR-4	S-146, Ichinose, Kenmochi. Chinese White
1995s	Kanava-2, S36, S54, S13, MR-2, Viswa, V1, S1635, RFS-175, RFS-135		

Table 2.3: Mulberry varieties released and authorized by Central Silk Board for commercial use

Variety	*Developed at*	*Climate*	*Potential yield /ha/yr (MT)*
K2	DOS Karnataka	Tropical	30.0
S797	CSR&TI Berhampore	Tropical humid	25.0
S799	CSR&TI Berhampore	Tropical humid	26.4
C776	CSR&TI Berhampore	Tropical humid	29.6
C763	CSR&TI Berhampore	Tropical humid	32.0
S1	CSR&TI Berhampore	Tropical humid	27.4
TR-10	CSR&TI Berhampore	Tropical humid	19.3
BC259	CSR&TI Berhampore	Tropical humid	22.7
S30	CSR&TI Mysore	Tropical	41.3
S41	CSR&TI Mysore	Tropical	34.0
S54	CSR&TI Mysore	Tropical	40-50
RFS135	CSR&TI Mysore	Tropical	40-50
MR2	DOS Tamil Nadu	Tropical	25.0
S1635	CSR&TI Berhampore	Tropical humid	31.2
S34	CSR&TI Mysore	Tropical	17.0
S13	CSR&TI Mysore	Tropical	16.0
S36	CSR&TI Mysore	Tropical	45.0
S146	CSR&TI Berhampore	Temperate wet/tropical humid	22.0
Chak majra	RSRS Jammu	Sub-tropical	15.2
Chinese (White)	CSR&TI Pampore	Temperate	12.0
V1	CSR&TI Mysore	Tropical	60-65

climatic regions, shows high rate of growth, good response to pruning and producing more biomass.

MULBERRY SOILS AND FERTILIZERS

The land has been divided into various agro-climatic zones depending on the types of soil, topography of land, rainfall pattern, temperature and humidity fluctuations etc. This was done based on the requirements of various agricultural crops so as to plan cropping pattern for the best advantages of mankind. Similar is the case with silkworm food plants, which show different kinds of

Table 2.4: Popular mulberry varieties of some of the sericultural countries of the world

Country	*Mulberry variety*
China	Heyebai, Thantou Heyebai, Tongxiangqing, Husong No. 197, Yu No.2, Lun No. 40, Za Zhangsang, Damudo, Heyesang
France	*Murier sanvageon, M. rose, M. rebelaire, M. colombassa, M. colombasette*
India	
South	Mysore Local, Kanava-2, S54, S36, MR2, S13, S34, Viswa, Victory-1 (V1)
North East	Kajjali, Matigara Black, Mandalaya (S1), TR4, TR10, BC259, S776, S799, Chosen
Jammu & Kashmir	Goshoerami, Tsukasaguwa, Sujanpuri, S146, Ichinose, Chinese White, Kenmochi
Indonesia	*Morus multicaulis, M. nigra, M. lambing, M. cathayana*
Italy	*Gelso della valtellia, G. della acchio, G. montorao, G. romano, G. morettiana, G. ihon, G. trentin*
Japan	Ichinose, Kairy, Oshimaso, Roso, Akagi, Kenmochi, Ichihei, Kairyo roso, Enshutakasuke, Shinso No.2, Kokuso No.21, Kokuso N. 20, Kokuso No.27, Atsubamidori, Tokiyutaka, Aobanezumi
South Vietnam	Dau bau Trang, Dau bau Den, Dau duoi, Dau cay
Thailand	Baipoe, Chiang, Daeng kam, Jark, Noi, Plong, Tadam, Yuork, BR8, Tark, Soi
USSR	Paiwandi, Zarif Toot, Kol Toot, Tadjik, Pioneersky, Azari Toot, Khanlar Toot, Firudin Toot, Russian Local, Hybrid mulberry

responses to certain types of agro-climatic conditions. This is the reason due to which some of the sericulture activities are restricted to specific zones of the country. Even in case of mulberry, which is well adapted to different climatic conditions, plant variety behaves different in varied agro-climates. On the other hand, the silkworm is a sensitive insect, which can tolerate narrow range of fluctuation of temperature and humidity. However, this could be managed to some extent by manipulating the room conditions in case of *Bombyx mori*. Therefore, it is most essential to plan the sericultural activities, particularly pre-cocoon activities based on the agro-climatic conditions of the region.

Mulberry: Soil-plant interaction in a particular climate is the key to success of any agricultural crops and it is not an exception to sericultural practices also. The Indian soil has been divided into various agro-climatic zones depending on the origin, types, topography, rainfall, temperature and humidity. As such, sericulture activities are either restricted or limited to specific zones of the country. Though rearing of silkworm is also influenced by varying climatic conditions, however, mulberry cultivation essentially field activity needs special references from agro-climatic point of consideration while planning for sericultural activity.

Soil: On the basis of physical properties of soil, Indian soils have been classified into 14 types viz., red sandy soil, loamy soil, red and yellow soil, laterite soil, sub-mountain soil, desert soil, gray and brown soil, black soil, mixed red and black soil, mountain soil, alluvial soil, terai soils, skeletal soil and glacier soil. The total sericulture area of the country (232076 ha), which is distributed in different states, has different types of soil. Soil physiochemical properties influence the quality and quantity of leaf produced. The nature and characteristics of surface soil and sub-soil both greatly affect growth and development of mulberry plant. Therefore, it is essential to determine the soil physiochemical properties before the establishment of mulberry garden. Chemical problems can be rectified with lime, fused phosphate or organic matter but physical problems such as soil texture, available soil depth, porosity, structure, hardness and water table in quite difficult to change.

Soil texture: Mulberry growth is greatly influenced by soil texture. The most vigorous growth occurs in sandy loam and loam soils. In clayey, sandy or gravel soil, the number of branches, the growth of plant, the length of branch etc are poorer than on loamy soil.

Soil depth: Since mulberry is deep rooted, soil depth affects growth and development of plant. Harmful factors such as high water table, coarse sand layer, and a layer with over 50% gravel; clay pan or rock bed should be avoided within 50 cm of soil surface to ensure proper growth. The ratio of solid, air and liquid phases in soil also affects growth and development of plant. Under bad soil conditions such as over 55% solid phase, lower than 15% liquid phase or over 40 per cent liquid phase and less than 10% air phase is not suitable for optimum growth of plant and hence should be improved by deep soil crash, irrigation or drainage. The optimum requirement for growth of mulberry plant is within the range of 40-55% solid phase, 15-40% liquid phase and 15-25% air phase.

Rainfall: Water content of soil influences not only quantity but also quality of leaf produced. The transpiration coefficient of mulberry is 350-400, which is much higher than that of even rice (178-284). This indicates that mulberry consumes large quantity of water in the production of dry matter. The evapo-transpiration rate in mulberry is about 4-5 mm/day for the initial growth stage, 5 mm/day from the vigorous growing stage and 7 mm/day in maximum. Therefore, water management is very essential for the vigorous growth of the mulberry plant.

Temperature: Temperature is a crucial factor that influences the growth and development. Extreme high or low temperature is injurious to both silkworm and their food plants. The summer temperature is extremely high in northern western states of Rajasthan, Punjab, Haryana,

Uttar Pradesh, parts of Gujarat, coastal Tamil Nadu and south coast of Andhra Pradesh with an average temperature above 30°C and hence sericulture in this season is ruled out. The temperature is also high (28-30°C) in Gujarat, south Rajasthan, northern parts of Madhya Pradesh, northern and eastern Uttar Pradesh, major parts of Bihar, Orissa and West Bengal and Andhra Pradesh, northeastern states except northern parts of Arunachal Pradesh and parts of Tamil Nadu. Central India, Deccan plateau and west coast covering the states of Kerala, Karnataka, Goa and Maharashtra have an average summer temperature of 25-27°C while south and central parts of Karnataka and parts of Maharashtra have an average summer temperature of 20-25°C. J & K, Himachal Pradesh and Himalayan ranges have average summer temperature falling below 20°C. The average winter temperature falls below 10°C at the Himalayan ranges, between 10-15°C in Punjab, Haryana, west Uttar Pradesh and north Rajasthan, between 10-18°C in central and eastern Uttar Pradesh, south Rajasthan, north Madhya Pradesh, north and west Bihar, Assam, Nagaland, parts of Arunachal Pradesh and Manipur. The area between 21°N and 22°N altitude experiences an average temperature of 18-20°C. A major portion of Maharashtra, Madhya Pradesh and Orissa and small patches in Karnataka and Andhra Pradesh experiences an average winter temperature of 20-23°C. Coastal Maharashtra, a major portion of Karnataka, Andhra Pradesh and northern Tami Nadu experiences an average winter temperature of 23-25°C. The rest of Kerala, coastal Karnataka, south coastal Maharashtra and southern Tamil Nadu get an average winter temperature of 25-27.5°C. The highest average winter temperature of 28-30°C is found in central Kerala. Temperature between 24-28°C is suitable for silkworm rearing and hence only those regions where temperature falls within the optimum range, sericulture can be practised.

regions: Based on the varied climatic factors, India has been divided into six climatic regions viz., Highland, Humid Sub-tropical, Semi-arid, Arid, Tropical

Wet & Dry and Tropical Wet. J&K and the area falling in the Himalayan ranges are classified as Highland. The remaining part of North Eastern states, Uttar Pradesh, Himachal Pradesh, northern Punjab, Haryana, West Bengal, northern Madhya Pradesh and a major portion of Bihar fall under humid sub-tropical region. West of Rajasthan and north of Gujarat fall under arid region and a strip of land on the eastern and southern side of arid region corning under Punjab, Haryana, Uttar Pradesh, Madhya Pradesh, Rajasthan and Gujarat and a strip of land stretching from central Maharashtra to the southern-most strip fall under semi-arid region. Kerala, coastal Karnataka and south coastal Maharashtra fall under tropical wet and dry region.

Based on the soil types and climatic conditions, several seri-zones suitable for sericulture activities have been identified and suitable silkworm strains and mulberry varieties are evolved, recommended and authorized for these seri-zones. Central Silk Board has broadly classified four seri-zones in the country viz., Tropical Humid, Tropical Dry, Temperate Dry and Temperate Wet.

Fertilizers: Mulberry leaf is the sole food for rearing of the silkworm and its quality exerts very important influence upon cocoon yield. The leaf quantity and quality depend on solar energy, temperature, 0_2 and CO_2 concentration, water, mechanical support, nutrients and harmful conditions of soil. Among these factors, fertilizers and soil amendments can improve only nutrient status and harmful conditions of soil while other factors are almost impossible to be rectified.

Mulberry is perennial foliage plant. They are pruned and harvested round the year, which takes great amount of nutritive elements away from the soil. If no or insufficient fertilizer is applied to the field after leaf is harvested and or plant is pruned, the ensuing plants will grow poorly and will result in low leaf yield. However, on the contrary, leaf yield rises with the increase of fertilizer application provided other factors are favourable but excessive manuring should be avoided as it may not be economical on the one hand and lead to curve of parabola or "S" shaped on the other.

Types and properties of fertilizers

(a) **Organic fertilizers:** Organic fertilizers are those that contain organic matter such as livestock dung, farm yard manure (FYM), compost, green manure (sun hemp, cowpeas, soybeans etc), human wastes, sludge, silkworm faeces etc. Neem cake and groundnut cake are also used to a limited extent. All these fertilizers have the common characters of containing all-round nutritiveness such as N, P, K, Ca, Mg, Fe, S and various microelements and growth substances as well.

(b) **Chemical fertilizers:** Chemical fertilizers are of many types. They contain nitrogen, phosphorus, potassium and microelements and compound fertilizers. Each fertilizer has its own characteristics. However, the common characteristics are -

- With single nutrient
- With easiness to dissolve
- With high content of certain nutrients
- Without organic matter

The chemical fertilizers in common use in mulberry field are Ammonium sulphate, Urea, Calcium super phosphate, Calcium magnesium phosphate, Ammonium bi-carbonate, Potassium chloride and Sulphate etc.

(c) **Compound fertilizers**: Compound fertilizers are those commercial fertilizers which contain two or more than two nutrients. They are also called complex or multiple nutrient fertilizers. It is the major form of fertilizer under industrial production and are put in use in agriculture as well as in sericulture in both developed and developing countries in the world.

PROPAGATION OF MULBERRY

Mulberry propagation is one of the important techniques in sericultural production. There are two methods of propagation:

(i) Sexual propagation (seedling)

(ii) Asexual propagation (vegetative propagation, grafting, cuttings layering etc.)

(i) Sexual propagation: Mulberry is generally so heterogeneous that it is difficult to produce a pure line or an individual of the same characters as their parent. Therefore, seedlings are usually used as stock for grafting. Mulberry seeds are harvested from ripened fruits of 10-year-old trees with uniform quality. Care must be taken to collect the seed from the same variety. Exposure of seed to sunlight should be avoided and the seeds containing sieve are rubbed and washed within 1-2 days, air dried in time to preserve vitality. If these seeds are kept in damp place for 3-5 months, they lose their vitality. Air-dried mulberry seeds are to be sown in time. Quality mulberry seeds are yellowish brown, plump and flat-egg shaped. Generally one kilogram contains 6,50,000-7,00,000 seeds or in other words, one gram contains 650-700 seeds. Seeds should be properly cleaned for the purpose of storing.

Quantity of seeds required: If normal seeds occupied 80% of the total number of seeds produced, and its 85% of the normal seeds germinate, then its worth use will be only 68% ie. 80 × 85 ÷ 100. The quantity requirement then is calculated as:

$$X = \frac{100}{68} = 1.47$$ i.e. 1.47 fold quantity of seeds are required to be sown of the actual requirements.

Conditions required for seed germination

Temperature: The optimum temperature for mulberry seed germination is 30 ± 2°C. Temperature below 15°C or above 39°C impedes the germination. The germination takes approximately 10 days at 27°C, 8 days at 30°C, 6 days at 33°C and thus indicating that the number of days taken for germination decreases with the increase in temperature.

Light: Mulberry seeds are photosensitive and illumination increases germination ability of the seeds. Type of illumination also influences the germination conditions. Germination is affected if the germination bed is exposed to violet, blue or bright light rays.

Water: Water is another essential element in the germination of seeds. Mulberry seeds absorb water accounting for 55-60 per cent of their weight to initiate germination and metabolic activities.

Atmosphere: Germinating mulberry seeds respire vigorously and require sufficient oxygen supply in the soil to decompose and transport the nutrients in the endosperm. Mulberry seeds can be sown in spring, summer or autumn. In order to avoid unfavorable climate and to achieve a good and even germination, the seeds are often verbalized and then sown into nursery.

Sowing methods: There are three methods of sowing the seeds in nursery beds:

(a) **Drilling:** It can be divided into two patterns i.e. cross and parallel. The seeds are first mixed with four-fold dried fine soil and then sown into the ditches evenly. The characteristic of sowing in lines includes requirement of less quantity of seeds in comparison to broadcasting method. The method has the advantage of good ventilation and lighting, the seedlings produced are stout and nursery management is better.

(b) **Scattering or broadcasting:** Seeds are mixed with dry soil and then scattered evenly in the nursery beds. It is simple and productive. The characteristics of broadcasting are—the amount of seeds used per unit area is large, 2-3 gm seed is required for each square meter and will produce 400-450 seedlings. Since their density is very high, the seedlings become weak.

(c) **Dribbling:** This method requires less seeds and provides convenience in management. Seedlings grow evenly. However, it produces fewer seedlings over drilling and broadcasting.

Management after sowing: Once the sowing is completed, the bed is covered with soil. The thickness of covering soil should be such that it completely covers the seeds (about 2-3 mm thick). Finally, a thin layer of sawdust or straw or other proper stuff is spread over the bed. The bed is then supplied with sufficient water. After sowing and till the time of seed germination, water is sprinkled once or twice every day on the bed. After germination water is supplied, depending on the requirement. The sawdust or covering is removed once all the seeds germinate after 10-14 days of sowing. The thinning out operation is carried out after 2-3 leaves have sprouted. The mulberry seedling growth can be divided into four stages -

(a) **Germination stage:** This stage starts from the sowing to the sprouting of two cotyledons from the seed.

(b) **Slow growing stage:** This stage starts from the emergence of two cotyledons to the appearance of 4-5 leaves.

(c) **Vigorous growth stage:** In this stage, the aerial portions of seedlings grow rapidly. Biomass of aerial portion accounts for 90% of the total biomass at the end of the year.

(d) **Dormant stage:** Dormant stage refers to the period that the seedling's shoot apices stop growing, leaves become yellow and begin to fall.

Management operations such as irrigation, seedling thinning and setting, top dressing, loosening soil, weeding and pest control should be conducted at appropriate time for better growth of the seedling. However, propagation of mulberry through seed is not popular in India,

(ii) **Asexual propagation:** Asexual propagation is also called vegetative propagation. In asexual propagation, the inherited characteristic of the parent stocks can be retained. In reality, the new plant is the continuation of the growth and development of the parent stock. Asexual propagation can be practised in four ways i.e. grafting, layering, tissue culture and cuttings. Of these methods, propagation through cutting is the simplest form of asexual propagation, where a fragment of a plant's vegetative organ will grow out new roots and shoots and become a new plant. This method is simple in operation and quick in producing saplings. Rooting in cuttings is influenced by mulberry variety, availability of nutrition, age of parental plant etc.

Mulberry sapling propagation through cutting can be divided into two types i.e. hard woodcuttings and soft woodcuttings. Hard woodcutting is popular and is usually used in mulberry propagation. For hard woodcutting, one-year-old plant or mature branch is selected which is cut horizontally or diagonally just below the leaf scar. The cuttings should be 12-15 cm long. The top of the cutting should be cut at the same level as the apex of the terminal bud. The cuttings are transported and planted in the nursery bed leaving only the terminal bud above the surface of the soil. In order to prevent them from drying, straw mats or husk are spread on the soil. By spraying water at regular intervals sprouting and root development occur in about 2-3 weeks. However, sprouting and rooting capacity of cuttings are dependent on the quality of soil, temperature, moisture etc. If soil are sandy loam or sandy, the rooting capacity will be good. Further, high temperature and high moisture is essential for better rooting capacity. This method of raising saplings through cuttings is known as 'common cutting method' and is very much popular in India.

(a) **Grafting:** Grafting is a method where the bud or the branch having the bud of a plant is grafted into the root or the shoot bearing the root of another plant, so as to prepare an independent plant that is a plant with independent physiological activities. The plant bearing the root is called the stock and the plant having the bud, which is grafted, is called scion. The method of grafting is classified into indoor grafting and field grafting. The indoor grafting practised in India includes scion grafting, bud grafting, root grafting etc. The field grafting includes low grafting, top grafting and approach grafting. Besides these, there are selection grafting, ventral grafting and bark grafting.

Merits of grafting

- Good adoptability of the stock to the circumstances.
- Easy mass production of saplings with a same variety.
- Can be performed at any time of the year.

Demerits of grafting

- Necessity of highly trained skill.
- Requirement of 2 years for growing stocks and grafted plants.
- This method is not popular because it is not economical besides time-consuming.

Establishment of mulberry garden: The mulberry plant is perennial and arboraceous. Although Mulberry plant will grow well in flat and fertile land but there is great pressure on these types of land for agricultural and horticultural crops and, therefore, mulberry plantation is mostly established in marginal and slop lands where other crops cannot be grown easily. Since it is difficult to replant the mulberry for many years once planted, every effort should be taken in order to harvest large quantity of qualitative and quantitative leaves for production of stable quality cocoon crop. The location for mulberry plantation should be carefully selected after considering various factors such as climate and topography of the region, nature of soil, quantity of rearing, economic aspects etc.

Climate and topography: Mulberry can be grown under various climatic conditions ranging from temperate to tropical. A perusal of geographical position of mulberry growing countries of the world indicates that all of them except Brazil are located north to the equator. It is desirable to have mulberry garden as close as possible to the place of rearing house. This will reduce the labour required for transporting the mulberry leaves and also prevent the wilting or drying of leaves during the period between harvesting and supplying to the silkworm larvae.

Atmospheric temperature and rainfall: Atmospheric temperature ranging in between 24-28°C is optimum for good growth of mulberry. It can be grown in places with a rainfall range of about 600 mm-250 mm. Under low rainfall conditions, the growth is limited due to soil moisture stress resulting in low leaf yield. On an average 50 mm rainfall once in 10 days is considered ideal for growth of mulberry. However, for seed crop mulberry should be raised under irrigated conditions only.

Neighbouring environment: Quality of mulberry leaves and its growth are often affected by various factors viz., presence or absence of forest or woodlands, buildings, factories, mines, tobacco fields, orchards etc. as well as the presence or absence of grass fields. It will be safer not to set up the mulberry garden in and around these locations. In principle, grass should not be grown near the mulberry fields. Sometimes smoke from factories spoils mulberry leaves and make it unsuitable as feed to silkworm. Nicotine coming out from a tobacco plant will contaminate mulberry leaves and often poison silkworms.

In recent years, various kinds of agricultural chemicals are being used for control of pests and diseases of animals and perennial agricultural crops and most of these chemicals are harmful to neighbouring mulberry plantation and silkworm, if fed with these contaminated leaves, will die leading to crop failure. Therefore, care should be taken while spraying the pesticides on neighbouring agricultural crops to avoid the mulberry from contamination from these chemicals.

Elevation: Mulberry cultivation can be practiced at an altitude of about 1000 meters above MSL. However, 700-meter AMSL is considered desirable for luxuriant growth of mulberry. In the tropical climate, mulberry can be grown at a relatively higher altitude also.

Soil: Soil for mulberry fields has to maintain the mulberry plant for sustained productivity of quality leaves. It has to supply:

(a) The essential major and minor nutrient to the plant.

(b) Oxygen for root respiration.

(c) Mechanical support or anchorage to plant.

(d) As a storehouse of water.

Since mulberry is a deep-rooted perennial and long standing crop, soil should be capable of supplying sufficient water, air and nutrients even in the deep layer where the root system penetrates. Therefore, physical and chemical properties of soil such as pH, total nitrogen, content of effective phosphoric acid and potassium, absorbent coefficient of phosphoric acid and nitrogen, composition of grain size, water holding capacity, water permeability and soil water and pore space relation etc. are checked in different layers of soil before establishment of mulberry garden. Soil is tested when there is nc crop in the field and also prior to application of any manure or fertilizer. For sampling of soil extreme corner of field, areas recently manured or fertilized, old bunds, irrigated channels, marshy spots and non-representative areas should be avoided. Soil samples should not be collected immediately after rain, irrigation, fertilizer application, manuring, burning of crop residues etc. Further, for collecting the soil samples, fertilizer bags without washing should not be used.

Soil should be deep, fertile, well drained, clay loam to loam in texture, friable, porous and good capacity of holding moisture for the establishment of mulberry plantation. Slightly acidic soil (pH: 6.2-6.8), which is free from injurious salts, is ideal for good growth of plant. Saline (pH below 6.2) and alkaline (pH above 8.3) soils should be avoided. For good growth of mulberry plant, the saline and alkaline soil can be improved by the application of gypsum, sulphur or green manure and acidic soil by application of lime and green manure.

Soil acidification: Cereals, grasses and potatoes take up little calcium, while sugarcane, mulberry and leguminous plants take large quantity of calcium for their growth and development. Calcium has dual functions in soil. It is an essential nutrient in soil and it is a dominant base, which keeps soil neutral in reaction. In soil saturated with Ca ions, the negative charges are neutralized. If calcium ions lost by leaching is not replaced, positively charged hydrogen ion takes their place and soil becomes acidic in nature and pH falls below neutral. Acidity in soil causes:

(i) Deterioration of structure of heavy soils.

(ii) Iron, aluminium and manganese becomes more soluble and may become toxic to plant growth.

(iii) Phosphates become less soluble.

(iv) Many soil organisms do not survive in acidic soil, particularly the organism, which convert nitrogen reserves to nitrates and those that decomposes plant remains.

(v) The use efficiency of fertilizers decreases with the decrease in pH (Table 2.5).

(vi) At low pH, the quantity and quality of mulberry leaves decreases resulting in poor yield of cocoons.

Table 2.5: Fertilizer-use efficiency with pH (index)

pH	*N (%)*	*P (%)*	*K (%)*	*Average*
7.0	100	100	100	100
6.0	89	52	100	80
5.5	77	48	77	67
5.0	43	34	52	46
4.5	30	23	33	29

Acidic conditions of soil can be corrected by addition of lime material like dolomite, calcite lime stones, burnt lime, hydrated lime, marl, lime sludge and slags. In India lime stone application for reclamation of acidic soil is very popular. The quantity of limestone required for reclamation, varies according to the texture and degree of acidity of soil. The quantity of lime stone required could be estimated as indicated in Table 2.6.

Table 2.6: Relationship between soil texture and quantity of lime required for ratification

Soil texture	*Quantity of lime stone required (tones/ha) to bring soil pH to 5.5 from*	
	pH. 4.5	*pH. 5.5*
Sandy	5.00	2.50
Sandy loam	7.50	3.75
Loam and slit loam	10.00	5.00
Clay loam	15.00	7.00
Clay	16.50	8.25

The efficiency of limestone increases significantly if it is grind to fine particles of 60-80 mesh size. If application is carried out before plantation, fine dust of limestone can be broadcasted on the land and incorporated into soil by ploughing. Lime application is to be repeated in 4-5 years based on soil pH. Following precautions are to be taken into consideration in selection and broadcasting of lime material:

(a) Select locally available and cheap liming material.

(b) Apply liming material in very fine powder form.

(c) Mix lime with soil to the required depth through repeated ploughing.

(d) If required, lime application can be repeated in every 4-5 years, based on soil pH test results.

Reclamation of alkaline soil: Alkalinity of soil is due to the presence of salt (carbonates of calcium, magnesium and sodium) in comparatively higher quantity. These soils usually occur in semiarid and arid regions and the conditions of soil do not permit the growth of mulberry. Generally, such soils are deficient in nitrogen content. In alkaline soil, the organic matter content is extremely low with high pH and exchangeable sodium percentage causes reduction in the availability of plant nutrients.

Alkali or sodic soil contain high quantities of exchangeable sodium (>15%) and show electrical conductivity less than 4 m mohs/cm and high pH (>8.5). Organic (press mud or compost) and inorganic (sulphur or gypsum) materials are applied for the correction of pH of alkaline soil. Press mud or compost should be applied @20-40 MT/ha in two or more split doses. Application of sulphur is advantageous when sodium carbonate content is high in the soil. It is applied @ 0.5-1.0 tones/ha. Application of gypsum is recommended when the soil has high content of caustic carbonates. It is applied @ 2-4 tones/ha only at the topsoil and not ploughed deep. After the application of sulphur or gypsum, the soil should be well drained to leach out the soluble salts.

Reclamation of saline soil: Saline soils are those which contain high quantity of soluble salts and show electrical conductivity above 4 m mohs/cm, pH below 8.5 and exchangeable sodium percentage of < 15. High water level with high salt content, low rainfall with high evaporation rate, irrigation with saline water, poor drainage, use of salt producing fertilizers are some of the reasons causing saline condition of the soil. To reclaim such soil for healthy growth of mulberry plant, it is recommended to irrigate the garden and use green manuring or straw as surface mulch. Moreover, for better results, the reclamation work should be taken up during rainy season. Salt concentration and composition of irrigated water should be known. Only good quality water should be used for flooding and leaching the dissolved salt.

RAISING OF MULBERRY GARDEN

Mulberry plants can be propagated through seedlings, cuttings, grafting, air layering or saplings. Cuttings are most commonly used. But sometimes cuttings fail to establish and survive, due to poor rooting behavior of mulberry variety besides soil conditions. Initial establishment of mulberry plant is important to ensure good growth and high yield per unit area. Therefore, planting of rooted cuttings or saplings is ideal over the planting of direct cuttings to ensure good establishment of mulberry garden.

Raising of mulberry sapling

Sapling is rooted cutting of specific age (4 or 6 months)

and height (1.0-1.5 meters) raised in a nursery to establish low bush, or high bush or tree mulberry plantation. The saplings get established quickly, grow vigorously and uniformly and ensure high survival. Saplings should be raised to match its availability during the regular planting season. Therefore, 4 or 6 months in advance of the planting season, preparation should start for raising saplings.

A flat land nearer to water source is preferred as nursery site. Well drainable land with loamy soil is ideal for nursery. The land must be ploughed or dug 45 cm to 60 cm deep. Allow the soil for weathering in sun for 2-3 weeks. Land is again ploughed two or more times to bring the soil to fine tilt. Rootstocks, pebbles and weeds should be removed at the time of ploughing and the land should be leveled. Generally, the nursery area accounts for about 5% of the total area to be brought under regular plantation.

Land prepared is divided into a number of small units in order to prepare the nursery bed. The size of the bed can vary according to the need, requirement of sapling besides management system. A bed size of 240 cm (L) × 120 cm (W) can accommodate 180 cuttings (row to row 20 cm distance and cutting to cutting in a row at 8 cm distance) to raise 3-4 months old saplings. To raise 5-6 months old saplings the same bed can accommodate 100 cuttings (row to row 30 cm and cutting to cutting 10 cm distance). Each bed on all sides should be separated by a bund of 20 to 30 cm width and height and provided with irrigation channel of 20 cm-30 cm width and 15 -20 cm deep. The following measures are required before planting cuttings in the bed:

- Add 20 kg of organic manure (FYM) to each bed and mix thoroughly with soil.
- In case of clay or black cotton soil add 50 kg of sand per bed and mix with soil uniformly.
- Mix 10 gm of BHC per bed to avoid possible termite infestation.

Preparation of cuttings: Plants selected for preparation of cuttings must be healthy and free from scale insect, tukra infestation etc. The shoots should be 6-9 months old and should have attained a thickness of 10-15 mm diameter. The shoot lower portion and tender-green upper portion of the stem are not fit to be used for cuttings. The middle portion of uniform thickness is used. Cuttings of 15-20 cm length with 3-4 good buds are necessary for raising 3-4 months old saplings. For raising 5-6 months old saplings, cuttings are made a little longer of 23-25 cm size. Sharp knife must be used to get clean-cut ends without damaging the bark.

Availability of cuttings from one plant:

- Weight of one cutting = 10 gm approximately
- One plant has at least 3 branches and one plant has at least 5 cuttings. Therefore, one plant has 3 × 5 = 15 cuttings.
- Weight of 15 effective cuttings = 15 × 10 = 150 gm
- Weight of non-effective cuttings 25% i.e. 150 × 25% = 37.5 gm
- Total weight of cuttings available from one plant = 150 + 37.5 = 187.5 or 190 gm

Availability of cuttings in different spacing from one acre of land is indicated below (Table 2.7):

Table 2.7: Availability of cuttings in different spacing

Spacing (feet)	*No. of plants per acre*	*Total cuttings weight (kg)*	*Effective cuttings weight (kg)*	*No. of effective cuttings*
2 × 2	10900	2070	1635	163500
2 × 3	7250	1378	1088	108750
3 × 3	4850	920	728	72750

Transportation and storing of cuttings: Cuttings are to be planted immediately after preparation. Due to unavoidable circumstances, if mulberry cuttings are to be transported over long distances or stored for 2-3 days, the same should be done carefully so that the cuttings should not dry. Keep the cuttings in wet gunny cloth, if they are not planted immediately after preparation. Dressed shoots are preferred for transportation in comparison to whole shoot or stem as such, as the volume can be reduced considerably more than prepared cuttings, which dry too fast. Dressed shoots are transported during cooler hours, especially during night over long distances. Prepared cuttings, if required to store, should be bundled with all buds in one direction and kept over a wet sand bed with the buds pointing upward under shade. It can be covered with a thin layer of hay. The sand bed and hay covering must be sprinkled with water daily to avoid drying of cuttings. Cuttings can be stored in this way for 2-3 days.

Planting: Nursery beds can be adequately watered and made wet one or two days earlier to planting. Make each row at a distance of 20 cm or 30 cm as required with the help of a rope. In each row by using a pointed stick make small hole at 8 cm or 10 cm distance to insert cuttings. To avoid fungal attack, cuttings may be dipped in 0.2 per cent Bavestin solution for 10-15 minutes. Cuttings must be planted in the hole in a slightly slanting position, bud turned up, exposing only one bud above the surface of the soil. The soil around the cutting must be pressed firmly after planting.

Irrigation: One irrigation must be provided immediately after planting, by light flooding of each bed. Subsequent irrigation is given once in 3-5 days in case of sandy loam, silt loam or red soil and once in 7-8 days in case of black cotton soil or clay soil.

Weeding: Nursery bed must be kept free from all kinds of weeds. At least two rounds of manual weeding are required, first after 25-30 days and second after 55-60 days of planting. Only light harrowing using weeding sickle or weeding fork should be attempted without disturbing the sprouted cuttings. Walking or sitting on the bed should be avoided.

Fertilizer application: Chemical fertilizer must be applied in the nursery when sapling attains 25-30 cm height in about 55-60 days after planting, preferably after the second round of weeding operation. Urea @ 0.5 kg can be applied per bed, followed by light irrigation.

Plant protection: Leaf spot is the most common disease in nursery. Application of 0.1 per cent Bavistin twice at an interval of 15-20 days is recommended. Spraying of 0.1 per cent Rogor to control thrips and 0.1 per cent Melasystax to control mites are recommended, incase infestation occurs.

Uprooting and planting of saplings: Three to four months old saplings are ready for transplantation to establish bush system of plantation in 60 cm × 60 cm or 90 cm × 90 cm or Indo-Japanese type of spacing. For tree plantation or for raising high bush adopting wider spacing and high crown height, 5-6 month old saplings are used. Good saplings will attain a height of 90 cm to 120 cm in 3-4 months and about 150 cm in 5-6 months in nursery beds. Plot should be made ready before uprooting of sapling from nursery bed. Two or three days before uprooting of saplings, nursery bed should be adequately watered for easy removal. Nursery bed is loosened with the help of crowbar or guddali and saplings are taken out one by one, without damaging the main roots. After uprooting, preservation of saplings should be avoided as far as possible and must be taken to the planting site immediately. If long distance transportation is required, saplings must be packed in bundles, covered with wet gunny cloth and taken to the planting site during cooler hours. Saplings should be planted immediately after uprooting and as soon as they are received at the planting site, in the pits prepared for regular plantation. Only one sapling per pit should be planted. Under bush system of plantation (60 cm × 60 cm or 90 cm × 90 cm), after planting the sapling, the stem is cut at a uniform height of 30 cm above the ground level. In high bush or tree plantation the stem is cut at the height of the crown to be maintained.

Mulberry being a perennial plant, its initial establishment is important to ensure continuous high yield of leaves over the years. Direct cutting plantation does not ensure good establishment and gap filling of failed pits in established gardens is not successful practically, especially in close system of cultivation. Sapling ensures successful establishment of garden. It is therefore a viable proposition to raise saplings in large scale commercially and make them available to farmers at appropriate time. Saplings can be raised directly in nursery bed or in polythene bags of 20-25 cm height and 10-15 cm diameter, filled with mixture of soil, organic manure and sand. The polythene bags should be provided with holes at the bottom to drain excess water. Saplings in polythene bags are easy to maintain and transport.

Chawki mulberry garden

Among the several factors that contribute to successful young age silkworm rearing such as temperature, humidity, disease-free seed, hygiene etc. supply of highly nutritious leaves suitable to the age and stage of silkworm plays an important role in the harvest of stable cocoon crop. Though the requirement of leaf at this stage is only about 6 per cent of the total quantum, but need nutritive, soft and succulent leaves or high moisture protein and carbohydrate content. Mostly, the general mulberry garden raised commercially for rearing silkworm crops do not produce such specific high quality leaves. Therefore, a separate package has been developed to raise mulberry garden exclusively for producing chawki leaves for rearing young age silkworm larvae to harvest successful cocoon crop.

Selection of site: The plantation should be taken up in flat lands of porous and fertile soil. Land preparation procedure is same as that of general mulberry garden.

Mulberry varieties: Mulberry varieties viz., S54, K2, S36 and S30 are preferred for chawki rearing and thus raising for chawki garden.

Plant spacing and establishment of garden: Plant spacing recommended is 60 cm × 60 cm. Therefore, existing mulberry garden of S30, S36, S54 or K2 variety with plant spacing of 60 cm × 60 cm can also be converted to chawki garden, following the recommended manure and fertilizer application and pruning schedules. In case of new garden, land preparation, pit making or trench opening (45 cm deep) and other procedures are same as in general plantation. Three to four months old saplings must be used as planting material. It is ideal to take up the plantation during rainy season. Weeding, fertilizer application, irrigation and other cultural operations are followed as recommended for establishment of general mulberry garden. However, Farm Yard Manure (FYM) is applied @ 40 MT/ha/yr, in two split doses of 20 MT before planting and 20 MT after 6 months of establishment. Though the garden will be ready for light leaf harvest after 6 months of planting, it is advisable not to go for either regular leaf harvest or pruning till the completion of one year and full establishment of garden. After completion of one year, plants should be pruned by giving the base cut at 30 cm above ground level.

Schedule of activity: In the establishd chawki garden, training schedules and leaf harvests are planned to obtain 8 harvests in a year. The schedule of activity is indicated in Table 2.8:

Table 2.8: Schedule of activity for chawki garden

Activities	*Period (Progressive days)*
Base cut or bottom pruning	'0' days
Start leaf harvest after 35 days of basal cut	35 days
1st leaf harvest (10 days)	45 days
Completion of 1st leaf harvest, clip the terminal bud	45 days
25 days from top clipping, start harvesting of shoot -lets	70 days
1st shoot-let harvest (10 days)	80 days
After completion of shoot-let harvest give basal pruning	80 days

Repeat this cycle 4 times a year to have total 8 crops. Out of 8 crops, I, III. V and VII, crops are by leaf plucking and II, IV, VI and VIII crops by shoot let feeding,

Manure and fertilizer schedules: FYM is applied @ 40 MT/ha/yr, in two split doses of 20 MT each after base cut (1st and 5th or 3rd and 7th crop). Fertilizer dose recommended is 225 kg N: 150 kg P: 150 kg K per hectare per year and it is applied in 8 equal split doses. Thus, NPK input may be calculated as 28 kg N: 19 kg P: 19 kg K per crop. If the soil is found to be alkaline, ammonium sulphate, single super phosphate and sulphate of potash may be applied.

Table 2.9: Commercial straight fertilizers to be mixed for application

Area	*Ammonium Sulphate (20.5% N)*	*Single super Phosphate (16.5%P)*	*Sulphate of Potash (48% K)*	*Total quantity per dose (kg)*
Hectare	137	115	40	292
Acre	55	46	16	117

Irrigation requirement: Mulberry leaves meant for young age silkworm rearing should have high moisture content of above 75 per cent. To ensure this, frequent irrigation at 4 to 7 days interval @ 1.5 to 2.0 acre-inch should be provided depending upon the soil conditions. Light sandy soil requires frequent irrigation at fewer intervals and heavy clay loam soil requires less frequent irrigation at long intervals. Roughly, 34,000 to 45,000 gallons of water are required per acre per irrigation. This can be provided through ridges and furrows system or sprinkler.

Leaf yield: Adoption of the above method will ensure roughly 28 MT of chawki leaf per hectare per year in 8 crops. Leaf yield per crop ranges from 3000 kg to 4000 kg. All the leaves produced are fit for chawki rearing, unlike in regular mulberry garden where only about 20 per cent of total leaf yield is fit for chawki rearing, which is about 7 MT/ha/yr. Leaf yield in exclusive chawki garden raised is adequate to rear 1,40,000-160,000 laying/yr/ha or roughly 17,000 to 18,000 laying per crop or 64,000 Dfls/acre/year.

Leaf quality: Qualitatively, the leaves produced in chawki garden are far superior with 75-80 per cent moisture content, 25 per cent leaf protein and 13 per cent leaf sugar in comparison to leaves obtained in general mulberry garden, with 70-74 per cent moisture, 20-21 per cent leaf protein and 11% leaf sugar.

PACKAGE OF PRACTICES FOR SEED CROP REARING

Though mulberry is a hardy plant capable of thriving under different agro-climatic zones and soil conditions but it responds extremely well to optimum irrigation and appropriate fertilizer application. The leaf yield can be stepped up to 40 MT and over /ha/yr. The recommended package of practices for mulberry cultivation under irrigated conditions for seed crop rearing involves use of high-yielding mulberry varieties, proper establishment of mulberry plantation, optimum inputs by way of irrigation, fertilizer application and organic manure, inter-cultivation, moisture conservation measures and plant protection from diseases and pests. Mulberry is a perennial crop and once it is properly established during the first year, it can come to full yielding capacity in the second or third year and lasts for about 15-20 years, without significant reduction in quality and quantity of leaf production. It is therefore of utmost importance that initial planting and establishment of the crop are ensured.

Selection and preparation of land

Flat or slightly sloping land is suitable for mulberry cultivation. More sloppy or steep land in hilly tracts needs proper soil conservation steps through contour bunds, drains and even bench terracing. Loamy to sandy loam and clay loam soil are ideal for mulberry cultivation. Too acidic (pH: < 5) and too alkaline (pH: > 8) soils need corrective measures bring the pH nearer to neutral (pH = 7) level through application of lime or gypsum respectively,

Before the onset of monsoon, land should be ploughed deep followed by 2 to 3 times light ploughing to bring the soil to a fine tilt and free of weeds. Land is then leveled. Finally, Farm Yard Manure (FYM) @ 40 MT/ha/yr should be applied and incorporated in the soil. Land is then divided into plots of convenient sizes. Optimum spacing recommended is 60 cm × 60 cm in the plains and 90 cm × 90 cm in hilly areas.

In the close system of plantation (60 cm × 60 cm), ridges (15 cm height) and furrows (15 cm deep) are made alternatively at a distance of 60 cm. When spacing of 90 cm × 90 cm is adopted in hilly areas, pit system of plantation is ideal. For this purpose, pits of 35 cm × 35 cm

× 35 cm are dug and then filled with a mixture of FYM and soil. Mulberry plant grows luxuriously in wider spacing because of more aeration and space when compared to closer spacing. S36 mulberry variety with Indo-Japanese (paired row) system of plantation [(90 + 180) + 60 cm] is recommended for seed crop. This system of plantation accommodates same number of plants as in existing spacing and also facilitates partial mechanization by power tiller. As the recommended varieties are not still very popular in the field, newly evolved improved mulberry variety V1 may be utilized for popularization. The variety S36 and V1 are having better moisture content, protein (%) and sugar (%) than other existing varieties in the field.

Planting material and planting

High yielding mulberry varieties recommended for commercial exploitation should be selected for planting. The cutting of 3 to 4 months old saplings can be used as planting material. When cuttings are used, it should be made from mature shoots of 6 to 8 months old. Each cutting should be 15-18 cm in length, 1-1.5 cm in diameter with 3-4 buds. Two cuttings are planted along at each spot. The distance between two such spots is kept at 60 cm in order to achieve 60 cm × 60 cm spacing. When saplings are used, one sapling at each spot is adequate.

In hilly areas, in pit system of plantation, three cuttings of 20-22 cm length with 4-5 buds and about 1.5 cm in diameter are planted per pit with a spacing of 15 cm between cuttings in a triangle. Cuttings should be inserted deep in the soil leaving just only one bud exposing above the ground level. Soil around each cutting should be pressed well to keep it firmly in the soil. When saplings are used for planting, one sapling per pit is adequate. In general, plantation work is carried out during rainy season for better establishment. Irrigation should be provided just after plantation, through furrows in close system (60 cm × 60 cm) and through inter connected basins in pit system (90 cm × 90 cm). Filling is carried out where cuttings or saplings do not sprout/survive after 2-3 weeks' time, to ensure optimum plant density.

Initial care and input during establishment period

Regular irrigation must be provided at an interval of 9-10 days. A light hoeing and weeding is carried out about two months after plantation. In close system, when the plantation is 3 months old, the first dose of fertilizer, NPK @ 50 kg: 50 kg: 50 kg per hectare is applied. After 6 months of planting, the first crop through light harvest is possible. The second weeding and second dose of fertilizer @ 50 kg N/ha should be given after 3 weeks of first leaf harvest. After the third leaf harvest, bottom pruning is carried out at height of 20 cm above ground level.

In hilly areas, weeding is done through light hoeing after 2 and 4 months of planting. After 5 months of planting, the first dose of fertilizer is given @ NPK 50 kg: 25 kg: 25 kg per hectare. The first crop harvest can be taken when plantation is 6 months old. Weeding and second dose of fertilizer @ 50 kg N/ha is given after first leaf harvest. Weeding and application of third dose of fertilizer @ NPK 50 kg: 25 kg: 25 kg are carried out after second leaf harvest. Irrigation must be provided regularly at an interval of 8-10 days, through inter connected basin in a row. Where slop is more, either sprinkler or drip irrigation is recommended. After completion of third leaf harvest, bottom pruning is carried out at a height of 30 cm above ground level.

Maintenance of mulberry garden

Systematic cultivation practices for maintenance of mulberry garden from second year of planting onwards are briefly described below:

(a) **Irrigation:** Irrigate the mulberry garden in 10 days in loamy soils and once in 15 days in clayey soils. Quantum of water should be 1.5 acre inch (34,000 gallons or 148,500 liters) per irrigation. In furrow irrigation, it is necessary to maintain the depth of channel at 15 cm deep, to ensure full quantum of irrigation. In 90 cm × 90 cm spacing also, furrow irrigation can be followed from second year onwards. In case of sprinkler method, irrigation @ 80 mm/week is suggested. During mulberry growth, the plot should be free from weeds for quality leaf production.

(b) Manure and fertilizer schedule: With the start of monsoon FYM/compost should be applied @ 40 MT/ ha/yr in two split doses (I & III crop). Chemical fertilizer is applied in 5 or 6 split doses depending upon the number of shoot/leaf harvests. Recommended NPK dose is @ 350 kg: 140 kg: 140 kg in shoot harvest system (5 crops) or leaf plucking system (6 crops) per hectare per year.

Table 2.10: Fertilizer and manure schedule in close system of plantation

Crop No.	*FYM (MT/ha/yr)*	*Fertilizer (kg/ha/crop) Shoot harvest*		
		N	*P*	*K*
1	20	70	28	28
2		70	28	28
3	20	70	28	28
4		70	28	28
5		70	28	28
Total	40	350	140	140

In hilly areas, where wider spacing is recommended, FYM is applied @ 40 MT /ha/yr. However, the chemical fertilizer is applied @ NPK 250 kg: 100 kg: 100 kg /ha/yr in 5 split doses as shown in Table 2.11.

Table 2.11: Fertilizer and manure application in pit system of plantation

Crop No.	*FYM (MT/ha/yr)*	*Fertilizer dose (kg/ha/crop)*		
		N	*P*	*K*
1	20	50	50	50
2		50		
3	20	50	50	50
4		50		
5		50		
Total	40	250	100	100

(c) **Leaf yields and harvest:** Quantum of leaf produced varies depending upon the mulberry variety, season of harvest, system of cultivation and region. In the plains, the expected leaf yield is 40 MT/ha/yr through 5 shoot harvests or 6 leaf plucking. In the hilly region, the leaf yield is roughly 25 MT/ha/yr through 5 leaf plucking

Table 2.12: Schedule of operations for maintenance of mulberry garden for shoot harvest

Activities	*Schedule*
1st pruning combining with shoot harvest	With the commencement of South-West monsoon rains (early June)
1st weeding and inter-cultivation	Within a week after pruning (2nd week of June)
Application of FYM @ 20 MT/ha	Within a fortnight after pruning (mid June)
1st dose of fertilizer application	Within a month after pruning (early July)
1st shoot harvest	By pruning (mid August)
2nd weeding and inter-cultivation	Within a month of pruning (2nd fortnight of August)
2nd dose of fertilizer application	Within a month of 1st harvest (mid September)
2nd shoot harvest	By pruning (mid October)
Application of FYM @ 20 MT/ha	Within a fortnight after pruning (2nd fortnight of October)
3rd weeding and inter-cultivation	Within a month of 2nd harvest (2nd week of November)
3rd dose of fertilizer application	Within 4 weeks of 3rd weeding (1st week of December)
3rd shoot harvest	By pruning (mid January)
4th weeding and inter-cultivation	Within a week of 3rd harvest (3rd week of January)
4th dose of fertilizer application	Within a month of 3rd harvest (mid February)
4th shoot harvest of leaves	By pruning (late March)
5th weeding and inter-cultivation	Within a month of 4th harvest (1st week of April)
5th dose of fertilizer application	Within a month of 4th harvest (late April)
5th shoot harvest	By pruning (early June)

followed by shoot dressing at 45 cm height from ground level. In North East and North, the yield is about 20 MT/ha/yr through three leaf harvest followed by shoot dressing at 60 cm height from ground level. In North

Table 2.13: Schedule of operations for maintenance of mulberry garden for leaf plucking

Activities	*Schedule*
1st Bottom pruning	With the commencement of South-West monsoon rains (early June)
1st weeding and inter-cultivation	Within a week after pruning (2nd week of June)
Application of bulk organic manure @ 20 MT/ha	Within a fortnight after pruning (3rd week of June)
1st dose of fertilizer application	Within a month after pruning (early July)
1st harvest of leaves	By leaf plucking (mid August)
2nd weeding and inter-cultivation	Within a week of 1st harvest (3rd week of August)
2nd dose of fertilizer application	Within 3 weeks of last harvest (2nd week of September)
2nd harvest of leaves	By leaf plucking (Early October)
3rd dose of fertilizer application	Within 3 weeks of 2nd harvest (4th week of October)
3rd harvest of leaves	By leaf picking (Late November)
2nd bottom pruning	Immediately after 3rd leaf harvest (late November)
Application of FYM @ 20 MT/ha	Within a fortnight after pruning (1st week of December)
3rd weeding and inter-cultivation	Within a fortnight after 2nd pruning (1st week of December)
4th dose of fertilizer application	Within a month after 2nd pruning (3rd week of December)
4th harvest of leaves	By leaf picking (early February)
5th dose of fertilizer application	Within 3 weeks after 4th harvest (4th week of February)
5th harvest of leaves	By leaf picking (1st week of April)
4th weeding and inter-cultivation	Within a week of 5th harvest (2nd week of April)
6th harvest of leaves	By leaf picking (late May)

East including West Bengal, where shoot harvest is followed, it is done at 15 cm height from ground level. In the South, the same is practised at 20 cm height from ground level. In the above region, step shoot harvest has been recommended by pruning at 20 cm (basal pruning), 50cm, 40 cm and 20 cm (basal pruning) for the 1st, 2nd, 3rd and 4th shoot harvest, to facilitate shoot rearing.

Table 2.14: Schedule of operations for maintenance of mulberry garden in hilly areas

Activities	*Schedule*
Annual basal pruning	After commencement of South-West monsoon rains (4th week of June)
1st weeding and inter-cultivation	1st week after pruning
Sowing of green manure crop like horse-gram	2nd week after pruning
1st dose of fertilizer application	One month after pruning (4th week of July)
1st leaf harvest	Mid August
2nd dose of fertilizer application	Within 3 weeks of 1st leaf harvest (late September)
2nd leaf harvest	Mid October
Weeding and mulching of green manure crop	Within a week of 2nd leaf harvest (3rd week of November)
Sowing green manure seeds	Within 3 weeks of 2nd leaf harvest (4th week of November)
3rd dose of fertilizer application	4th week of November
3rd leaf harvest followed by middle pruning	1st week of January
Application of FYM	3rd week of January
4th dose of fertilizer application	Within 3 weeks of 3rd leaf harvest (1st week of February)
4th leaf harvest	1st week of March
Weeding/mulching of green manure crop	Within a week of 4th leaf harvest (2nd week of April)
5th dose of fertilizer application	Within 3 weeks of 4th leaf harvest
5th leaf harvest	Mid May
Basal pruning at crown height	June

Schedule of activities for maintenance of mulberry garden: Schedule of operations depends upon the system of cultivation, number of leaf or shoot harvests, season of harvest and the region of cultivation. These activities are described separately below for different systems as applicable in Indian sericultural States.

PRUNING AND HARVESTING OF MULBERRY

Mulberry is the perennial plant and in order to improve leaf yield, quality and repeated leaf harvesting, it is necessary to train it into a definite shape by artificial pruning. Pruning is one of the cardinal principles of mulberry leaf production technology. Trimming or shaping of plants into a definite form is essential in mulberry cultivation for easy harvest and inter cultivation. If mulberry plants left to grow freely they become trees. In such cases harvesting of mulberry leaves becomes poor and it becomes very difficult to pluck the leaves. Also it is difficult to employ preventive measures against pests and diseases. Pruning helps to divert the energies of the plant for optimum production of leaf. Usually more branches grow on the top of any mulberry plant than can persist, therefore, there is overcrowding. By pruning, the residual branches receive more energy and hence make quicker growth and yield more and quality leaves. Therefore, it is essential to maintain definite shape and size of the plant for easy harvest and also to carry out management activities to accelerate uniform growth in order to harvest increased quantity of leaf during the required period. By adopting proper trimming and method of pruning, it is possible to get three harvests in sub-temperate region in a year and up to five to six harvests under tropical climates. Every year a certain pattern of pruning should be followed to harvest good quality of mulberry leaf in large amount.

Types of pruning: The pruning is classified by the height of the mulberry stump into four forms viz., ground/ basal pruning, middle pruning, half height pruning and top clipping.

(i) **Ground/bottom pruning:** In this type of pruning, branches are cut at the base of the stem at ground level. Under the Kolar system and strip system of cultivation, the whole shoot is cut to the ground level at each harvest. In all, five harvests are made in a year and thus plant receives five prunings. This is suitable only for the areas where mulberry sprouts throughout the year with no dormant period for bud sprouting. This type of severe pruning, however, needs heavy fertilizer doses and irrigation. Therefore, it is adopted in areas with high rainfall, comparatively high temperature and high densely planted areas.

In tropical climate of India, where mulberry sprouts throughout the year, mostly pruning season depends on rainfall conditions and plant is pruned only once in a year 10-15 cm above the ground level during June-July just at the onset of the monsoon.

(ii) **Middle pruning:** Middle pruning is a method of cutting the branches of bush mulberry at the height of 45-60 cm above the ground level during December-January. Middle pruning stimulates sprouting of the lower buds in the bush mulberry during winter season. This method is adopted in areas with less rainfall, flood susceptible fields, border mulberry fields and sparsely planted gardens.

Merits and demerits of ground and middle pruning

Ground level pruning	*Middle level pruning*
Merits	
➢ Easy to harvest leaves	➢ Can be saved from damages of snow, flood and frost
➢ Easy to control diseases and pests	➢ High viability of plants leading to adequate yield
➢ Early 1st harvest	➢ Strong against dwarf diseases and drought damage
➢ High yield	➢ High life expectancy

Demerits

- More chances of dwarf diseases and cold damage
- Leaves at lower part of the branch becomes usually dirty and hence unfit for silkworm feeding
- The plant can not grow easily if the land is not rich in nutrient
- Economic age of plant is usually less
- Takes longer time to grow to reach to the level of a tree
- Much effort is needed to harvest leaves and to control diseases
- Many noxious insects prevails as pests

Pruning should be done simultaneously or immediately after harvesting as soon as possible so that latent or auxiliary buds will be promoted to sprout and grow fast. Otherwise, the buds will be delayed to sprout causing decrease leaf yield. In any pruning system it is important to maintain the mulberry plant in proper shape, size, height and form. Therefore, it is necessary to carry out systematic pruning together with trimming of unnecessary and dead branches.

(iii) Top clipping: Top clipping is a type of training of mulberry plant in order to produce more branches and leaves for rearing of silkworm. It consists of clipping off the top of the branch but not the whole branch. It is practised usually during winter season. It has more advantages in the production and harvestation of quality mulberry leaves. It is only a kind of branch training and hence does not alter the shape of the plant.

Harvesting: Choosing the proper method of harvesting is important not only for obtaining good food for the silkworms but also for achieving full productivity potential of the plant. The harvesting methods of mulberry leaves depend on the rearing practices in vogue. Leaf is either fed to the silkworm as a whole or in the cut form and in some cases or areas whole shoot or branch is used for feeding. With the advancement of technology, in some parts of the country, the whole shoot is provided as feed to the late stages of the silkworm. This system of rearing is known as shoot rearing. This type of rearing is practised to suit the availability of labour and intensity of rearing practices. However, for rearing of young silkworm larvae, individual tender leaf has to be harvested necessarily. There are three methods of mulberry leaf harvesting followed in different parts of the country -

(i) Leaf plucking

(ii) Whole shoot harvest

(iii) Branch harvest

(i) Leaf plucking: Leaf plucking is the most common method of harvesting of leaves for feeding to the silkworm larvae. In this method, leaf is picked individually from the mulberry plant. In tropical regions of India, because of continuous rearing throughout the year, harvesting through leaf picking can be done 6-7 times from the same mulberry field. After taking 6-7 harvests, the plants are pruned almost at the ground level during monsoon. Leaf picking takes more time to harvest leaves besides leading to employ more labourers. When individual leaves are picked from the mulberry plant, the tender ones are fed to the young silkworms and matured ones to the late age silkworms. In India, leaf picking mostly starts about 10 weeks after bottom pruning and subsequent picking at an interval of 7-8 weeks, thus obtaining 6-7 harvests in a year.

There are various types of plucking of leaves. For example, the leaves are plucked leaving behind a part of the leaf blade. In another method, the leaves are plucked close to the center of the stipule either by finger or using leaf pluckier. In the third method, leaves are plucked by hand at random. During harvesting, half of the leaf petiole is left on the branch itself, which protects the auxiliaries bud from getting damaged. This results in improved sprouting of buds. Since a large amount of leaves are required for rearing grown-up silkworms, the third method is often adopted.

(ii) **Whole shoot harvest:** In this method, young shoots are harvested one by one. Harvested shoots are chopped and provided as feed to the later stages of the silkworms. Sometimes, whole shoots are given as feeding to the 4th and 5th stage of the silkworms. However, whole shoot rearing is not very common in India and hence shoot harvest is also not popular. Whole shoot harvest method is practised in Kolar region in Karnataka state and in Malda district of West Bengal. The branches are cut almost close to the ground level. Shoots are generally harvested at an interval of 10-12 weeks and thus 4-5 harvests can be obtained in a year. However, with the advancement of rearing technology and adoption of shelf/shoot rearing, this method of harvest of mulberry leaf is becoming more and more popular.

(iii) **Branch harvest:** Entire branch with leaves on it is harvested and fed to the silkworms especially during 4th and 5th instars of silkworm rearing. The annual branches and shoots are cut off together from the base of the branch. Feeding the silkworms directly with the branches is called 'branch rearing'. Sometimes, after harvesting the branches, persons may also pick off the leaves from the branches to feed to the silkworms. It has certain advantages viz.:

- Easy in low-cut formed pruning
- Saves labour in harvest
- Help in maintaining hygienic conditions in rearing room
- Better quality of leaves as they are attached to the branches maintaining prolonged succulence of leaves
- Requirement of rearing equipments is reduced because of shelf or floor rearing where the branches along with leaves are provided directly as feed to the silkworms.

Influence of harvesting on physiology of mulberry plant: Harvesting of leaves affects the physiological functions of plant and causes a drastic loss of mulberry plant organ (leaf) required for photosynthesis, consequently a corresponding loss of rootlets leading to a reduction of storing capacity of nutrients needed for recovery. If the leaves are removed either by plucking or branch/shoot harvest, then corresponding loss will lead to a diminished leaf yield in the subsequent-generation. It takes about 45 days for the root system to recover its original conditions. By retaining some leaves on the top of the branches, stress to the plant can be alleviated to certain extent. Thus maintaining of proper harvesting method together with balanced harvesting and efficient management practices ensure the maintenance of plant

Harvesting and yield of mulberry: The harvesting amount of mulberry can be expressed by quantity of leaf harvested, amount of mulberry shoots cut, amount of young shoots collected etc. However, the ratio of various parts of mulberry shoots collected for rearing of silkworms varies according to the mulberry variety, plant density, the age of the plant, amount of manuring, the climatic conditions of the region, training method and the system adopted for the cultivation of the plant. However, the usual standard is:

- The young shoots covers about 50%.
- The ratio of leaf blades with petioles account for 75% of the total harvested yield and the shoot-lets contribute about 20-25%.
- The ratio of leaf blade to cut shoots covers about 40%.

The amount of leaf harvested is closely related to the age of the plant. There is rapid increase in the quantity of leaf following few years of planting, but after the plant achieves its maturity, the increasing ratio of harvesting amount somewhat decreases. There is gradual decrease in the yield with the aging of the plant. The duration after planting up to the period of aging differs according to the variety, manuring, nature of harvesting, quality of soil, climatic conditions, training of the plant etc. However, the common standard is 15-20 years in basal pruning and in case of medium and high level pruning it is even more than 30 years, after which the harvesting decreases to less than half of the maximum harvesting amount.

Time of harvest: Harvesting time influences the quality of leaves. Fresher the leaves better to the feed value for the silkworm. Therefore, every effort is to be made to harvest quality leaves and keep them in fresh conditions for longer period. The leaves harvested in the afternoon wither more rapidly in comparison to leaves harvested in the morning due to comparatively less water and more carbohydrate content. Therefore, it is generally recommended to harvest leaves early in the morning and preserve it properly to maintain its quality and feed value for the vigorous growth of the silkworm.

Preservation of leaves: Generally, the leaves are harvested in the morning and are preserved for successive feedings up to 24 hrs as per necessity. During this period leaves should be preserved in moist, cool and clean places in order to preserve their succulence. The individual leaf harvested should be collected in bamboo baskets covered with wet gunny cloth and transported to the preservation room. Heaping up of leaves leads to fermentation and high storage temperature. Therefore, to avoid this, the leaves should be spread loosely in layers and covered with gunny cloth. The ideal condition for preservation of leaf is below 20°C atmospheric temperature and over 90% of relative humidity.

If leaves are stored for longer period, considerable nutritional changes take place. The proteins are broken down to amino acids and carbohydrates to simple sugars in the harvested leaves, which are utilized by leaves during storage for respiration. Thus leaves become poor in their nutritive value. Therefore, long storage of leaves should be avoided in order to preserve nutritive value of leaves to harvest successful stable cocoon crop.

Yield estimation: The production of mulberry leaves is the only basis for determining the number of Dfls of silkworms to be reared. A precise estimate of leaf yield is the only basis for planning a balanced programme of leaf harvest and rearing of silkworm. Production of leaf yield is influenced by the variety of mulberry cultivated, planting density, age of plant, manuring and culturing, time and method of harvesting, training of plant etc. Leaf output can be estimated as indicated below:

(a) Estimation according to total shoot length: Yield of mulberry can be approximately estimated from the total shoot length of the plant. According to the growth conditions mulberry fields are classified into different categories before sprouting. For the purpose, length of branches per plant is measured and total length per unit area based on number of plants is calculated. The output of leaves per unit area can be computed by using the leaf yield per meter of branches as follows:

$$\frac{\text{Total branch length of plants investigated}}{\text{Number of plants investigated}} = \text{Average total branch length per plant (m)}$$

Average total branch length per plant (m) × leaf yield per meter of branch (kg) = leaf yield per plant (kg).

Leaf yield per plant (kg) × actual number of plants in the field = Total leaf yield of whole field (kg).

(b) Estimation by practice: Select 20-30 plants or certain number of plants in a unit area. Find out the leaf yield per plant by harvesting all leaves from these plants and then calculate the output per unit area of the whole mulberry field. Add 2-3% more yield in the total per day under normal conditions to the day of actual harvest.

Output of leaves (kg) = Average leaf yield per plant (kg) × actual number of plants per unit area

However, the best way to estimate the leaf yield is by accumulating experiences from continuous practices. On the basis of past experiences, the silkworm rearer works out the increase or decrease in the yield of mulberry as compared to the condition of the previous years with reference to the actual yield and the conditions of the mulberry grown.

3

SILKWORM AND ITS RACES

CLASSIFICATION OF SILKWORM

Mulberry silkworm (*Bombyx mori)* is the common silkworm belonging to the phylum Arthropoda, order Lepidoptera; class Insecta belonging to the family Bombycidae. It is under division Endopteregota and undergoes complete metamorphosis with egg, larva, pupa and adult (moth) in its life cycle.

Systematic Position

Phylum	Arthropoda
Class	Insecta
Sub-class	Pterygota
Division	Endopteregota
Order	Lepidoptera
Super family	Bombycoidia
Family	Bombycidae
Genus	*Bombyx*
Species	*mori*

Salient features

Insecta

- Body is metamerically segmented.
- Body is bilaterally symmetrical.
- Body is divided into three distinct regions i.e. head, thorax and abdomen.
- Head bears one pair of antennae and usually one pair of compound eyes.

- Thorax consists of three segments, bears three pairs of jointed legs, usually with two pairs of wings which may be sometimes one pair and rarely absent (louse).
- Insects are the only invertebrates that can fly.
- Abdomen is divided into 7-11 segments, which are without ambulatory appendages in the adult.
- Sexes are separate (diocious).
- Fertilization is usually internal.
- Insects are also known as hexapoda due to presence of six legs (3 pairs).

Lepidoptera

- Insects with two pairs of membranous wings.
- Body, wings and appendages covered with minute overlapping scales forming coloured pattern.
- Metamorphosis complete.
- Fore wings always larger than hind wings.
- Larvae are typical caterpillars with biting mouthparts, three pairs of thoracic legs (true) and five pairs of abdominal legs (pseudolegs).
- Adult mouthpart is of sucking type, maxillae modified into coiled proboscis.

Bombycoidea

- Proboscis absent or rarely developed.
- Antennae pectinate.
- CU_2 absent from both the wings.
- Maxillary palpi and tymphanal organs absent.
- Chetosema absent.

Bombycidae

- No proboscis.
- Antennae pectinate in both the sexes.
- Larvae elongated with mediodorsal horn (caudal horn) on the eighth abdominal segment.
- Producing silk.

Species of silkworms

The insects which are utilized for the production of commercial silk includes the following species:

(a) Mulberry silkworm *(Bombyx mori* Linnaeus)

(b) Japanese tasar silkworm *(Antheraea* yamama Guerin)

(c) Chinese tasar silkworm *(Antheraea pernyi* Guerin)

(d) Tasar silkworm *(Antheraea mylitta* Drury)

(e) Muga silkworm *(Antheraea assama* Heifer)

(f) Eri silkworm *(Philosamia cynthia ricini* Boisduval)

Life cycle and external morphology of silkworm

Among the caterpillars, which can produce silk, the mulberry silkworm (*Bombyx mori*) is the one that produces most beautiful product. Silkworm is a holometabolous insect and passes through a complete metamorphosis from egg to the adult stage. The two other stages between egg and adult are larva (caterpillar) and pupa (cocoon).

Egg: The silkworm eggs are tiny and measure approximately 1-1.3 mm in length and 0.9-1.2 mm in width. Eggs may be ovoid, flat, ellipsoid or oval with micropyle at the anterior pole and slightly off-centre. Mostly, the freshly laid eggs are pale yellow or dark yellow in colour. The colour of hibernating eggs laid by bivoltine or multivoltine races changes and becomes dark brown or purple.

Larva: Larva is popularly called silkworm caterpillar. It is the developmental stage of ingestion and nutrient accumulation to begin from newly hatched larva and end before spinning. Newly hatched silkworm larvae are black or dark brown in colour. It has a large head and body. The body is covered with bristles. There are four pairs of tubercles i.e. sub-dorsal, supra-spiracular, infra spiracular, and basal tubercle, each of which carries three to six setae. Young larvae soon after hatching start feeding on mulberry leaves and grow. This period is called first instar. After 3 days, larvae stops feeding and after 20-30 hrs they undergo ecdysis. The period of ecdysis is called the first moulting. After moulting, larvae starts feeding again, grow in size and weight and repeat the moulting process. In the common silkworm race, there are four moults and five larval instars. The duration of larval instars varies with the breed, temperature, humidity etc. Silkworms from first to third instars are referred as young (chawki) age silkworms and fourth and fifth instars as advanced (late) age silkworms. The fifth larval stage is the longest larval stage and shows maximum consumption of leaf. The growth rate during this stage is also extremely high. At the end of 5th stage, larvae stops feeding and start spinning from spinneret. In appearance, the larvae at this stage become lustrous and translucent. This stage is known as mature silkworms. From this stage onwards, the larvae spin cocoon and once the cocoon formation is over, the larvae moults inside and transforms itself into pupae. This is known as pupation. The body of silkworm is divisible into head, thorax and abdomen. The thorax is composed of three segments and abdomen 11 segments. Inter-segmental membranes join the successive segments. The head is composed of six segments, which are fused together. The second, fourth, fifth and sixth segments carry appendages, which are modified into antennae, mandibles, maxillae and labium respectively. There are six pairs of ocelli or larval eyes, which are located behind and a little above the base of antennae. The antenna is five segmented and is used as sensory organ. The mandibles are well developed and powerful and are adopted for mastication. Maxillae consist of cardo, strips, maxillary lobe and maxillary palpi. Maxillary lobe and maxillary palpi discriminate the taste of food. The thorax, which consists of three segments are called pre, meso and meta-thorax. Each of the three thoracic segments has one pair of legs. Each leg is composed of three jointed segments, which carries sharp distal claws. These legs are referred to as true legs. The claws help in holding the mulberry leaves while the larvae are feeding on it. The abdomen consists of eleven body segments, wherein last three segments i.e. 9th, 10th and 11th are fused together to form 9th segment, anal plate and the caudal legs. Thus, only nine segments can be distinguished in the abdomen. Each 3rd, 4th, 5th, 6th and 9th abdominal segment bears a pair of abdominal legs. These legs are fleshy, unjointed muscular protuberances and are known as pseudo-legs. Eighth abdominal segment on the dorsal side carries caudal horn. The abdominal legs at the extremity form a sort of disc with a series of inwardly curved hooks, which are arranged in semicircle and helps in crawling of the larvae. The abdominal segments on the ventral side of 8th and 9th segments carry sexual markings, which develop distinctly in 4th and 5th instars. In the female, the sexual markings appear as a pair of milky white spots, one each on the right and left side in 8th and 9th abdominal segments. These spots are known as Ishiwata's glands. The anterior pair situated in the 8th abdominal segment is known as Ishiwata's foregland and the posterior pair in 9th segment is referred as Ishiwata's hind glands. When the female larvae pupate had transformed in to an adult, the anterior Ishiwata gland becomes a pair of bursacopulatrix, recepticulum seminis and its duct while the posterior Ishiwata glands are modified to form the posterior part of oviduct and accessory gland. The reproductive gland in the male silkworm appears as a small milky white protuberance at the center of the ventral side between 8th and 9th abdominal segments. The gland is known as Herold's gland. When the larva transforms into an adult, the Herold's gland develops into seminal vesicle and ejaculatory duct. The male and female can be distinguished based on these glands during early 5th instar larvae. There are nine pairs of spiracles placed laterally on either side of the body. They are found on the first thoracic segment and from 1st to 8th abdominal segments. The spiracles are the part of respiratory system. Between the first and second thoracic segments, there is a pair of rudimentary spiracle. The size of the spiracles varies from breed to breed, individual to individual and from segment to segment. The spiracles on the 8th abdominal segment are the largest whereas those on the 2nd, 3rd and 4th are the smallest.

Pupa: The pupal stage is generally called resting or inactive stage in the life cycle of the silkworm, when it is incapable of feeding. This is a transitional stage during which definite changes take place. The mature silkworm larva passes through a pre-pupal stage before transforming into pupa. During pre-pupal stage the dissolution of the larval organs takes place and this is followed by formation of adult organs during the pupal stage. At the pupal stage, a pair of large compound eyes, a pair of large antennae, fore and hind wings and legs are prominent and it is much easier to differentiate male and female in the pupal stage than in the larval stage. The female pupa on the ventral side has a fine longitudinal line joining the 8th and 9th abdominal segment, while such a marking is absent in the case of male, which has a small opening in the 9th segment. Usually female is bigger and heavier than the male. Various tissues and organs present in the larva undergo histolysis in pupal stage and tissues and organs of the adult are in the process of histogenesis in this stage. There is no ocelli, abdominal appendages, silk glands, moulting glands etc. The cuticle of a freshly formed pupa is very soft and pale yellow in colour and gradually becomes darker.

Adult: The adult moth emerging from the pupa is called silk moth, which is incapable to fly because of its domestication for more than four thousand years. It does not feed during its adult life. The body of the moth is composed of three distinct segments viz., head, thorax and abdomen. The antennae are prominent, bipectinate and serrate. Two compound eyes are situated on either side of the head below the base of the antennae. In normal silk moths, compound eyes are usually black in colour due to tryptophane metabolites. The ocelli are absent. The mouthparts are located between the two compound eyes. The thorax consists of three segments namely prothorax, mesothorax and metathorax. The mesothorax is the largest and is pentagonal. All the segments are covered with hard chitinous scelrites. Each of the thoracic segments bears a pair of legs. Each of the thoracic leg is composed of five segments. The meso and meta thorax bear two pairs of wings—the forewings and hind wings. The forewings are larger, triangular in shape and are attached to the mesothorax. The forewings overlap the hind wings when the moth is in the resting position. The hind wings are smaller and are attached to the metathorax. The surfaces of wings are covered with fine scales. Thorax bears a pair of spiracles. Morphologically, male and female moths can easily be distinguished in the adult stage. In male silk moth while eight abdominal segments are visible, female has only seven such segments. There are six pairs of spiracles situated laterally on either side of the body. Female is less active than male and has smaller antennae, large blunt and fatter abdomen. At the caudal end, the male moth has a pair of hooks 'harps', while the female has knob like projections covered with sensory hairs.

Body temperature

As silkworm is poikilothermic, their body temperature fluctuates with changes in external environmental conditions. With the progress of development, the body temperature increases. Temperature is higher during the peak period of feeding and decreases thereafter. The factors affecting the body temperature of silkworm is ambient temperature, humidity, ventilation, supply of mulberry leaves and accumulation of waste materials in the rearing bed and population of density of larvae per unit area. Body temperature of pupa is low compared to 5th instar larvae but as soon as pupa metamorphoses into adult, the body temperature again increases. However, temperature of 24 –28°C and humidity of 75-85% is ideal for all activity of silkworm. Higher or lower temperature than the optimum affects crop stability in various ways.

Nature of Classification

Silkworms are classified in different ways. For example, the classification may be based on distribution, number of generations in a year (voltinism) or even the number of larval moults. Silkworms are also being classified according to the pattern of larval markings, body colour of larva and cocoon besides colour of eggs etc.

I. Classification based on distribution

Broadly the silkworms are classified into two categories, viz., temperate and tropical races. Based on geographical distribution, the silkworm's races are grouped into Japanese races, Chinese races, European races and South East Asian races.

(i) **Japanese races:** Japanese races are univoltine and bivoltine having robust larvae and spin peanut shaped cocoons. These races can withstand bad quality leaf but are weak against high temperature. Cocoon filament is thick. Average cocoon weight is 2.3 gm; shell weight 0.55 gm, SR 24%, and filament length 800-1500 meters and raw silk yield is 19%.

(ii) **Chinese races:** Chinese races are uni, bi and even multivoltine. Larval growth is quick. Larvae are usually plain and robust. It can withstand high temperature but are weak against high humidity, as well as low temperature. Shape of cocoon is elliptical or spherical in many races but some are spindle in shape also. Average bivoltine cocoon weight is 2-2.5 gm, shell weight 0.44-0.55 gm, SR 22% with 16% raw silk yield. Polyvoltine cocoon weighs 1.1-1.2 gm, shell weight 0.15-0.16 gm, SR 14% with raw silk yield of 10-11 %. The cocoons are white, golden yellow, green or even pink in colour. The fibers are thin and their reeling is good.

(iii) **European races:** European races are only univoltine. Larvae show light normal markings. Races are weak against high temperature and high humidity. Cocoons are large with mild constriction. Average cocoon weight is 2.0-2.4 gm, shell weight 0.46-0.61 gm, SR 23-25%, filament length 1700 meter, raw silk yield 20%. Generally the eggs, larvae and cocoons are larger than those of Japanese and Chinese races. Larval period is longer. Cocoons are white or buff coloured and fiber is longer with good reeling.

(iv) **South East Asian races:** Usually multivoltine are hardy and have tremendous ability to survive and reproduce under fluctuating climates. Economic characters are poor. Cocoon shape in most cases is spindle. Cocoon weight is 0.9 gm, shell weight 0.1 gm, SR 12%, filament length 350 meter and raw silk yield is 6%.

II. Classification based on moulting

During larval period at certain interval silkworms stop feeding, become inactive and shed their skin. This process is called moulting and the classification can be based on number of moults. These are:

(i) **Trimoulters:** Primitive type and is usually noticed in wild silkworm exhibited by three moults, short larval duration, small body and cocoon and fine silk filament.

(ii) **Tetramoulters:** Almost all present commercial silkworm races are tetramoulters, characterized by four moults with normal larval duration. They are reared for commercial exploitation.

(iii) **Pentamoulters:** These races are characterized by five moults, longer larval duration and large size filament. Occasionally few trimoulters or pentamoulters also appear in tetramoulting races. The dominance relationship is:

Tri > Tetra > Penta

Moreover, these moulters are under the control of M^3 allele series. These alleles are M^3, +M and M^5. Besides ecdysone hormone secreted by prothoracic gland also plays an important role in determination of moulting.

M^3 allele
↓
Brain ⇒ Prothoracic gland ⇒ Ecdysone ⇒ Moulting

III. Classification based on cocoon colour

Various varieties of silkworms are known producing different colours of cocoons such as white, yellow, golden yellow, green, greenish yellow, pink etc. These are broadly classified into white and coloured. The white ones are of two types—inferior white and superior white. Among the white cocoons some are pure white, while others are dirty white. Coloured cocoons are of different types viz., yellow, buff, straw, green, and golden yellow and so on,

Two main pigments are responsible for these colours, namely, carotenoids and flavonoids. Carotenoids are responsible for yellow and pink colour of cocoons. Carotenoids found in cocoon shell of silkworms are β-carotene, neo β-carotene, lutein, tetraxanthin, violaxanthin and sarcinaxanthin. All these carotenoids are being reportedly present in mulberry leaf and hence it is being assumed that the pigment found in cocoon-shell might have derived from the mulberry leaves. Flavonoids are responsible for green and light green colour of the cocoon. The pigment 'flavone' is abundantly contained in mulberry leaves.

Yellow cocoon races have permeability only for carotenoids or its derivatives while greenish colour cocoon races have permeability only for flavonoids. But in white cocoon races, the intestinal wall is impermeable to all kinds of pigments. The genes which control the permeability are:

Y gene: Colour pigment (carotenoids and flavonoids) passes to haemolymph from intestinal mucosa (alimentary canal).

I gene: Colour pigments are not allowed to pass to haemolymph. Haemolymph is colourless and hence the cocoons produced are white.

Y gene (silk gland cells): It allows carotenoid to pass to silk gland cells and hence yellow cocoons are produced.

Ga, Gb and Gc gene (silk gland cells): It allows flavonoids to pass to silk gland cells and hence light green or greenish colour cocoons are produced.

IV. Classification based on rearing period

Based on rearing period silkworms are classified into spring, summer and autumn races. The summer-autumn is further classified as summer, early autumn, late autumn and very late autumn silkworms.

V. Classification based on larval markings

According to larval markings, silkworms are classified into two categories—plain and marked. Three pairs of spots on the body represent normal marked silkworm larvae. These spots are located on the 2nd thoracic (mesothorax) segment (eye spot), 2nd abdominal segment (crescent or lunules) and 5th abdominal segment (star spots). Besides these, the other types of larval markings are stripes, dark colour, zebra bands, brown spots, quail marks, multistar, multilunar etc.

VI. Classification based on voltinism

Voltinism is defined as a number of broods or generation in a year produced under natural conditions. Though genes located at different loci control the phenomenon of voltinism, it is also under the control of temperature, photoperiod, humidity and nutrition. India has the unique distinction of being the only country in the world producing all the four commercially known varieties of silk. On the basis of voltinism, these silkworm races are classified as univoltine, bivoltine and multivoltine producing respectively one, two and many generations in a year. Different types of voltinism exhibited by silkworms are presented in Table 3.1.

Mulberry silkworm *(Bombyx mori)* generally produces two types of eggs. These are hibernating and non-hibernating. In hibernating eggs, the embryo enters diapause after partial development and hatches out during the following spring while in non-hibernating eggs; the embryo develops without any interruption and hatches out in about 10 days. Univoltine lay only hibernating eggs, which are also called Kurodane eggs while multivoltine lay only non-hibernating eggs, which are known as Nemadane eggs. The behaviour of bivoltine eggs is intermediate which lay non-hibernating eggs during first generation and hibernating eggs in the next generation which hatches out in the following spring and thus produce only two generations in a year.

Table 3.1: Types of voltinism in silkworm

Common name	Family	Scientific name	Voltinism
1. Mulberry silkworm	Bombycidae	*Bombyx mori*	Uni, Bi and Multivoltine
2. Tasar silkworm			
(a) Tropical	Saturniidae	*Antheraea mylitta*	Uni, Bi and Multivoltine
(b) Temperate	Saturniidae	*Antheraea proylei*	Bivoltine
3. Muga silkworm	Saturniidae	*Antheraea assama*	Multivoltine
4. Eri silkworm			
(a) Domesticated	Saturniidae	*Philosamia ricini*	Multivoltine
(b) Wild	Saturniidae	*Philosamia cynthia*	Uni and Bi

VOLTINOGENESIS AND SILKWORM RACES

Though the status question of origin of different voltinic forms in silkworm has attracted many investigators but still no concrète information is available on the line. Prof. Yasikada, an eminent scientist of Tokyo University Japan, who collected some 250 original silkworm races from different parts of world including univoltine, bivoltine and multivoltine stated the origin as:

Univoltine → Bivoltine → Multivoltine

The study was primarily based on acid phosphotase and esterase in haemolymph and epidermis. He found in total 15 types of phosphotase and esterases. Of these he noticed five types of phosphotase (A, B, C, D and O) and four types of esterase (A, B, C and O) in haemolymph and 6 types of esterases (A, B, C, AB, AC and O) in epidermis. He found all these 15 types only in Chinese bivoltine races. Other silkworm races lacked one or the other esterases. Genetical theories also explain that ancient and wild type varieties would preserve most divergent genes in their genotypes. As the seasonal, environmental besides location affects the life strategies of living organism, univoltine races through mutational changes might have lost one or more genes corresponding to the missing esterases. Accordingly, Prof. Yasikada stated that univoltine silkworm is the earliest race originated about 5000 years ago in North China. This original race moved towards South China and got converted into bivoltine some 4000 years ago. When these voltinic forms moved to middle China (tropical zone) they got converted into polyvoltine.

Famous Chinese sericulture scientist Prof. Tang Wai Leo of South China Agricultural University, Ghonzhou, expressed a different view on voltinogenesis. His explanation is based taking environmental conditions into consideration. According to him North China was a part of tropical and subtropical region. Due to drastic environmental changes, the tropical hot weather became cool and North China became a temperate zone. Tropical weather started shifting towards south. Polyvoltine races also moved to South China but the indigenous polyvoltine in North China must have converted to bivoltine and stayed there. But continuous cooling of north ultimately compelled these bivoltine to change into univoltine to continue in the same region. The bivoltine, which were not able to survive there, were shifted to mid-China, while polyvoltine have been further pushed to South. According to him as univoltine races passed through divergent environmental conditions, has compelled them to develop divergent genes in their bodies to synthesize fifteen phosphotase and esterase. Thus the finding what was stated by Japanese scientist was advocated as correct but the explanation put forth was contradicted. Hence, according to Prof. Leo, the original direction suggested by Prof. Yasikada was proved reverse.

Polyvoltine → Bivoltine → Multivoltine

Indigenous Indian silkworm races

(a) **Barapolu:** It was the only univoltine silkworm race indigenous to India (Bengal). The larvae spin flossy cocoons of greenish white or pure white colour. One end pointed and compact cocoon has short filament length. The race has now degenerated.

(b) **Chotopolu:** It was a univoltine race of Bengal. Larvae spin characteristically small, flossy, white or yellow cocoons. The race has now degenerated.

(c) **Pure Mysore:** Multivoltine race of Karnataka. Larvae spin greenish yellow, soft and flossy cocoons. Larval period is quite long (27-28 days). It is said to have originated in China and brought to India in 1795.

(d) **Sarupat:** Multivoltine race reared in North Eastern part of India (Assam). Plain larvae spin small, flossy, light creamy white spindle cocoons.

(e) **Moria:** Multivoltine race of North Eastern India. The plain larvae build flossy and creamy white spindle cocoons. The cocoons are very small with only 15 kg yield/100 Dfls. It is not a very good combiner with existing races and hence not in use.

Table 3.2: Evolution of silkworm breeds over the years in India

Year	Multivoltine		Bivoltine	
	Breed	Breeder	Breed	Breeder
1920s	Pure Mysore Nistari Sarupat, Moria	Karnataka West Bengal Assam		
1950s	Nistid, Nismo, Ichot, Itan HS6	CSR&TI, Berhampore DOS Karnataka		
1960s	Kollegal Jawan, Kolar Gold, Mysore Princes	CSR&TI, Mysore	KA, KPG-B, PLF, BL1, SH6	RSRS Kalimpong RSRS Pampore
	MBD-IV, MBD-V, A4e, D14b	CSR&TI Berhampore	S21	RSRS Dehradun
1970s	Hosa Mysore Tamil Nadu (white)	CSR&TI, Mysore DOS Tamil Nadu	NB4D2, NB7, NB18	CSR&TI, Mysore
1980s	G.CB2, CB5, Nistari (SL), A23. A25	CSR&TI. Berhampore	CC1, CA2, YS3, SF19	CSR&TI, Mysore RSRS, Dehradun
	MY1, P2D1, RD1, PCN	CSR&TI, Mysore	NP2, SP2	KSSRDI, Bangalore
1990s	BL-23, BL-24, BL-43 MU1, MU11, MU303	CSR&TI, Mysore Mysore University	CSR series, 1HT, 2 HT PAM101, PAM 111, KS01, KS02, MG 408, MG414, MG854, SK3, SK4. CNR3, CNR4, CNR14	CSR&TI, Mysore CSR&TI, Pampore KSSRDI, B'lore Mysore University CSR&TI, Berhampore RSRS Coonoor
	APM1	APSSRDI, Hindupur	APS8, APS4, APS5	APSSRDI, Hindupur

Table 3.3: Authorized silkworm hybrids for commercial exploitation

Sl. No.	*Hybrids*	*Combinations*	*Seasons*	*State/region*
	1	**2**	**3**	**4**
1.	P2D1 × NB18	MV × BV	Winter Spring Summer/Early autumn	Andhra Pradesh West Bengal, Assam, Bihar, Orissa, M.P. Uttar Pradesh
2.	MY1 × NB18	MV × BV	Spring /autumn	West Bengal, Assam, Bihar, Orissa, M.P.
3.	N × (NB18 × P5)	MV × BV	Autumn Summer/autumn	West Bengal Assam. Bihar, Orissa, M.P.
4.	PM × NB18	MV × BV	Summer	Assam, Bihar, Orissa, M.P.
5.	RD1 × NB18	MV × BV	Summer/early winter	Uttar Pradesh
6.	BL23 × NB18	MV × BV	Spring/autumn	Rainfed areas
7.	BL24 × NB18	MV × BV	Spring/ autumn	Irrigated areas
8.	SH6 × KA	BV × BV	Spring/autumn/winter	West Bengal, Assam, Bihar, Orissa, M.P.
9.	SH6 × NB4D2	BV × BV	Spring	Uttar Pradesh, J & K
10.	CA2 × NB4D2	BV × BV	Spring Spring, autumn/early winter	West Bengal, Assam, Bihar Orissa, M.P., Uttar Pradesh, J& K
11.	NB18 × P5	BV × BV	Winter	Assam, Bihar, Orissa, M.P.

12.	YS3 × SF19	BV × BV	Spring	J & K, Uttar Pradesh
13.	PAM101 × NB4D2	BV × BV	Autumn/early winter	J & K, Uttar Pradesh
14.	CC1 × NB4D2	BV × BV	Autumn/early winter	J & K, Uttar Pradesh
15.	PAM111 × SF19	BV × BV	Autumn /early winter	J & K, Uttar Pradesh
16.	CSR12 × CSR6	BV × BV	Spring /autumn	Temperate & tropical zones
17.	CSR18 × CSR19	BV × BV	Autumn	Temperate & tropical zones
18.	CSR16 × CSR17	BV × BV	Spring /autumn	Temperate & tropical zones
19.	CSR3 × CSR6	BV × BV	Spring/autumn	Temperate & tropical zones
20.	CSR2 × CSR4	BV × BV	Spring /autumn	Temperate & sub- tropical zones
21.	CSR2 × CSR5	BV × BV	Spring/autumn	Temperate & sub-tropical zones
22.	KSO1 × SP2	BV × BV	Spring	Temperate & tropical zones
23.	SKUAST-1 × SKAUST-6	BV × BV	Spring	J & K
24.	APM1 × APS8	MV × BV	Spring & Autumn	South Zone
25.	BL-43 × NB4D2	MV × BV	Spring & Autumn	South Zone
26.	APS5 × APS4	BV × BV	Spring & Autumn	North Zone

(f) **Kashmiri race:** It is now extinct, which once produced famous Kashmiri silk. This race was univoltine yielding yellow elongated oval cocoons.

(g) **Nistari:** Multivoltine race introduced in India in the year 1780-81 from China. The larvae of this race are small and spin soft and flossy golden yellow spindle cocoons. The race is very popular with the sericulturist of West Bengal. It is resistant to high temperature and high humidity. The yield/100 Dfls is low which, ranges from 15-22 kg only. It is very good combiner with many evolved multivoltine and bivoltine breeds.

Both multivoltine and bivoltine races evolved over the years in India are presented in Table 3.2 and silkworm hybrids authorized for commercial use in Table 3.3. The table also shows the seasons and regions of the country, where these authorized hybrids are to be reared by the sericulturists.

4

DISINFECTION AND HYGIENE

The silkworm is affected by a large number of diseases caused by virus, bacteria, fungi and protozoa. These diseases are known to occur in almost all sericultural regions of the world. The adverse environmental factors like temperature, humidity and poor quality of mulberry leaves reduce the tolerance of the host to the pathogen and hence increases susceptibility to infections. Disinfections and hygiene forms an integral part of healthy and successful silkworm rearing. Crop loss due to incidence of diseases is one of the major problems encountered by silkworm rearers in India. The incidence of silkworm diseases and crop losses is greatly influenced by rearing practices, frequency of cropping; conditions of rearing houses, general hygiene and environmental conditions favourable for pathogen build up and spread.

Cocoons arriving in the grainages from different sericultural areas can form a continuous source of pathogen entry into seed production units. Processing of batches continuously without providing sufficient time gap, leads to inadequate disinfection and thereby favours pathogen build up in the grainages. Some of the facts about silkworm diseases are:

- All the infectious diseases of silkworms are caused by pathogens.
- The adverse environmental factors like temperature, humidity and poor quality of mulberry leaf reduce the tolerance level of host to the pathogen and hence increase susceptibility to infections.

- The diseases of silkworms are highly contagious and spread fast.
- There is no silkworm breed, which is resistant to all the diseases.
- The silkworm pathogens survive longer in the rearing environment and remain infective.
- The diseases have atypical and typical morphological symptoms.

Disinfection forms an integral part of healthy and successful crop harvest. It is the total destruction of diseases caused by pathogens. There is no curative method for any of the silkworm diseases and hence they can best be prevented and cured. This can be achieved by adoption of proper and effective methods of disinfection before and after every silkworm crop. Therefore, to prevent crop losses due to diseases, disinfection is inevitable.

Since, the species of microorganisms vary and the situations in which they may occur differ greatly, no one or two methods are generally applicable. Each situation is a problem in itself and the methods employed depends on the knowledge, ingenuity and purposes of the operator. There are four main reasons for killing, removing or inhibiting microorganisms to maintain hygienic conditions. They are:

(a) To prevent infection to man, his animals and plants.

(b) To prevent spoilage of food and other commodities.

(c) To prevent interference by contaminating microorganisms in various industrial processes that depend on pure culture.

(d) To prevent contamination of materials used in pure culture work in laboratories (diagnostics, research, industry etc.).

Common methods of killing or removing microorganisms are:

(i) Destruction by heat (boiler, oven etc), chemical agents (disinfectants), radiation (X-ray,

ultraviolet rays etc.), mechanical agents (crushing, shattering by ultrasonic vibration etc.).

(ii) Removal (especially bacteria) by filtration, high seed centrifugation etc.

(iii) Inhibition by low temperatures (refrigeration, dry ice), desiccation (drying process), high osmotic pressures (lymph, brines etc), chemicals and drugs.

Selection of disinfectants: Several disinfectants are available in the market but only a few are widely used. The disinfectants available in the market can be grouped as:

- Halogens: (Chlorine, Iodine etc.).
- Heavy metals ($HgCl_2$, Mercurochrome, Metaphen, Protargol, etc.).
- Phenol compounds (Lysol, Crecsols etc.).
- Alcohols (Ethyl and Isopropyl).
- Formaldehydes (strong reducing agent which inactivates even enzymes).
- Ethylene oxide (Carboxide, Cryocide etc.).

Qualities of an ideal disinfectant: Ideal disinfectant must posses the following qualities:

- Highly effective against a wide variety of micro-organisms in concentration as low as to be economical for use as well as non-toxic for animals and plants.
- Non-injurious and non-staining to materials like fabrics, furniture or metal wares and non-offensive to odour or taste.
- As specific as possible for microorganisms.
- A good surface tension reducer (have good waiting and penetrating properties).
- Stable in storage.
- Readily available and not expensive.

- Easily applied under household or other practical conditions of use.
- Completely microbicidal within a few minutes or an hour at the most, and not inducing macrobiotics, leading to a false sense of security.
- Non-corrosive.

But, no single disinfectant has all these ideal properties. Some agents may be ideal under some conditions but not under others, e.g., Cresol may be ideal for floors or sanitary purposes but harmful to infants.

Conditions necessary for effective disinfect

It is established that disinfectants respond better under some specific conditions whereby disinfection becomes perfect and effective, such as:

(a) **Hydration:** Considerable quantity of water is required to facilitate the action of disinfectants, e.g., dehydrated protein to coagulate is difficult since it will turn brown or char. Moreover, resistance of bacterial endospore to heat is probably caused in part by their extremely dehydrated conditions.

(b) **Time:** No disinfectant, as ordinarily used, acts instantly. Sufficient time for contact must be allowed for whatever chemical and physical reactions to occur. The time required will depend on the nature of the disinfectant, concentration, pH, temperature, nature of target organism and existence of the bacterial population of cells having varying susceptibilities to the disinfectant.

(c) **Temperature:** With respect to the microbicidal action of heat, temperature is inversely related to time. In case of chemical microbicides, as a rule, the warmer a disinfectant, the more effective is its action. Higher temperatures generally reduce the surface tension, increase acidity, decrease viscosity and diminish adsorption.

(d) **Concentration:** Effectiveness of a disinfectant is generally related to concentration exponentially, but not linearly. For example, doubling a 0.5% concentration of phenol in aqueous solution does not merely double the killing rate. Doubling the concentration again may increase the effect by only a negligible amount. There is clearly an optimum concentration of phenol at about 1%. Thus, a concentration of a disinfectant beyond a certain point accomplishes increasingly less and is wasteful.

(e) **pH:** As a general rule, the lethal or toxic action of harmful agents involving physical and chemical actions is increased by increased concentration of H or OH- ions.

(f) **Osmotic pressure:** Fluids of high osmotic pressure (e.g. food preserving syrups and brines) tend to dehydrate the cell contents and so increase resistance of microbial cells to heat and chemical disinfectants.

(g) **Surface tension:** Surface tension is of basic importance in disinfection. There are two aspects of this factor, adsorption of surface disinfectants or interfering substances on the surface of the cells and the effect of disinfectants on the wetting and spreading properties of the solution. Both affect contact between disinfectants and microorganisms.

Method of disinfections

A. Physical methods (burning, burying and exposure to sunlight)

Exposing the rearing and grainage equipments to bright sunlight for 8-10 hrs is a very economical method of disinfection under Indian conditions. However, this could be supplemented with chemical disinfection.

B. Chemical methods

(a) **Formalin:** It is the most commonly used disinfectants in all sericultural countries. It is commercially available in the form of 35-40% formaldehyde. A mixture of 2% formalin + 0.5% staked lime is very effective solution that can be used for disinfection purpose. Formaldehyde upon storage polymerizes into trioxymetylene, which is ineffective as spray. The action of formalin takes place under wet conditions and therefore, the surface of equipments and walls should be drenched with the solution. The action of formalin is faster and more pronounced at temperature above 25°C. The action is greatly reduced at temperature below 20°C. This mixture is more effective only if rearing houses/rooms/buildings could be closed to near airtight conditions.

(b) **Bleaching Powder:** Bleaching powder is also called chlorinated lime. It is white amorphous powder with a characteristic of pungent smell of chlorine. The efficacy of bleaching powder is very much dependent on the level of active chlorine in the compound. For effective disinfection, a high-grade bleaching powder with active chlorine content of 30% and above must be used. Bleaching powder when comes in contact with water and weak acid releases nascent oxygen which has strong oxidizing action on germs. It should be stored in sealed bags, away from moisture, failing which it will be rendered ineffective. A 2% bleaching powder in 0.3% slaked lime is used for disinfection as spray.

(c) **Slaked Lime:** It is very widely used disinfectant in sericulture. It absorbs moisture and can be used to regulate bed humidity and maintain hygiene in rearing/grainage buildings. It has strong antiviral action. Application of lime dust alone or in combination with bleaching powder in and around rearing/grainage houses and premises improves hygiene in the environment.

(d) **Paraformaldehyde:** It is white crystalline substance with a strong odour of formalin formed by polymerization of formaldehyde. It is effective for fumigation purpose. On heating, it sublimates and releases formaldehyde gas, which inactivates the pathogens in wet condition and therefore the humidity of the room should be simultaneously increased to maintain the optimum level of requirement for silkworm rearing.

(e) **Chlorine dioxide:** It is an ideal disinfectant suitable for all types of rearing/grainage houses. In combination with slaked lime, it is effective against all silkworm pathogens. It is a strong oxidizing agent, 2.5 times stronger than chlorine and two times stronger than sodium hypo-chloride. It is effective at broader ranges of pH and less reactive with organic compounds. It is least corrosive and non-hazardous. Chlorine dioxide (Sanitech) 500 ppm in 0.5% slaked lime may be used for disinfection. It is stable and may be activated at the time of its use.

Quantity requirement of disinfectants

Quantity requirement of disinfectant is estimated based on the surface area of the building or trays to be disinfected. The quantity requirement may be estimated as:

a. Room: (Total area in square meter)

Area of roof and floor	:	L × B × 2
Area of two opposite walls	:	L × B × 2
Area of two other side walls	:	L × B × 2
b. Wooden Trays	:	L × B × 2 × Number of trays
c. Chandrikes	:	L × B × 2 × Number of chandrikes
d. Bamboo Trays	:	II r^2 × 2 × Number of trays

The disinfectant solution should be prepared @ one liter per 2.5 square meters.

$$\text{Solution required in liters} = \frac{\text{Total area in square meters}}{2.5}$$

Preparation of disinfectant solution

Disinfectant solution should be prepared a fresh before use.

(i) **2% Formalin solution:** Commercial available formalin contains 40% formaldehyde. This is diluted to prepare 2% solution of formalin as follows:

$$\frac{\text{Concentration of available formalin} - \text{Concentration of formalin required}}{\text{Concentration of required formalin}} = \text{Parts of water to be added in one part of formalin}$$

i.e. $\frac{40-2}{2}$ = 19 parts of water

Or $N1V1 = N2V2$ or $V1 = \frac{N2V2}{N1}$ i.e $V1 = \frac{2\text{x}100 \text{ (ml)}}{40}$

100 — 5 = 95 ml water; Ratio = 95: 5 or 19: 1

Where;

N1 = Given strength of solution

N2 = Desired strength of solution

V1 = Volume of stock chemical required

V2 = Desired volume of solution to be prepared

Practically, for all purposes, one part of formalin can be mixed with 19 parts of water to prepare 2% formalin solution (Table 4.1).

Table 4.1: Preparation of 2% formalin solution of different quantities

Sl. No.	*Total volume of solution required*	*Quantity of formalin required*	*Water to be added*	*Ratio of Formalin: Water*
1.	1.00	50 ml	0.950	1: 19
2.	5.00	250 ml	4.750	1: 19
3.	10.00	500 ml	9.500	1: 19
4.	15.00	750 ml	14.250	1: 19
5.	20.00	1000 ml	19.000	1: 19
6.	25.00	1.250 liter	23.750	1: 19
7.	30.00	1.500 liter	28.500	1: 19
8.	35.00	1.750 liter	33.250	1: 19
9.	50.00	2.500 liter	47.500	1: 19
10.	75.00	3.750 liter	71.250	1: 19
11.	100.00	5.000 liter	95.000	1: 19

If commercial available formalin contains 40% formaldehyde, ratio of formalin and water in preparation of solution of different concentration of formalin will be as follows (Table 4.2).

Table 4.2: Preparation of different concentrations of formalin

Sl. No.	*Concentration of formalin required*	*Concentration of available formalin (%)*	*Ratio of Water and Formalin*
1.	1	40	39.00: 1
2.	2	40	19.00: 1
3.	3	40	12.33: 1
4.	4	40	9.00: 1
5.	5	40	7.00: 1
6.	6	40	5.67: 1
7.	7	40	4.71: 1
8.	8	40	4.00: 1
9.	9	40	3.44: 1
10.	10	40	3.00: 1

(ii) Formalin 2% + 0.5% slaked lime mixture: After preparation of 2% formalin solution, slaked lime is added to it @ 5 gm in one liter of formalin solution. Slaked lime is prepared by sprinkling water on burnt limestone and pulverized it into fine powder of 200–250-mesh size.

Estimation of quantity of disinfectant required

The quantity required for disinfection may be calculated adopting the following procedure (example):

Length of floor (L) =20'

Breadth of floor (B) = 15'

Floor area for disinfection = L × B = 20' × 15' = 300 square feet or 28 m^2

The disinfectant required for disinfection of rearing house is 2 liter/square meter floor area or 185 ml/sq.feet floor area.

Disinfection solution required = Total area × @ 2 liter/ sq. meter or 28 m^2 × 2 = 56 liter

Disinfection for outside the rearing house and appliances is to be added in this quantity. Additional disinfectant required for appliances is estimated to be 25%

of the solution required for floor area i.e. 56 × 25% = 14 liters.

Additional disinfectant required for outside the rearing house is estimated to be 10% of the solution required for floor area i.e. 56 × 10% = 5.6 liters.

Total quantity of disinfectant required = 56 + 14 + 5.6 = 75.6 or 75 liters. See Table 4.1 for preparation of 75 liters of 2% formalin solution.

(iii) 5% Bleaching powder solution (Stable 30% chlorine): 5% solution of bleaching powder is prepared by dissolving 50 gm of the chemical in one liter of water (ratio; 1: 20). The mixture is agitated well. It is filtered through a layer of muslin cloth and the clear solution is used for spraying/disinfection. A ready recknor for preparation of 5% bleaching powder solution of different volumes is detailed in Table 4.3.

Table 4.3: Preparation of different quantities of 5% bleaching powder solution

Sl. No.	*Total Volume of solution required (liter)*	*Bleaching powder required (gm)*	*Water to be added (liter)*	*Ratio of Bleaching powder: Water*
1.	1.00	50	1.00	1: 20
2.	5.00	250	5.00	1: 20
3.	10.00	500	10.00	1: 20
4.	15.00	750	15.00	1: 20
5.	20.00	1000	20.00	1: 20
6.	25.00	1250	25.00	1: 20
7.	30.00	1500	30.00	1: 20
8.	35.00	1750	35.00	1: 20
9.	50.00	2500	50.00	1: 20
10.	100.00	5000	100.00	1: 20

The ratio of powder and water to be mixed for preparation of different concentrations of bleaching powder solution is presented in Table 4.4.

Table 4.4: Requirement of bleaching powder for preparation of different concentrations of solution

Sl. No.	*Concentration solution required (%)*	*Quality of water (liter)*	*Quantity of powder (gm)*	*Ratio of Bleaching powder: Water*
1.	1.00	1.00	10.00	1: 10
2.	2.00	1.00	20.00	1: 50
3.	3.00	1.00	30.00	1: 33
4.	4.00	1.00	40.00	1: 25
5.	5.00	1.00	50.00	1: 20
6.	6.00	1.00	60.00	1: 17
7.	7.00	1.00	70.00	1: 14
8.	8.00	1.00	80.00	1: 13
9.	9.00	1.00	90.00	1: 11
10.	10.00	1.00	100.00	1: 10

$$\text{Quantity of chemical required} = \frac{\text{\% of solution to be prepared} \times \text{quantity of solution required}}{100}$$

Example: (a) 2% of 1 liter solution $= \frac{2\% \times 1000 \text{ (ml)}}{100} = 20\text{gm}$

(b) 5% of 1 liter solution $= \frac{5\% \times 1000 \text{ (ml)}}{100} = 50\text{gm}$

(c) 2% of 75 liter solution $= \frac{2 \times 75{,}000 \text{ ml}}{100} = 1500\text{gm or } 1.5\text{kg.}$

(iv) Bleaching powder-slaked lime mixture: High-grade bleaching powder is mixed with finely powdered slaked lime @ 100 gm per 900 gm of lime.

(v) Slaked lime powder: Burnt rock lime (limestone) or shell lime is procured, water is sprinkled and it is allowed to become powder. This is further pulverized, sieved and made into the form of fine powder, which can be readily used.

(vi) Chlorine dioxide (Sanitech 2,00,000-ppm stable): It is powerful, user-friendly, safe and effective disinfectant for silkworm rearing house and equipments. It is capable of successfully destroying microbial and all silkworm pathogens. Sanitech is 25 times more potent than chlorine and 50 times more effective than hypochlorites. Demands no airtight conditions of rearing and grainages houses for its action. There is no limitation of temperature and humidity for its action. Do not have corroding action on metallic items and rearing equipments at the recommended concentration. Sanitech is effective on a broad pH range (pH: 5-10). 500-ppm chlorine Dioxide in 0.5% slaked lime can be prepared as:

Solution A: Add 50 gm of activator crystal to 500 ml Sanitech (CIO_2) solution stir and allow 5 minutes for complete dissolution of crystals. Colour changes to light yellow. Add the prepared 500 ml yellow solution to 19 liters of water to get 19.5 liter of solution

Solution B: Dissolve 100 gm of slaked lime powder in 500 ml water in another container and allow to stand.

Mix solution A and B to obtain a total of 20 liters of disinfectants. One liter of Sanitech makes 40 liters of disinfectants. For disinfection of one square meter of area, two liter of Sanitech solution is required.

To prepare 2.5% Chlorine Dioxide + 0.5% slaked lime solution of different quantities, the requirement will be as detailed in Table 4.5.

Disinfection of rearing houses, appliances etc.: Drench all parts of rearing house inside and outside and appliances uniformly using gutter or jet sprayer with required quantity of disinfectant (@ 2.0 liter/m^2 floor area of rearing house + 25% of disinfectant solution for appliances + 10% for outside of rearing house). After disinfection, rearing houses must be closed for a minimum period of 24 hrs. Bamboo mountages must be disinfected with 2% formalin solution. Bleaching powder should not be used for disinfection of mountages. Rearing trays should not be smeared with cow dung. Disinfected rearing houses must be opened at least 24 hrs before initiation of rearing.

Table 4.5: Preparation of 2.5% Chlorine Dioxide + 0.5% slaked lime solution

Sl. No.	Volume Solution Required (liter)	Quantity of Sanitech Required (liter)	Water to be added (liter)	Activator crystal required (gm)	Quantity of Lime to be added (gm)
1.	5.00	0.125	4.875	12.50	2.50
2.	10.00	0.250	9.750	25.00	5.00
3.	20.00	0.500	19.500	50.00	10.00
4.	30.00	0.750	29.250	75.00	15.00
5.	40.00	1.000	39.000	100.00	20.00
6.	50.00	1.250	48.750	125.00	25.00
7.	60.00	1.500	58.500	150.00	30.00
8.	80.00	2.000	78.000	200.00	40.00
9.	100.00	2.500	97.500	250.00	50.00

Dipping the appliances in disinfectant: Disinfect the rearing appliances in 2% bleaching powder in 0.3% slaked lime solution by dipping for at least 10 minutes in disinfection tank. The disinfection tank of 2 feet depth and 4 feet diameter is considered suitable for disinfection purpose. Prepare the disinfectant solution of required quantity and concentration and fill half of the tank. To determine the volume of the tank and the disinfectant solution to be prepared the formula llr^2h is used. Example:

The volume of tank of 4 feet diameter and 2 feet height

Diameter = 4 feet and therefore radius (r) = 4 ÷ 2 = 2; as only half of the tank is to be filled, the height of solution in the tank will be 2 ÷ 2 = 1'

Therefore, llr^2h = 3.14 × 2 × 2 × 1 = 12.56 cubic feet

One cubic feet holds 28 liters of solution, therefore 12.56 cubic feet will hold 12.56 × 28 = 352 liters of solution.

To prepare 352 liters of 2% bleaching powder in 0.3% slaked lime solution, the requirement will be as follows:

Requirement of water = 352 liters

Requirement of bleaching powder = 352 × 20 gm = 7.040 kg.

Requirement of 0.3% slaked lime = 352 × 3 gm = 1.056 kg.

Prepare 352 liters of solution and fill in the disinfection tank. Dip the appliances as many as possible to submerge in the solution. After 10 minutes the appliances are removed from the disinfection tank and carried directly to the disinfected rearing houses. Afterwards, another set of appliances is dipped in the solution. This system will continue for 8-10 times. The solution is discarded after using 10 times and fresh solution is prepared for the purpose.

Maintenance of hygienic conditions for silkworm is ensured by rigorous practice of disinfection on the vulnerable foci of infection. Disinfection of rearing room and appliances to prevent vertical transmission of pathogens is very much essential which is to be carried out before rearing/grainage with available disinfectants to destroy pathogens. Disinfection of other sources of contamination /infection to prevent horizontal transmission of pathogens is -

- Surface sterilization of silkworm eggs.
- Disinfection of mounting rooms.
- Disinfection of mulberry leaf storage room.
- Mulberry leaf sterilization.
- Disinfection of surrounding areas of rearing/ grainage room.
- Disinfection of litter storage.
- Rearing bed disinfection through dusting.
- Disinfection of rearing/grainage appliances and storage room.
- Personal hygiene.

Before using the disinfectants, it is of utmost importance to think about the residual effect of the disinfectants towards environmental pollution and positive side-effects on the persons who are handling the disinfectants as also their pets. As no disinfectant is absolutely free from the above, only those disinfectants are to be selected where the side effects are minimal. At

Disinfectants and their requirement for 200 sq. ft. floor area of rearing house (100 Dfls capacity)

Item to disinfectant	*Mode of disinfection*	*Quantity*	*Quantity of disinfectants required*			
			Bleaching powder (kg)	*Slaked Lime (kg)*	*Formaline (kg)*	*Detergent (kg)*
Rearing house (200 sq. ft. or 18.58 sq. mtr.) and appliances (8 rearing stands and 160 trays)	Spray disinfection cleaning and washing with 2% bleaching powder in 0.3% slaked lime + 50 % for appliances	Floor area of rearing house x 2 liters/sq. mtr. + 50% for applications	1.02	0.126	–	–
Disinfection of rearing appliances by soaking trays, plastic sheets and collapsible mountages etc.	2% bleaching powder in 0.3% slaked lime solution	500 liters	10.00	1.500	–	–
Spray disinfection of rearing house and surroundings	0.03% slaked lime solution + 25% for surroundings	37 liters + 7.00 liters =44 liters	–	0.105	–	–
Spray disinfection of 60 mountages@ 28ml/sq. ft.	(a) 0.3% slaked lime solution (b) 2% formalin	60 liters 60 liters	–	0.180	–	–
Spray disinfection of rearing house and appliances	2% formalin +0.5% detergent 50% for appliances +25% for rearing house and sorroundings	37 liters + 14 liters + 7 liters = 58 liters	–	–	2.882	0.025

present Chlorine dioxide ranks first being the most eco-friendly and user-friendly disinfectant available to the sericulture industry. Regular practice of disinfection in all possible ways has proved to be very much effective to maintain hygiene of silkworms and its successful implementation in the field will minimize crop loss due to diseases.

5

SEED PRODUCTION

SEED ORGANIZATION AND SEED MULTIPLICATION

The term 'silkworm seed' connotes seed cocoons and silkworm eggs. Disease-free seeds especially the seeds free from pebrine disease play a vital role in determining the level of production and productivity. Production and productivity are also dependent upon the silkworm races reared. Broadly, the silkworm races are classified into univoltines, bivoltines and multivoltines. Whereas bivoltine gives better yield of cocoons and silk, multivoltine is a poor yielder of cocoons and inferior quality of silk. Another factor that influences production and productivity is hybrid vigour or heterosis. Hybrids generally behave better than either of the parents in survival rate, stability of crop and productivity.

Japan, China and USSR have organized multiplication of silkworm seed on scientific lines and introduced three-tier seed multiplication system viz., P3, P2 and P1. Farmers with the help of technical personnel raise cocoons of P1. Important activities observed in advanced countries regarding seed productions are -

- Research stations concentrate on the evaluation of silkworm breeds/hybrids.
- The 3-tier system of seed multiplication is being practised. Stock released for multiplication is not continued for more than 3 generations.
- The grainages play a vital role in transforming

the technology suit to the rearers, which helps in the production of quality P1 cocoons.

- Higher incentive prices are given for seed cocoons.

Silkworm seed is the sheet anchor of sericulture industry. A sound silkworm seed organization governs the production and productivity of silk. In order to maintain vigour, health and purity of parental stocks, the multiplication of basic seed is conducted at three levels in India viz., P3 (Great Grand parent), P2 (Grand parent) and P1 (parent). Strict close watch at every stage from cocoon to silkworm egg production is necessary to maintain the stock in sound health and purity. The breeder who supplies authorized silkworm breeds to P3 centers in small quantities as and when required maintains P4 stock. Since multiplication at P3 and P2 levels are very important and crucial for maintaining the purity, vigour and disease-freeness of the seed, they are exclusively kept under the direct control of government. At P1 stage, the government produces a small portion and the major production is from the seed areas and from selected seed rearers in other areas.

It is necessary that the organizations and institutions responsible for seed production, processing, storage and distribution should review periodically and assess their internal quality control system besides seeking support from statutory functionaries such as seed certification agency, law enforcement agency, seed testing laboratory etc. which are integral part of the system.

Quality control is a very complex process and there are many factors affecting seed quality viz., genetical quality, physical quality, physiological quality and health quality, which independently and or in interaction with one another constitute the overall quality of the seed. Breeds evolved by the breeders are authorized and released for multiplication by National and Provincial Race Authorization Committees. The morphological, genetical and economic characteristics should be maintained in subsequent generations (P3, P2 and P1). Each breed is identified by its distinguishing characteristics and it is checked from one generation to another generation whether it conforms to the standard prescribed genetic purity. It is expected that the breeder seed should have cent per cent genetic purity. Such high standard of genetic purity at different levels of seed multiplication can be achieved by following the scientific principles of breed maintenance and multiplication procedure at each level.

- ➢ The physical quality of seed includes its appearance and luster and is dependent on post-harvest technology and handling of seeds.
- ➢ The physiological quality of seed relates to its vigour and viability and is affected mainly by exposure of seed-lots to fluctuating temperatures and relative humidity conditions of the environment.
- ➢ Seed should be free from all kinds of diseases in general and pebrine in particular to maintain the health of the seed.

Production of superior quality hybrid silkworm seed involves two aspects viz.:

(a) Parental seed cocoon production.

(b) Commercial seed cocoon production.

Parental seed cocoons are the essential raw material for the preparation of commercial seed. Stability in production is an essential component for the economically viable grainage. The very existence of sericulture as commercial crop depends on the planned programme of preservation of silkworm stock. In India, a separate three-tier seed multiplication is lacking in most of the states. In these states, the silkworm stocks are raised for more than three generations leading fall in standards and quality. In Karnataka, which is the major silk and seed producing state in the country has three-tier system of seed organization, multiplication and seed production. It is a well known fact that breeding depression in insects is very high. In order to check this deterioration and its bad effect on the hybrid egg production, a three-tier multiplication programme of parent seed cocoon is practised in almost all the countries. This enables stock multiplication of three generations only and fresh stocks are replenished from P3 stations periodically. The basic stock is maintained at P3 stations. These stocks are maintained on highly scientific and hygienic conditions and are manned by competent breeders.

Factors affecting seed quality

Seed quality is influenced by numerous factors. These can be broadly classified into ecological influence, production technology influence and handling technology influence.

(a) **Ecological influence:** The quality of seeds is strongly influenced not only by genetical factors but also by the environmental conditions in which the production is undertaken. These environmental factors include temperature, photoperiod, humidity etc. Although, these factors are natural, many of them can be modified and controlled to a great extent to the optimum level for the production of quality seed.

(b) **Influence of production technology:** Application and adoption of recommended production packages are very essential for getting good seed crop. One may make broad general recommendations to be adopted but to raise a healthy and pure seed crop, these are required to be suitably modified on the basis of experiences. Emphasis should always be laid on those factors, which contribute and affect seed quality viz., the seed source, protection of seed, control of pests and diseases etc.

(c) **Influence of handling technology:** The time, energy and money spent in growing genetically pure and disease-free seed crop may go waste if the end products are left to the vagaries of the weather conditions or if steps are not taken to complete its processing such as winnowing, drying, cleaning, grading, seed treatment, packaging, labeling and later transportation and preservation etc.

Production and supply of required quantity of disease free silkworm eggs to the sericulturists on time is one of the prerequisites for achieving sustained cocoon production. 'Quality seed' is often defined as entirely free from diseases, having more number of viable eggs and assuring stable cocoon crop. To meet the large quantity of commercial hybrid seed, it is necessary to have adequate quantity of parent seed, which is achieved through systematic and scientific multiplication of seed at different levels ensuring the purity and vigour of the breed so as to exploit heterosis in sericulture (see chapter 9). The multiplication of basic seed is a very important aspect in breed maintenance and hybrid egg production. The organized set-up comprising maintenance of breeder's stock and its multiplication forms the 'seed organization' with an ultimate aim to produce large-scale healthy silkworm seed.

Seed organization comprises the maintenance of breeder's stock and its multiplication for the ultimate production of large quantity of commercial hybrid seed and thus forms the backbone of sericulture industry.

Multiplication of silkworm breeds at P4 & P3 level: The breeder's stock (P4) maintenance is the responsibility of breeders of research institutes that in turn supply the basic seed for multiplication. A three-tier system is considered more ideal and efficient for Indian conditions, which is followed in almost all sericulturally advanced countries.

- Plan and programme the basic seed production based on the requirement of eggs in next level of multiplication. There should be an integrated programme to supply the eggs to various multiplication centers.
- Prepare a PERT chart and supply programme for a year in advance for effective monitoring and supply of basic seed.
- Brush individual Dfl at P4 and P3 and mass (2 -5 Dfls) at P2 level (Table 5.1).
- Obtain P3 laying from P4 stock for every rearing.
- Perform cellular rearing at P4 and P3 and mass rearing at P2.

Table 5.1: Rearing of silkworm at different levels of seed multiplication

Particulars	*P4*	*P3*	*P2*
Brushing	Individual (cellular)	Individual (cellular)	Mass (2-5 Dfls)
Chawki	Individual (cellular)	Individual (cellular)	Mass (2-5 Dfls)
No. of larvae after 3rd moult	250-300	250-300	All larvae
Late age rearing	250-300	250-300	All larvae
Mounting	250-300	250-300	All larvae @ 300 per mountage

- Retain 250-300 larvae per batch at random after III moult at P4 and P3 and all larvae at P2. Adopt tray rearing at P4, P3 and P2 level.
- Mount 250-300 larvae per mountage in P4 and P3 and @ 300 larvae per rnountage at P2.
- Carry out individual batch harvesting, deflossing, sorting of defective cocoons and calculation of pupation rate at P4 and P3 level (Table 5.2). Mass cocoon harvesting, deflossing, sorting of defective cocoons and pupation rate is calculated from 1 kg per tray of sample cocoons at P2 level.
- Assess batchwise 10 female and 10 male cocoons for cocoon weight, shell weight and shell ratio at P4 and P3 level and 50 female and 50 male cocoons in each race for cocoon weight, shell weight and shell ratio at P2 level.
- Select 50 to 60 cocoons in each selected batch at P4 and retain all good cocoons after rejecting of defective cocoons at P3.
- Remove inferior cocoons and retain remaining cocoons at P2 level for P1 production.
- Selected cocoons at P4 and P3 and sorted cocoons at P2 are to be cut, opened and arranged in grainage boxes (Table 5.3) for egg production.

Table 5.2: Harvest and cocoon assessment

Particulars	*P4*	*P3*	*P2*
Harvest	Individual batch	Individual batch	Mass
Defloss	Individual batch	Individual batch	All cocoons
Sorting of defective cocoons	Individual batch	Individual batch	All cocoons
Calculation of pupation rate	Individual batch	Individual batch	1 kg cocoons
Cocoon assessment/batch (Male + female)	10 + 10	10 + 10	50 + 50
Batch selection	Good batch	Bad batch rejection	
Selection of cocoons	50-60	Defective cocoons rejection (remaining good cocoons are retained)	Inferior cocoons rejection (remaining good cocoons are retained)

Table 5.3: System of egg production

Particulars	*P4*	*P3*	*P2*
Cocoon cutting	Selected cocoons (50-60 from each selected batch)	All good cocoons of selected batch	All good cocoons
Sex separation	Necessary	Necessary	No sex separation
Crossing system	Inter batch	Males- mixing Females -separate	Random
Mother moth Examination	Individual (all) moths	20 moths together (one sheet) for all moths	20 moths together (one sheet) for all

- For inter-batch crossing at P4. Batchwise female and male pupae are kept separately. All males are mixed and females are kept batchwise at P3. At P2 level separation of female and male pupae is not necessary.
- Preserve the cocoons in single layer in trays.
- Examine individually mother moth at P4, while 20 moths of each sheet together at P3 and P2 for incidence of diseases.
- Surfaces disinfect and preserve layings properly.
- To carry out inter-batch crossing, prepare a chart as mentioned in Table 5.4 to 5.6 to ensure uniform maintenance of racial characters and to avoid inbreeding depression.
- The female and male pupae of each selected batch are counted and reserved separately.

Table 5.4: Inter batch-crossing system (example)

Crossing plan

Batch No. Male/Female	*31*	*33*	*36*	*40*	*46*	*47*
31		X	X	X	X	X
33	(X)		X	X	X	X
36	(X)	(X)		X	X	X
40	(X)	(X)	(X)		X	X
46	(X)	(X)	(X)	(X)		X
47	(X)	(X)	(X)	(X)	(X)	

Table 5.5: Number of pupae from selected batch

Batch No.	*Male Number*	*Female Number*
31	30	30
33	30	30
36	20	30
40	20	30
46	30	30
47	30	30

Table 5.6: Inter-batch crossing

Male	*31*	*33*	*36*	*40*	*46*	*47*
Female (F)						
31		10F	10F	10F		
33			10F	10F	10F	
36				10F		10F
40					10F	10F
46	10F		10F			10F
47	15F	15F				

- ➢ Inter-batch crossing is effected by dividing the female and male pupae of designated batches.

Production of P1 seed cocoons: This is the last stage of multiplication of the parent stock in three-tier silkworm seed organization programme. The production of P1 seed cocoons needed for commercial hybrid seed production is organized under private sector with selected seed cocoon growers either in seed areas or with adopted farmers in hybrid seed areas. There are separate seed areas in almost every state in India for the production of bivoltine and multivoltine seed cocoons. In these areas, farmers are selected as seed cocoon growers. They are trained in rearing pure races, the behaviour of silkworm races, care at different stages of rearing, feeding, moulting and mounting. Incentives are also given to these farmers in the form of special subsidies for improving their plantation, rearing houses, purchase of equipments etc. Government also ensures that all the cocoons produced by these farmers are purchased at higher rate, if they fulfill the norms of seed cocoons fixed by the government from time to tome.

Parent seed cocoon production can also be organized through selected seed rearers by the respective seed production centers. These farmers need not be in seed areas. On the other hand, they may be located in the areas where hybrids are reared. But these rearers are selected considering their mulberry garden for growing good quality leaf, a good spacious rearing house enough for pure race rearing and technical knowledge. After supply of pure seed, the technical staff periodically visits the rearers' house and guides the farmer in rearing pure races. They also check the growth of the larvae and incidence of diseases if any. The farmer has the responsibility to produce cocoons as per norms and demand for quality. The grainage officers select those farmers who are away from the industrial areas to avoid contamination of diseases. After purchasing the cocoons for the preparation of cross breed laying, all the cocoons are sorted out and defective cocoons are discarded/removed. Generally, 80-85% of the cocoons can be used for F1 hybrid preparation. Rearing of P1 should be well planned to produce synchronizing batches of cocoons. The crop should be screened for pebrine disease by microscopical examination during larval and pupal stages and the cocoons raised should conform to the breed characteristics.

Mostly, the supply of silkworm seed in India is taken by the following agencies:

(a) Grainages run by State Department of Sericulture.

(b) Grainages run by Central Silk Board.

(c) Other institutes recognized by government like KSSRDI, Asian Institute of Rural Development etc.

(d) Private seed producers who are licensed for the preparation of commercial silkworm eggs.

Government of Karnataka notified seed areas for the production of seed cocoons under the Karnataka Silkworm Seed Cocoon Regulation (Production, Supply and Distribution) Act 1943. For the quality commercial silkworm seed supply (F1), a well-organized Basic Seed Farms (BSFs) maintained on scientific lines for the authorized breed is a must. Specific qualitative and quantitative characters to be taken into consideration for maintaining the breeds at optimum level are already standardized and recommended.

All the guidelines for silkworm rearing at different levels of seed multiplication are described in Chapter 8. Correlation between production of Dfls at different levels of seed multiplication is presented in Table 5.7.The norms for irrigated Basic Seed Farms i.e. leaf productivity, manpower requirement/ha, leaf requirement for 100 Dfls, quantity of Dfls to be reared/ha/yr and leaf cocoon ratio is also presented.

Table 5.7: Correlation in production of Dfls at various levels of multiplication

Voltinism/ level of multiplication	*P3*	*P2*	*P1*	*Cocoon*	*Bi × Bi laying*	*Result*
Bivoltine						
P3	1	50	2500	575000	175000	P3 × P2 × P1 × Dfls
P2		1	50	11500	3450	
P1			1	230	70	1 × 50 × 50 × 70 = 175000
Multivoltine						
P3	1	50	2400	564000	1,69200	
P2		1	48	11280	3380	
P1			1	235	70	1 × 50 × 48 × 70 = 168000

Multivoltine × Bivoltine hybrid preparation

560000 + (575000 ÷ 4) = 560000 + 143750 or 140000 = 700000 cocoon
Recovery @ 24 % of the total cocoon i.e. 700000 × 24% = 168000 Dfls

or Recovery @ 30% of female parent cocoon i.e. 560000 × 30% = 168000 Dfls

Correlation of acreage at various levels of seed multiplication

Voltinism/level of Multiplication	*P3*	*P2*	*P1*
Bivoltine			
P3	1	50	2200
P2		1	45
Multivoltine			
P3	1	40	1700
P2		1	43

Norms for irrigated Basic Seed Farms

1. **Leaf productivity**

   Irrigated : 30,000 Kg (30 MT)/ha/year

   Spacing : 3' × 3'

2. **Manpower requirement/ha.**

Rearing + Maintenance of garden = Total
2.62 + 2.62 = 5.25

3. **Leaf requirement for 100 Dfls**

Bivoltine : 1300-1600 kg

Multivoltine : 700-800 kg

4. **No. of Dfls to be reared/ha/year**

Race	P3	P2	P1
Bivoltine	1750	1875	2000
Multivoltine	2500	3000	3500

5. **Leaf cocoon ratio**

Bivoltine P3, P2, P1: 22: 1

Multivoltine P3, P2, P1: 25: 1

CALCULATION: Correlation in production of Dfls at different levels of seed multiplication in both bivoltine and multivoltine silkworm breeds

A. **Bivoltine**

1 P3 Dfl→500 fecundity→90% hatching→450 larvae→85% ERR →380 P2 cocoons→70% selection→265 P2 seed cocoons→20% recovery→53 P2 Dfls or 50 P2 Dfls

1 P2 Dfl→450 fecundity→90% hatching→405 larvae→80% ERR →325 P1 cocoons→75% selection→245 P1 seed cocoons→20% recovery→50 P1 Dfls

1 P1 Dfl→400 fecundity→85% hatching→340 larvae→75% ERR →255 cocoons→90% selection→230 seed cocoons→30% recovery→70 Dfls

Total: P3 × P2 × P1 × Dfls = Hybrids Dfls produced

1 × 50 × 50 × 70 = 175000 hybrid Dfls

B. **Multivoltine**

1 P3 Dfl→450 fecundity→95% hatching→430 larvae→85% ERR →365 P2 cocoons→70% selection→250 P2 seed cocoons→20% recovery→50 P2 Dfls

1 P2 Dfl→450 fecundity→90% hatching→405 larvae→80% ERR →325 P1 cocoons→75% selection→240 P1 seed cocoons→20% recovery→48 P1 Dfls

1 P1 Dfl→400 fecundity→90% hatching→360 larvae→75% ERR →270 cocoons→90% selection→240 seed cocoons→30% recovery→70 Dfls

Total: P3 × P2 × P1 × Dfls = Hybrid Dfls produced

1 × 50 × 48 × 70 = 168000 hybrid Dfls

METHODS OF EGG PRODUCTION

The success of sericulture industry depends on quality of silkworm eggs. At the egg production centers, the eggs are collected with the aim of:

1. Producing heterozygotic hybrids for commercial rearing.
2. Producing eggs, which can be used to produce seed of parent variety.

The process of egg collection in these two methods is completely different. In the case of collection of eggs meant for utilizing eggs for P2 and parent variety, each and every moth is strictly tested to prevent transovarian transmission of pebrine infection. In case of commercial rearing meant for producing reeling cocoons, mass mother moth examination is carried out. Therefore, the method of egg collection can be divided into two categories:

(a) Segregated egg laying

(b) Mixed egg laying.

(a) **Segregated egg laying:** The segregated egg laying method is performed in production of grand parent eggs of F1 hybrids and of parent race where every moth is tested for pebrine disease. Segregated egg laying method is sub-divided into two groups:

(i) Pasteur method

(ii) Cellular method

(i) **Pasteur method:** This method is adopted for the production of parental silkworm strains and grandparent silkworms of F1 hybrids. In this method, one thick sheet of egg laying paper of size 32 × 18 cm^2 is divided into 28 partitions. In each partition, one moth is allowed to lay eggs. Enough space is provided between two egg laying moths with the help of cellule/rings to prevent the mixing. After oviposition the moths are transferred to another moth box with the same number of partitions labeled with their serial numbers for microscopic examination. This method is convenient for individual mother moth examination and is less expensive compared to cellular bag method, convenient to eliminate inferior laying but in this method large quantities of thick sheet of papers are required besides being more labourious.

(ii) Cellular method: This method was also devised by Pasteur in France with the idea of avoiding pebrine infection and hence belongs to a type of segregated egg laying. In this method, small cellular bags of thin cloth or paraffin paper perforated with small holes in which female moths are allowed to lay eggs individually are used. Female moth after copulation is kept in this bag individually and tied. After oviposition, the moths are subjected for microscopical examination. In this method, there is no confusion about the female moth and also the numbers of eggs laid are more, because moths are left free besides perfect pebrine examination. Moreover, this method is more labourious, time consuming, more expensive and requires lot of space. Therefore, this method is not popular.

(b) Mixed egg laying: This is also known as collective moth egg collection method and is adopted for production of commercial F1 hybrid eggs. Mixed egg laying method is sub-divided into two groups:

(i) Flat card method

(ii) Loose formed method

(i) Flat card method: In this method, certain number of moths is permitted to lay eggs in a definite area of a sheet of craft paper. Generally, the egg laying area is about 400 cm^2 (20 × 20 cm) but somewhat different in moth number for laying eggs according to varieties, fecundity capacity of moths, productive seasons, rearing environment, quality of seed cocoons etc. The principle is that the area is full and flat without overlapping eggs. This method is simple, convenient and labour-saving but does not permit individual selection or elimination of inferior laying. After oviposition, all the moths are collected and put together for moth examination. It is more convenient in washing, disinfections, incubation and brushing/ collecting newly hatched larvae. This method can be practised only in places where pebrine is not prevalent because if even one moth is affected with pebrine in a sheet, the entire egg card is rejected. This method is popular for collecting eggs to be diverted for commercial rearing.

(ii) **Loose formed method**: Loose eggs are free eggs not attached to the sheet and the production of such eggs by detaching them from the sheet is known as loose egg production. For production of commercial silkworm eggs, the loose-formed method is a more advanced one in advanced silk producing countries. In Europe this method is obligatory because of varietal characteristics of the breed. In Japan, all silkworm eggs for commercial rearing are produced employing this method only. This method is commonly used in Eastern Provinces of China also. But, in India the concept of loose egg production has not percolated to the desired magnitude. Experiences have shown that the reasons for non-acceptance or reluctance from both the egg producers and farmers are basically due to lack of technical knowhow and inadequate infrastructural facilities and difficulties encountered when brushing. The loose eggs are packed in boxes and each box contains approximately 12 gm of eggs. For preservation of loose eggs, either starched cotton cloth or starched thick craft paper is selected so that they could be used repeatedly and make loose egg production more economical. Generally, 40-50 gm of starch is required to prepare one liter of paste in which 10-15 gm of boric acid is added to prevent mould attack. One liter of paste is sufficient to smear 20 m^2 surface areas of sheets.

Size of egg sheet varies according to the size of the tray as oviposition is allowed in trays for convenience. Size of egg sheet should slightly be more than the size of the tray. As egg sheet of size 105 × 75 cm is more ideal to befit 90 cm × 60 cm oviposition tray.

Density of moth per sheet varies according to the strain of silkworm and its voltinism. Under Indian conditions, approximately 250-275 of bivoltine or 275-300 of multivoltine moths can be distributed in 0.50 sq. meter base area.

The female moths are allowed to lay eggs for 24 hrs on the starch paper. After egg laying, sheets are collected and soaked in cold water for about 20-30 minutes. As a result, the gummy substance of the starch dissolved in water. The eggs become loose now. The eggs are removed from the sheet by hand or soft brush gently. The removed eggs are collected into nylon bag (doubled layered, 35 cm × 25 cm with hard loops tied at the nose of the washing tray) and washed in water to remove starch. Each bag will hold 600-750 gm of eggs released from 8-10 sheets. To avoid clustering of eggs, 0.2-0.3% freshly prepared bleaching powder solution is used while washing. Water temperature during washing and collection of eggs should be in the range of 20-25°C. High concentration of bleaching powder should be avoided as it is detrimental and has ovicidal effect on silkworm eggs. Use fresh solution of 10 liters for every bag of 500-600 gm of eggs. After washing, splash the nylon bag gently to remove the excessive water contents.

For the removal of undesirable eggs viz., unfertile and dead eggs, salt solution of specific gravity 1.06-1.09 is prepared. Eggs are first dipped in 1.06 specific gravity salt-water solutions wherein unfertile eggs float on the surface while fertile and dead eggs sink to the bottom. The floating unfertile eggs are removed and eggs from the bottom are transferred to 1.09 specific gravity salt water solution.

Hence the fertile eggs float on the surface of the salt solution while dead eggs will sink to the bottom. The floating fertile eggs are collected and the sunken dead eggs are rejected. The fertile eggs are again washed in water to remove salt. The washed eggs are dried in shade and if hatching is required within 10-15 days in bivoltine, perform acid treatment as per schedule. For elimination of lighter eggs, feed the eggs into hopper of the winnowing unit and switch on the fan, discard the lighter eggs, which are blown away. Winnowing of hibernated eggs eliminate the unfertilized eggs satisfactorily. Regulate the speed of the fan of winnowing machine as per requirement for every lot winnowed. These eggs are ready for packing.

The weight of eggs varies from breed to breed, season to season, crop to crop and even day to day during incubation. A unit of 20,000 eggs equivalent to 50 Dfls @ 400 eggs per laying is considered as a standard unit. The box carrying loose eggs are made up of light wood frame, of which both sides are packed with thin cloth. On one side of the cloth at the top corner, a slit is made through which eggs are poured and slit is closed and sealed with sticker and an index slip is affixed on the frame. The index slip must indicate name of the grainage, lot number, breeds packed, quantity, laid on date, expected release of date, probable date of hatching etc. Before filling the eggs in the boxes, the standard weight of silkworm eggs is calculated. Bivoltine eggs generally weigh between 1500-1700 and multivoltine 1800-2100 eggs per gram. According to this one box of egg will contain approximately 20,000 ÷ 1600 = 12.5 gm of eggs or 50 Dfls. The eggs could be weighed and packed according to the weight. For this, weigh one gram of eggs on the electronic top loading balance and count them. Then calculate the weight of eggs to be packed i.e. weight of eggs to be packed = 20000 ÷ Number of eggs per gram e.g. if number of eggs per gram = 1600, then weight of eggs to be packed = 20,000 ÷1600= 12.5 or 13.0 gm/box.

Alternatively, instead of weighing every time, after determining the weight of 20,000 eggs, the weighed eggs can be filled in a narrow test tube and the level can be marked with a glass marking pencil. The same volume may be used for subsequent measurement for packing of eggs. Since, weight loss is observed with every day's development, the counting and packing should be done simultaneously on the day of packing. Preserve the boxes horizontally in ideal conditions.

Advantages of loose egg production: Eggs in loose forms are produced to ensure:

- Supply of quality eggs with higher hatchability.
- Supply of uniform and assured quantity of eggs independent of race/season/region/source of its production.

Production and distribution of loose eggs have many advantages both qualitatively and quantitatively, some of which are highlighted below -

- Facilitates elimination of unfertilized, dead, poor quality and defective eggs to ensure supply of only good quality eggs and hence increased hatchability and cocoon productivity.
- The egg recovery in grainages could be substantially increased as the healthy laying with low fecundity is also collected.
- Surface sterilization of eggs is performed effectively and completely.
- As loose eggs are supplied in standard unit by weight, distribution is considered more perfect with each and every indenter has equal number of eggs for same Dfls.
- Since there is uniformity in distribution of eggs, evaluation/comparison between different races and seasons on the performance of characters is more accurate and scientific.
- Handling is easy and space required during egg laying by moth is comparatively less.
- Acid treatment of bivoltine eggs, preservation, incubation and transportation of eggs is easy and more convenient.

- ➢ Quality of eggs can be judged more accurately.
- ➢ Economical seed production process.
- ➢ Easy for mass egg production.

Inspite of all these advantages, the production of loose eggs is not popular in India at commercial level. It has certain disadvantages also like:

- ➢ Calculation of hatching % is not accurate and at the same time difficult also.
- ➢ This method cannot be advocated for reproductive egg production.
- ➢ Techniques for separation of unfertilized egg are not accurate.
- ➢ Loose egg production is more laborious and time consuming if performed in smaller quantities.
- ➢ Since the minimum unit handled in each case is 50 Dfls, farmers have to inevitably take the eggs in multiples of 50 Dfls irrespective of their rearing capacity, which sometimes leads shortage of leaf at the later stage of rearing.
- ➢ Surface disinfections of eggs, though carried out at the time of production, cannot be repeated at chawki rearing centers before incubation. Handling of loose eggs is cumbersome as differentiation of non-hibernating and hibernating egg is difficult.
- ➢ Lack of expertise in loose eggs preparation and insufficient infrastructure also come in the way. Lack of user-friendly suitable equipments to simplify egg preparation.

Major differences between flat and loose egg production technology are furnished in brief in Table 5.9.

There are two other methods, which are used in the production of eggs in the past but are not in use at present. These methods are:

A. **Industrial method:** In this method, 50-100 cocoons from the lot is selected and preserved at 30°C and 70%

Table 5.9: Differences between flat and loose egg production method

	Flat card/sheet egg production	*Loose egg production*
I.	Ordinary craft sheet without starch coating is used for egg laying	Ordinary craft sheet coated with starch are used for egg laying
II.	Craft sheet used for egg laying is mostly 22.5 × 28 cm in size	Starch coated craft sheet used for egg laying is of 75 cm × 105 cm in size
III.	On each sheet 20 moths are left to lay eggs	On each sheet 250-300 moths are left to lay eggs
IV.	Cellules are placed over the moth to restrict the egg laying area	Cellules are not used but moths are spread uniformly on the sheet
V.	Eggs are supplied after surface sterilization and acid treatment (Bivoltine)	Eggs laid on sheets are loosened, surface sterilized, acid treated, quantity measured, packed in loose egg boxes and supplied
VI.	Followed for P3, P2 and P1 seed production and also for F1 commercial seed production	Followed only for F1 commercial seed production

humidity. The moths emerged are examined for pebrine disease. If pebrine infection is not noticed, the moths are allowed to lay eggs on card in groups. In this case, the moths are not subjected further to microscopical examination. This method is very simple, requires less equipment and labour besides saving time and thus reducing cost of production of laying. But this method is not popular because disease laying may be passed to the rearers. This method can be practised only in areas where pebrine is not prevalent.

B. **Biological method:** Prof. E.F. Povakov invented this method. As soon as larvae start pupating, they are subjected to high temperature of 33.8°C in a special compartment for 16 hrs a day at 55-65% humidity. High temperature reduces the chances of pebrine by activating phagocytes in the body of pupae. Moths emerged are allowed to lay eggs. These moths are not subjected for microscopical examination. But this method has many disadvantages viz., more number of unfertilized and dead eggs are produced, percentage of emergence is reduced due to high temperature treatment, increased occurrence of defective moths etc.

Preparation of egg laying

Preparation of egg laying is an intense and tedious job. Every arrangement is made well in advance to avoid any confusion, error or hindrance during preparation of laying. The grainage house must be composed of seed cocoon preservation room, low temperature room and silkworm egg preservation room. The rooms for emergence of moths, mating, egg laying and preservation of silkworm eggs should be equipped with air conditioning devices to regulate temperature, humidity and ventilation. The room should be uniformly bright during daytime and dark during night. Strong light and wind should be avoided. The perforated cotton cloth/paper for covering the cocoons, the trays for mating and egg laying should be cleaned and disinfected before use. All the materials should be in sufficient number/quantity which must correspond with the highest rate of daily emergence.

Techniques of egg production

Seed cocoons are the source to produce silkworm eggs. The quantity of seed cocoon is related to the quantity of silkworm eggs produced and success of rearing of parent seed. Therefore, seed cocoons harvested have to be subjected to strict microscopical examination. The cocoons that qualify the fixed norms should be preserved to ensure production of high quality eggs and better cocoon yield.

Transportation of seed cocoons

The seed cocoons produced at rearing centers are transported to seed cocoon market and from there to egg producing centers. These cocoons packed in plastic crates/ baskets are transported through automobiles. Do not transport seed cocoons packed in gunny bags. It is better to transport either early in the morning or late at night when outside temperature is slightly lower. Midday, when the temperature can be high should be avoided for transporting the seed cocoons. Pack only 10 kg of seed cocoons in each plastic basket.

Purchase of seed cocoons

Only after completion of pupation, the seed cocoons should be purchased. Seed cocoons should be free from all kinds of diseases in general and from pebrine disease in particular and there thorough inspection of disease freeness is required before purchase of cocoons for seed production. Purchase only those batches which fulfill the following norms:

- Pupation rate must be above 80%.
- Number of cocoons per kilogram in bivoltine must be 570-650 only.
- Average yield of cocoons/100 Dfls must be above 45 kg. If cocoons are not within the norms, such batches must be rejected and sent to reeling.

Selection of seed cocoons

After quality inspection, seed cocoons are subjected to individual selection, and those which do not conform to the racial characteristics of the parental races should be discarded. This maintains the uniform quality of cocoons for egg production. Defective cocoons which are to be rejected are thin shelled cocoons, malformed cocoons, fluffy cocoons, light yellow or yellowish or other coloured cocoons, melted cocoons, calceiform cocoons, stained cocoons, Uzi-infested cocoons etc. All defective cocoons which are unfit for seed preparations are stifled in hot air chamber and sent for reeling. If this is not done, such cocoon gives foul smell and contaminates the grainage. Further, such cocoons attract demestid beetles, which may also eat healthy moths in the grainages. Defective cocoons are formed mostly due to genetic characteristics or unfavourable environmental factors.

Preservation of seed cocoons

Improper method of preservation of seed cocoons leads to irregular emergence. The conditions required for preservation of seed cocoons are as follows:

(a) **Temperature:** Seed cocoons are to be preserved at proper temperature. Optimum temperature for preservation of bivoltine seed cocoon is 24-25°C, at which the emergence rate is high, number of eggs laid by female moth is maximum, and rate of dead and unfertilized eggs is lower. If seed cocoons are preserved at 30°C, the rate of moth emergence decreases, number of unfertilized eggs, dead eggs and non-hibernating eggs increases significantly besides affecting the preserved pupae with flacherie disease. Male pupae are more affected at high temperature. If temperature is lower than 20°C, moth emergence rate decreases, fecundity falls sharply, unfertilized eggs increase, synchronization becomes difficult due to prolongation of moth emergence and here female pupae suffers the most. The effect of different preservation temperatures during pupal stage on egg production is detailed in Table 5.10.

(b) **Humidity:** The optimum humidity for preservation of seed cocoon is 75-80%. Moreover, it is established

Table 5.10: Relationship between different preservation temperatures during pupal stage and egg production (Source: Ming *et al.*, 1989)

Preservation temperature (°C)		No. of eggs laid		No. of good eggs		No. of unfertilized eggs	
Before pupation	After pupation	Fecundity	Index	Per moth	Index	Per moth	Index
25	25	576	100	552	100	24	100
20	20	480	83	448	81	32	133
30	30	246	44	172	31	74	308
20	30	394	68	311	56	83	345
30	20	326	58	300	54	26	108

that humidity in the range of 65-90% has no evident effect on the health of moth, fecundity, and number of unfertilized eggs or on the voltinism of silkworm in the next generation. But when humidity is less than 60%, the pupal development becomes slow, percentage of emergence will decrease and number of moths failing to mate will increase. Therefore, humidity during preservation of seed cocoons should be adjusted to optimum recommended level.

(c) **Photoperiod:** Cyclical light and darkness are to be maintained i.e. care should be taken to make brightness in the daytime and darkness at night. It is important that the night be comparatively dark and the preserved cocoons are exposed to light before dawn on the day of eclosion/emergence.

(d) **Ventilation:** Preservation room should be such that no heavy winds and direct sunlight should fall on it. The rate of respiration of pupae inside the cocoons increases with the development. The rate of respiration and release of carbon dioxide are high when compound eyes of pupae become coloured. Air should be kept fresh through ventilation in the preservation room.

Correlation between pigmentation and development of pupae

Due to varying rearing conditions, non-synchronization of spinning dates and erratic moth emergence is very common. Therefore, to regulate synchronization of emergence of moths for mating, it is necessary to observe the morphological changes in growth and development of pupae regularly. Temperature should be regulated in accordance with the degree of pigmentation of the compound eyes, antennae and their body in order to synchronize the emergence of moths of two varieties simultaneously for hybrid preparation.

Generally, pigmentation and development of pupae are correlated (Ming *et al.*, 1989) as:

- The start of pigmentation of compound eyes marks the half wayı oint between mounting and emergence.

- The compound eyes become black at the two-thirds point.
- When the antennae turn dark black, moth will emerge in two or three days.
- When the pupae body becomes loose and soft, loses its luster and becomes shriveled, moths will emerge the following day.
- If non-synchronization is noticed, consign female pupae at 7°C for 1 or 2 days only, a day before moth emergence.

Quality inspection of seed cocoons

Seed cocoons purchased from the market for seed production are subjected for quality inspection as indicated below:

- Cut open half kilogram of seed cocoons and record percentage of defective cocoons viz., melted, Uzi infested and muscardine affected.
- Percentage of double cocoons.
- Percentage of male and female cocoons.

Arrangement of cocoons: Good cocoons selected are arranged in single layer either in wooden or bamboo trays. Bamboo trays of 105 cm diameter can hold 1000-1200 multivoltine or 800-900 bivoltine seed cocoons. Overcrowding of cocoons should be avoided as it leads to pupal mortality. After separating the cocoons according to sexes, they are arranged separately in preservation room/ chambers. For preservation of pupae corrugated sheet or paddy husk is used. In order to increase the efficiency of separating the cocoons and moths perforated paper/cloth is used to cover the tray a day before the expected date of start of emergence.

Developmental events that occur once in the life cycle of an insect have long been known to express at specific part of the day to manifest a population rhythm. Emergence can be predicted by recognizing the changes in the colouration and flexibility of the body of the pharate adult, dark pigmentation of the compound eyes, antennae and wings and loss of luster of pupal skin and its elasticity, soft nature of body and formation of wrinkles upon touch.

Emergence: During seed cocoon preservation, pupa develops and metamorphoses gradually until it finally emerges as a silkworm moth. Moths generally emerge on 10th day of spinning in multivoltine or 12th day in bivoltine. Emergence continues for approximately 3 days. When moths are allowed to emerge in a natural way from the cocoons, a kind of digestive fluid is secreted known as 'cocoonase' which dissolve the sericin and soften the silk filament of cocoon shell which allows the moths to emerge from the shell by pushing with its head. Just after emergence, the scaly hair on the body surface of freshly emerged moths is moist, the body flexible, wings small and curled. The moth stays motionless at this stage. Soon afterwards, the scaly hair gradually dries and wings begin to spread apart. Male moths start flapping their wings continuously and crawl around in an active state while looking for female moths to mate.

Shortly before the emergence, the pupae wriggle once in a while with an audible sound. When metamorphosis is complete, the moth body and pupal skin gradually separate from each other. Before emergence, the pupal body is delicate and soft to the touch. This is the chief characteristic of this development stage. Under normal preservation conditions, exposure of light begins at 4.00 hrs in the morning and emergence essentially ceases at 8.00 hrs on the same day. Light should not be bright. Even 2 lux of light is sufficient to induce moth emergence. Trained labourers pick the emerged moths. The male moths, which emerged first, are picked out immediately to avoid mating with the females because of error in sex discrimination if any. In case copulation is observed, the copulating female moth should be discarded.

Synchronization of moth emergence

For preparation of hybrid, the male and female moths should be essentially available simultaneously. For synchronization, the eclosion is adjusted by brushing schedules or by refrigerating the eggs/cocoons/moths. In principle, refrigeration of seed cocoons or pupae should be avoided since it has adverse effect on the overall reproductive efficiency. However, if it is inevitable, just a day prior to emergence, male and female cocoons can be refrigerated for 7 and 3 days respectively (Jolly, 1983). The ideal and widely accepted practice is to refrigerate the male moths for a period ranging between 7 days to 2 weeks at 5°C or 7°C (Tazima, 1978, Jolly, 1983). Bivoltines are more resistant to cold storage than multivoltines. Bivoltine virgin females can be preserved at 5°C for 3 days in summer and 4-5 days in rainy season to synchronize the mating but this should not be practised in winter season even for a day (Singh *et al.*, 1994). Cold storage should be restricted to any one stage of development to avoid deleterious effect thereafter.

Moth collection: In advanced countries, colours are sprayed on moths to identify the sex and breed at the time of crossing. In India, specific coloured crates are used for picking male and female moths of different breeds. The moths picked should be temporarily preserved in a cool and dark place to inhibit their activities, which reduce their energy consumption. When male moths smell the scent 'bombycol' secreted from the alluring glands of female moths, they will become highly stimulated which causes male moths to waste much of their energy and even many of them drop to the floor from the trays which creates difficulty in the work of picking of emerged moths. Therefore, two sexes are stored in different rooms, which are kept dark. Under normal conditions, the work of moth collection should be completed by 8.30 hrs in the morning.

Moth selection: Defective moths should be eliminated for improving the quality of silkworm eggs. Before mating, it is necessary to carefully sort and eliminate defective female moths. The major types of defective moths that are to be rejected are:

- Too long body segment, bulky body, abnormal body shape and vestigial or underdeveloped wings.

- Inert or dropped scaly hair.
- Inactive or incapable of copulation.
- Early and late emerged moths.
- Black marks or colour on abdominal segments and wings.

Copulation: After emergence of moths is over, the mating/crossing/copulation is carried out according to the plan of hybridization. Craft paper is spread over a wooden frame bearing the name of the breed. Generally emergence of moth occurs early in the morning. Male moths emerge first followed by females. When female moths emerge they take one or two minutes to spread their wings and prepare for copulation. Female moths are collected from the room and are evenly distributed on trays and then male moths are broadcasted over them and allowed to mate naturally. There should be about 20% more male moths than females. After about 10-20 minutes, pairing begins naturally. After pairing, unpaired moths are picked out and gathered in a separate tray. About 300-400 females can be accommodated in a wooden tray of size 60 × 90 cm and about 400-500 male moths are broadcasted over it. The paired moths in the process of copulation are arranged evenly with adequate spacing in between to avoid interruption and decoupling.

Sufficient time must be allowed for copulation. If it is too short, egg laying will be delayed and slow, fecundity will be less and more unfertilized eggs will be laid. On the other hand, if copulation is too long, decoupling will result in immediate oviposition and great loss. It is established by experience that pairing of 45 minutes at optimum temperature and humidity is sufficient for fertilization. However, for commercial egg production, copulation is allowed for 3-4 hrs since during this period at least two ejaculations occur. First ejaculation occurs during first 30 minutes and the second after one and half hours.

Duration of mating varies slightly with the temperature of oviposition room, silkworm races and number of mating to be allowed for male moths. Mating is little shorter at high temperature. It is best for the male moth to be allowed to mate once a day and should not be allowed for more than two matings. If mating is repeated on the same day, male moths should be refrigerated at 5 ± 2°C to rest for two hours between the first and second mating. Male moths should not be used for more than two times under any circumstances. If used for more than two times, it results in poor fecundity and more unfertilized eggs.

The optimum temperature during copulation should be 24-25°C for bivoltine and 27-28°C for multivoltines. The relative humidity in both the instances should be maintained at 75-85%. At high temperature of 30°C and dry conditions, the moths are naturally decoupled before completion of specific duration of mating. When mating is in progress, if decoupled moths are noticed, they should be removed and left to mate a new.

Male moth preservation

Before and after pairing, male moths have to be preserved at 7°C. Do not overcrowd the male moths. Keep 800-1000 male moths in each tray of standard size. If male moths have to be reused on the same day for second pairing, they should be rested at least for 3 hrs at 7°C.

Decoupling: After the time set for mating is over, male and female moths are detached. This process of detaching the male and female is known as decoupling. Decoupling/ depairing has to be done by experienced persons. Care must be taken not to apply force in pulling the moths apart, as reproductive organs could be damaged. The female moth is held between the thumb and middle finger and male moth is slightly pulled.

After mating, the female moth passes a considerable quantity of urine just before egg laying. The mother moth not having urinated or not having thoroughly urinated would not only have a late oviposition but also would contaminate eggs when they urinate during the course of oviposition. If urine is allowed to mix with eggs, it solidifies on the eggs and such eggs may die. In order to avoid such mortality, mother moths should be shaken to accelerate their urination. It is suggested to collect the decoupled female moths on a piece of soft cloth. Instead of in heaps, moths should be evenly dispersed on the cloth selected for the urination purpose. Then with two hands, the piece of cloth with moths on it should be lightly lifted and gently shaken up and down for 2-3 minutes. This will help the female moths to urinate thoroughly. Otherwise, the moths will delay laying their eggs and urine will spoil the craft paper and contaminate the eggs.

Oviposition: After decoupling and urination, female moths are collected and allowed to lay eggs on egg laying sheet, which are kept ready by the method described. The diversity of oviposition conditions of silkworm moth is closely related to differences of breed, duration of mating and temperature during oviposition and intensity of light. The earlier laid eggs are usually bigger than the late laid eggs in almost all the silkworm races. Also egg laying is quicker with prolonged mating and will be slow if mating duration is short. Oviposition can be accelerated, if temperature of oviposition room is high and will be slowed down if the temperature is low. In addition, fluctuation in temperature than the optimum level also affects the quality of silkworm eggs.

The temperature of 24 ± 1°C and humidity of 75 ± 5% are maintained in the oviposition room. This is very essential for good and optimum egg production. If humidity is less, the gummy substance secreted by female moths gets dried up on the ovipositor and obstructs egg laying. This results in less number of eggs laid by the female moth. To maintain humidity, humidifiers are used in oviposition room. During summer, wet gunny cloths are hung in the oviposition room and sand beds under the tray stands are also arranged.

Oviposition rooms are made dark for rapid egg laying. The doors and windows of oviposition room should be shaded with black curtains. Moths are kept in oviposition room till next morning by providing optimum environment. Usually the rate of oviposition reaches approximately 95% and sometimes surpasses 95% within 8 hrs of oviposition.

Moth collection after oviposition: Most of the silkworm eggs are laid in the same evening before 22.00 hrs. Therefore, female moths are usually collected on the following morning both in the case of multivoltine and those bivoltine, which are intended, for artificial hatching treatment. If, however, they are intended for hibernating eggs, there is no harm in postponing moth collection. However, it is being observed that most of the eggs laid on the second day of oviposition are unfertilized eggs. Moths collected for mother moth examination at later day are taken out and put into boxes indicating the date of oviposition, name of the breed, batch and serial number and stored in well-ventilated dry places. The moths should be well protected against insects or rat attacks or mould.

Harvesting of eggs: Harvesting of silkworm eggs is carried out after moth collection. The egg sheets are checked for poor layings in case of flat card method of egg production. Poor layings are those where the numbers of eggs in a laying are much less than the standard or norms fixed for a Dfl of a breed. These poor layings are scrapped and removed. Now the egg laying sheets are soaked in 2% formalin solution for nearly 15-20 minutes. This helps in surface sterilization of eggs. These eggs are washed in water and allowed to dry in shade. The certificate of disease freeness of seed is affixed. The egg sheets must carry the name of the grainage, hybrid combination/name of the breed, date of egg laying, signature of moth examiner and number of good Dfls on the sheet. In case of multivoltines, these eggs are ready for sale.

In case of bivoltines, eggs generally undergo hibernation within 48 hrs of oviposition. Therefore, if hatching is required within 15 days, the eggs must be treated with acid within 20 hrs of egg laying. In case hatching is required after lapse of more than one month, the healthy layings after washing with formalin are sent to cold storage for preservation.

6

OVIPOSITION AND EGG PRESERVATION

OVIPOSITION

Oviposition and egg laying behaviour has been at the centre of many of the major debates. Ever since Ehrlich and Raven (1964) report on co-evolution of butterflies and plants, Lepidopteron probably being the Texan in which the greatest number of species have been studied for some aspects of oviposition behaviour. The biological factors depending upon behavioural patterns and physiological conditions of male and female members of insects searching each other for mating and reproduction have been reported to be responsible for perpetuation of the population.

Oviposition is an important physiological and behavioural aspect in the life cycle of the silkworm, *Bombyx mori*. It is an act of reproduction through which viable eggs are laid by fertilized female moths. Number of factors and events are involved in the successful egg deposition which includes neural, hormonal, chemical, environmental, physical and behavioural. Besides these successful and viable eggs deposition by an adult female moth also depends upon various events of significance importance of reproductive physiology viz., mating, vitellogenesis, ovulation and oviposition etc.

Stimulation of oviposition

A range of adult behaviours is exhibited in succession after eclosion in the silkworm. The eclosion occurs during the opening of a particular gate. The insects that had completed development are able to emerge at this gate. If the insects are not competent enough to emerge from pupal case, must wait for the next open gate. The term 'gate' can be applied to such event that occurs only during a limited span of time. Thus a gate is being opened for a specific period of time once each day. In female moths, the calling behaviour (pheromone release) occurred after the expansion of wings. In 1959, Karlson and Luscher suggested the name pheromone for those substances 'secreted to out side by an individual and received by another individual of the same species, in which that releases a specific reaction'. The female moth secretes sex pheromone from the lateral glands of the last abdominal segment to attract male for mating. This pheromone is known as 'Bombykol' (10-12-hexa-decadien-1-ol) which in real sense is a primary alcohol with a chemical structure of $CH_3\ (CH_2)_2\ (CH = CH)_2\ (CH_2)_8\ CH_2OH$.

The scales of silk moth also serve as a releaser of copulation attempt followed by wing vibration and mating dance by male moths. Mating dance helps in determining the location of the consepecific female. The chemoreceptive abilities of male to bombykol produced by female are very high. Males react to bombykol at a concentration as low as 100 molecules of attractant per cubic centimeter of air. Even a single molecule of female sex pheromone is sufficient to trigger an impulse in the male receipt cells. This is due to presence of large number of sensilla (60,000) on the bipectinate antennae of moth, whose surface area with all the remi included is approximately 29 mm^2. During mating dance, male produces a strong air current with its wings, which flows parallel to body's longitudinal axis and could trace the pheromone source by testing the air. Further dancing male can draw air from the distance of 4 cm in front of its head while wing vibrations draw air from the sides of its area, thus improving the efficiency of antennae.

The response of male moths to the female secretion pheromone is not just a simple attraction but also a complex sequential series of events by anemotaxis, which occurs, in zigzag stages as:

- Reception-antennal elevation.
- Activation-wing fluttering.
- Orientation towards the source of pheromone (anemotaxis).
- Alighting-lending in an immediate vicinity of female moth.
- Copulation-mating.

For successful oviposition, three factors or events are of utmost importance:

a. The mating partner should be reproductively competent.
b. The mating should be at right time.
c. The mating should be followed by transfer of sperm and male factor (oviposition stimulating substance or fecundity enhancing substance) in the reproductive tract of the adult female.

Duration and frequency of mating

The mating length in silkworm essentially affects silkworm seed quality and quantity. In *Bombyx mori,* natural copulation continues for 6-12 hours and sometimes because of such prolonged copulation female moth dies without laying any eggs. The number of eggs laid by a female moth depends on its genotype and development, which increases in a proportion to the duration of mating (Askari and Sharan, 1984). Punitham *et al.* (1987) stated that mating duration up to 6 hrs increased the total egg output and reduced pre-oviposition period but subsequent increase in duration resulted in negative effects.

Moreover, mating lengths of 150-180 minutes is as optimal variants for enhancing productivity and quality of silkworm seed. Further, it is to be mentioned that for production of super elite, elite and reproductive seed, mating for less than 120-150 minutes should not be allowed, while for production of commercial seed, it should not be less than 90-120 minutes. A minimum period of 45 minutes is adequate to ensure normal egg laying with regard to both fertility and number of eggs laid and two matings can easily be adopted without affecting any of the commercial traits, such as number and viability of eggs, cocoon weight, shell weight and yield of good cocoons. By resorting to repeated mating of selected males, the cost of seed cocoons and consequently the cost of seed for commercial rearing can appreciably be reduced. Petkov and Mladenov (1979) observed that male silk moth could successively mate with 8 females of the same origin. Ram and Singh (1992) stated that a single male could mate with at least 11 females in bivoltine silk moths but higher percentage of viable eggs can be obtained only from the first mating. Gupta *et al.* (1986) stated that male of multivoltine and bivoltine can mate with 16 and 18 females respectively.

The mating capacity of males of *Bombyx mori* pure breeds as compared with hybrids was studied by Benchamin *et al.* (1990) with repeated mating (6 times a day) for six consecutive days (with rest periods at 5°C between mating) and stated that fecundity in multivoltine female parent was not influenced by the male but other characters including effective rate of mating, fecundity and fertility differed significantly among different crosses. All quantitative characters seem to decrease significantly with the increase in the number of matings. However, a male moth can mate to a large number of females but many-fold use of male silk moths for mating results in decrease in the basic biological characters, which include not only cocoon technological qualities but also the fertility of resulting moths. Further mating from 3rd fold onwards results in decrease of hatchability, viability, cocoon yield, cocoon weight, silk yield, filament length etc and hence future technologies should not allow more than two-fold mating for the production of silkworm seed to obtain better results not only in fertility but also for stable cocoon crop. Moreover, it is imperative to preserve the same male moth for 2 hrs at 5 ± 2°C for successful second-fold re-use.

Time of ejaculation

Mladenov (1990) stated that ejaculation occurs after 10 minutes of mating. At a shorter than 10 minutes mating duration, female moths could be utilized for production of hybrid silkworm seed with no risk of pure race contamination. Krishanaswami *et al.* (1973) reported that first ejaculation starts about 9 minutes after copulation and completed after 25 minutes of mating and hence optimum-mating duration of 30 minutes is adequate for obtaining desired number of viable eggs, which is sufficient to provide copulation stimulus essential for egg laying without impairing the percentage of fertility.

Although in silkworm *Bombyx mori,* the virgin female moths have fully developed eggs whose development takes place during pupal stage but lack of copulation reduces the number of eggs laid. The copulation provides some essential stimulus for oviposition and in *Bombyx mori,* the stimulus that incites egg laying is not the direct stimulus of copulation but is the stimulus by spermatozoa removing from the recepticulum seminalis to the vestibulum. Drastic biochemical events occurred in the spermatophore of the silkworm after mating. This assured the presence of normal sperm and or testicular fluid in the female reproductive organ (bursa-copulatrix/spermatheca) in sufficient number to induce the ovipositional bahaviour. On an average, normal male moths have 15.4×10^5 spermatozoa per head. It-is generally recognized that the male factors or the oviposition-stimulating substance (OSS) derived from the male reproductive tract are transferred to female during mating and these factors have the ability to accelerate the oviposition behaviour.

The male factor has been identified chemically in some insect order including Lepidopteron and is being termed as 'fecundity enhancing substance, or 'oviposition stimulating substance (OSS)'. These factors in the silkworm *(Bombyx mori)* have been identified as 'Prostaglandin'. Oviposition is stimulated in the female moth following the transfer of prostaglandin during mating. Hence, level of prostaglandin increases in mated females. Brady (1983) stated that prostaglandin increases egg laying in the silk moth by stimulating muscles in the oviduct in the same way as is being reported in egg laying vertebrates (Wechsung and Houvenaghel, 1976).

Vitellogenesis

It is a process through which the terminal oocytes grow unto final size before ovulation. This is achieved by incorporation of female specific protein 'vitellogenin' via haemolymph. The fat body and follicle cells of the ovary synthesize the vitellogenin at a specific age in the insect life cycle. These proteins have been found to be precursor of the egg yolk protein. The vitellogenin are termed 'vitellin' when deposited in the eggs. The vitellin and other similar yolk protein make up approximately 80% of the yolk proteins. The synthesis of vitellogenin is under the control of juvenile hormone and ecdysteroids. The juvenile hormone is secreted by Corpora Allata (CA) and is regulated (stimulated or inhibited) by neurosecretory cells of the brain and some other factors.

The ecdysone secreted from prothoracic gland and responsible for moulting also plays a major role in reproduction (Hoffmann *et al.*, 1980) and follicle cell, epithelium is the exact site of ecdysone biosynthesis. These ecdysteroids are either secreted into haemolymph or retained and accumulated in the oocytes to play a major role in vitellogenesis. During moth emergence, the brain stimulates synthesis of JH by CA. Juvenile hormone induces mating end and causes the ovary to become prepared to respond to a neurohormone, termed as 'Egg Development Neurohormone' (EDNH). EDNH triggers the synthesis and release of ecdysone from the ovary. Ecdysone, after its hydroxylation to 20-hydroxy ecdysone, stimulates vitellogenin synthesis.

Ovulation and oviposition

Ovulation is the process of expulsion of eggs from the ovary into the oviduct and oviposition is the passage of the eggs from oviduct through external genital opening of the female to the substratum/egg laying site. Ovulation and oviposition are related at least to the extent that ovulation is a prerequisite for ovulation. In other words, oviposition will not occur unless ovulation has taken place and in that oviposition frequently follows ovulation. Oviposition in silkworm is dependent on a number of intrinsic and extrinsic factors viz., neural, hormonal, environmental, physical, behavioural etc. It is a complex phenomenon involving multiplicity of coordinated events such as interaction between internal and external genetalia and the abdominal muscular system must be integrated in an orderly manner for systematic oviposition.

The mechanism controlling the switch from virgin to mated behaviour is not exactly known. Giebultowicz *et al.* (1990) reported that in *Lymantria* moth, the switch from virgin to mated behaviour could occur spontaneously in senescing virgin females. The same holds true also in *Bombyx mori* (Fugo and Arisawa, 1992). The bursa copulatrix and the spermatheca seems to be involved in the behavioural switching pattern from virgin to mated condition.

Mating provides a stimulus for activating ovulation. Information regarding mating is conveyed to the brain through 'spermathecal factor' released from spermatheca of mated females. This stimulation regulates the brain to release 'myotropic peptide' or 'ovulation hormone' or 'oviposition stimulating substance (OSS)', which affect the activity of the last abdominal ganglion of female moths for stimulation of oviposition. The female moths lay eggs in monolayer very compactly on the surface of the egg card. An actively ovipositing moth touches with its caudal tip the surface of the egg card or the margin of the previously laid eggs turning its abdomen from right to left or left to right. The long axis of the egg is mostly oriented radically. On the caudal tip, a pair of anal papillae is present and sensory hairs on them serves as mechanoreceptors to perceive the textural conditions of the oviposition substratum.

Temperature, humidity and oviposition

Considerably less is known about the effect of temperature and humidity on oviposition bahaviour. Virgin female requires optimum condition of environment for oviposition, which must be met; otherwise, it will lay only few eggs or none. Bliss (1927) was apparently the first to distinguish between the effect of temperature on the development of oocytes and its effect on oviposition behaviour. The rate of oviposition varies with temperature, which can be accelerated up to a point and then falls off rapidly. Nevertheless, the temperature limits between which oviposition can occur are often much narrower than the range of temperature over which the other activities of the same species remain normal.

The male seems often more sensitive than female to abnormal temperature. When 5th instar larvae were exposed to high temperature (32°C) for 72 hrs, the emerging males showed complete sterility. Maximum ovulation and oviposition with minimum retention of egg can occur at 25.36 ± 0.17°C (optimum) temperature and 80 ± 5% relative humidity. Any fluctuations of temperature from optimum level lead to decreased ovulation, oviposition rate, fecundity and increased retention of eggs. After mating, the female moths started to look for oviposition site. Female moths start to oviposit their eggs mostly at dusk and about 90% of the eggs that had matured are being deposited in a short span of time during night. Hardly, 9.65% egg laying took place from 24 hrs to 48 hrs, while less than 1% eggs in each hour are being laid from 16 hrs to 24 hrs of decoupling.

Photoperiod in insects serves as a clock indicating the seasonal changes and influencing its life cycle, distribution and abundance. Several workers have demonstrated the influence of photoperiod on the behaviour of silkworm *(Bombyx mori)*. Photoperiod plays an important role on oviposition and in that dark condition favours rapid oviposition, while bright has opposite effect. Maximum fecundity and minimum egg retention are recorded when the female moths are exposed to fluorescent light (80 lux) during day and darkness during night.

Oviposition and surface texture

Texture of the substratum has an influence on the egg laying behaviour in the silk moth, which includes the number of eggs laid, total time taken for complete egg laying and the rate of egg deposition. The sensory hairs (sensory receptors) on the ovipositor and on the anal papillae in silk moth influences oviposition through the sensory input received by these hairs. Maximum numbers of eggs are reported to be oviposited on a smooth surface (Gupta *et al.*, 1990) and this decreases with the increase in roughness of the substratum.

Responses to surface topography or texture by ovipositing females are mediated by tactile setae. In *Bombyx mori,* tactile setae on a pair of anal papillae are innervated from the last abdominal ganglion. Silkworm normally lay eggs in a monolayer and the ovipositing female keeps touching the surface or margin of the group of previously laid eggs with its anal papillae turning its abdomen from side to side. If the tactile hairs on the papillae are first cut and then burnt with acid, so that dendrites are destroyed, oviposition is disorganized and the eggs are often laid in piles instead of monolayers. Besides surface topography, the plane of inclination and preservation condition of pupae also played an important role in oviposition, while slightly inclined plane of oviposition site leads to higher fecundity.

Fecundity and weight of pupae or phorate adult

The number of eggs in the body of female silk moth depends on its genotype and development. Highly significant positive correlation of fecundity in some sericigenous moths, *Antheraea mylitta, Philosamia ricini* and *Samia cynthia ricini* with pupal weight has already been established. High level of linear relationship between female pupal weight and potential fecundity as well as pupal weight and eggs laid has also been studied in various insects.

In the silkworm *(Bombyx mori)* the heaviest pupae resulted in highest fecundity. Further, the maximum larval weight, cocoon, shell and pupal weights, moth emergence and fecundity in succeeding generation were also maximum in the progeny resulted from the heaviest female pupae. Highly significant positive correlation (Table 6.1) between female pupal weight and fecundity has been demonstrated in *Bombyx mori*. Though the selection of individuals for higher fecundity depends on its pupal weight but extreme heavy weight should be avoided as it may lead to bottleneck phenomenon. Therefore, selection of moderate pupal weight should only be encouraged for egg production as it determines increased larval weight, survival rate, filament length etc in the successive generations. Female pupal weight, which is positively correlated with fecundity, has also been reported positively correlated with larval weight and shell ratio, cocoon weight and moth weight (Table 6.2).

Table 6.1: Correlation between female pupal weight and fecundity in the silkworm *Bombyx mori* (Source: Singh, 1994)

Female pupal weight (gm) Range	*Average*	*Average fecundity*	*Correlation Coefficient*
1.000-1.200	1.12308	443.600	+0.8720**
1.201-1.300	1.24280	468.040	+0.9209**
1.301-1.500	1.41356	487.880	+0.8646**
1.501-1.700	1 .54728	535.360	+0.8456**
1.701-1.800	1 .74440	559.280	+0.8366**
Pooled data			
1.000-1.800	1.41422	498.831	+0.7820**

** Significant at 1% level of significance

Fecundity and larval density

Insect growth and development proceed optimally under certain population density. Larval population density has a great impact on biology, morphology and physiology of insects. Larval crowding due to inadequate rearing space has also been found to increase the larval duration and mortality; reduce the larval, pupal and imaginal weights and affects morphology, longevity, fecundity and fertility of the resulting moths in several representatives of the order Lepidoptera.

In silkworm, *Bombyx mori* the larval behaviour, yield of cocoons and cocoon features are determined by the space provided to the larvae especially during rearing of 5th instar. The space requirement for the larvae is maximum a day or two before spinning. At this stage, larvae increases by about ten thousand times in weight, seven thousand times in volume and four hundred times in body surface to become full-grown mature larvae. Under these circumstances, it becomes essential to provide adequate spacing in rearing bed to enable the larvae to eat enough actively in accordance with their growing stage to ensure successful harvest of bumper cocoon crop.

According to Hinton (1981), there exists a relation between larval density and fecundity. Further, the weight of female moth is directly related to its weight as a pupa and as a larva, and there is therefore usually a close relation between the fecundity of the adult and the weight of its pupa and larva. Positive effect of wider rearing space on larval growth, fecundity, hatchability and also on various economic characters of cocoons have been established from which it can be inferred that an increase in population density in rearing bed decreased fecundity and hatchability in mulberry silkworm.

Rearing space for 20,000 larvae (50 Dfls) of bivoltine silkworm *(Bombyx mori)* as adopted in different countries indicates wider spacing under Chinese schedule is better than Japanese and Indian for rearing of same number of larvae of any stage. The recommended Indian spacing for rearing of different stages is in between Chinese and Japanese. Studies conducted and comparisons made for three kinds of spacing schedule under Indian agro-climatic conditions reveal that recommended Chinese spacing holds better than both Japanese and Indian schedules. The 'Evaluation Index' (Singh and Rao, 1993) calculated also supports the view that wider rearing spacing has positive influence on various economic parameters.

While larval density has negative correlation with fecundity and pupal weight, its duration is negatively correlated with survival (Kasivishwanathan, 1976), reelability and neatness while positively with filament length and filament weight (Ohi *et al.*, 1970) (Table 6.2).

Table 6.2: Correlation between various economic parameters in silkworm influencing egg production

Correlation between	*Type of Correlation*
Fecundity and productivity	Negative
Fecundity and robustness	Negative
Fecundity and female pupal weight	Positive
Fecundity and moth weight	Positive
Pupal weight and larval weight	Positive
Pupal weight and shell ratio	Positive
Pupal weight and cocoon weight	Positive
Larval duration and filament length	Positive
Larval duration and filament weight	Positive
Larval duration, reelability and neatness	Negative
Larval duration and survival	Negative
Larval density and fecundity	Negative
Larval density and pupal weight	Negative

Following points are to be taken into consideration while preparing the laying for better results:

- Reproductively competent mating partner should only be allowed for perpetuation of population. The deformed, inactive, under-and over-sized moths should invariably be rejected.
- Mating duration should at least be 3 hrs for obtaining optimum productivity and quality of seed.
- Future technologies should not allow more than two-fold mating for production of seed. Moreover, male moths should be preserved at 5 ± 2°C for at least 2 hrs for successful second-fold reuse.
- Optimum temperature (25 ± 1°C) and relative humidity (80 ± 5%) during oviposition should be

maintained. Any fluctuation from optimum level affects ovulation, oviposition rate and fecundity.

- Dark conditions should be maintained during oviposition.
- For better egg recovery, mated female moths should be allowed to urinate by tapping/jerking/ shaking.
- Texture of the ovipositing site should be somewhat smooth.
- Too much high pupal/adult weight should not be allowed for egg production but only moderate weight should be encouraged.
- Wider spacing of rearing should be followed which has positive influence on various economic characters of paramount importance.

PRESERVATION OF SILKWORM EGGS

Preservation refers to the management and protection of eggs during the period from egg laying to hatching of the hibernating eggs. The success of silkworm crop depends on many factors like quality of seed, mulberry leaf, environmental factors, mode of rearing etc. Preservation of seed without affecting its quality and viability is an important factor in sericulture. The conditions under which eggs are preserved directly affect the hatching rate, rearing and quality of cocoon filament. The diapause and non-diapause characteristics of silkworm eggs are decided on the basis of the genetic traits and environmental conditions. In case of bivoltine silkworm, it is possible to make the eggs either to enter diapause or non-diapause through manipulation of incubation temperature. The cocoon quality of non-diapause eggs is usually inferior to that of silkworms that produce diapause eggs. Therefore, the preference of sericulturist is for diapausing eggs. These diapausing eggs can be made to hatch either through artificial treatment (hydrochlorization) or through preservation at low temperature for specific period. The changes of external conditions have direct influence on the development of diapausing eggs. If preservation is not done properly, more eggs will die, hatching will not be uniform, larvae of the next generation will be weak and sericultural production will be affected.

However, the preservation of eggs at low temperature is in practice from the last ten decades, but it is not known who has first initiated the cold storage of silkworm eggs. Yokoyama (1973) stated that first large scale practice of preservation of silkworm eggs was by Kisaburo Maeda who had used the natural caves situated at the footsteps of mount Fuji. The temperature in these caves was 0-4°C throughout the year.

The cold storage of silkworm eggs was improved by the use of refrigerator in 1902. Chotaro Yokota (1917) for the first time invented complex storage method. Mizuno (1920) suggested that safe duration of cold storage was dependent upon the storage of embryo, the temperature of storage and characteristics of silkworm variety. Considering these factors into account, several methods of storing of silkworm eggs for a long period without affecting the hatchability was reported (Yokoyama, 1973).

Conditions for egg preservation

Climatic conditions play a very important role during preservation of eggs. Once eggs are laid, they undergo maturation division, fertilization and nuclear division and in about week's time, embryo enters a state of stable diapause. Eggs when laid are light yellow in colour, which gradually changes into reddish brown and after one and a half days to two days, the colour continues to darken. On 5th day, the eggs display specific colour fixed for the breed. During this period development of eggs is very fast and rate of respiration is high. Therefore, eggs should be kept carefully to avoid shock, crush or rub. Again, the eggs should be preserved at 25°C and any change in this optimum temperature will influence development of silkworm eggs.

If newly laid eggs are preserved to a temperature of more than 30°C, it affects the physiological activity and may result more unfertilized eggs and non-diapause eggs.

The development below 20°C makes the diapause completion uncertain. Humidity should be maintained in between 75-85%, as too much drying will degenerate the development of eggs. At the same time, excessive humidity is also harmful, as it will give rise to the development of fungus either directly on the eggs or on the egg card. This will increase the number of dead and unfertilized eggs.

Substances harmful for development of silkworm eggs

There are many substances, which are harmful to the development of silkworm eggs. The most likely to be encountered in the preservation of silkworm eggs are moulds, tobacco, insecticides, oils, alcohols, perfumes, paste, mercury, alkaline substances, bad smells etc.

Washing and disinfection of eggs

In order to get rid of the scaly hair, urine and pathogenic microorganisms attach to the surface and also to allow silkworm eggs to adhere properly to the surface of egg card in case of sheet eggs, the silkworm eggs must be washed properly and disinfected. The disinfection is done before transferring the eggs into cold storage. For disinfection, silkworm eggs are dipped in 2% formaldehyde solution at 20°C for 20 minutes by turning egg cards up and down during immersion to disinfect eggs evenly. After disinfection, the egg cards are washed in clean running water and hang up individually to dry.

Preservation of hibernating eggs

Generally, bivoltine eggs are subjected to cold storage so that they can be used for rearing as and when required. The eggs produced in spring can be used for next spring or next autumn or next summer by adjusting the aestivation period after oviposition and cold storage. There is correlation between duration of aestivation (number of days preserved at normal room temperature) and refrigeration as indicated in Table 6.3.

Two-step cold storage (double refrigeration or intermediate care)

Sometimes, silkworm eggs should be preserved in cold storage for rather a long period. In this case, procedure of

Table 6.3: Relationship between aestivation (25°C) and cold storage (5°C) (Source: Narasimhanna, 1985)

Aestivation period (days)	*1*	*3*	*5*	*10*	*20*	*40*	*60*	*80*	*100*
Shortest cold Storage days	79	87	87	89	98	105	119	124	134
Longest cold storage days	139	165	168	178	193	202	196	161	145
Effective cold Storage period (days)	61	79	82	90	96	98	78	38	12

two-step cold storage is to be adopted for better results. This means that silkworm eggs undergo two times preservation in cold storage. It is very well established that the embryo of silkworm eggs has got the corresponding tolerance limit for optimum cold storing temperature at each stage of embryonic development. Therefore, eggs are cold stored for certain period at specific stage of embryonic development to retain the vitality of embryo. The method of two-step cold storage of silkworm eggs is detailed below:

Step-1: Step 1 consists of eggs being cold stored at a particular embryonic developmental stage. The cold storage temperature should be around 5°C. Time limit for cold storage is around 90-100 days.

Step-2: Step 2 consists of releasing the eggs from the cold storage when they have reached the time limit of the first step and further preserved for 3 days at 15°C or 10 days at 10°C and a relative humidity of 85% for allowing the embryos to reach the longest stage (stage-15). The stage of development of silkworm eggs should be confirmed by embryo tests. When the development of silkworm eggs reaches the longest stage, they are subjected to second step of cold storage at 2.5°C for 10-40 days depending upon the need of hatching for undertaking brushing. Although, the limit for the second stage cold storage may be as long as 100 days but it is safer not to exceed for more than 80 days.

Stage-11: The formation of mesoderm starts at central portion of the embryo and extends to caudal and head region. The mesoderm shows regional differences in thickness and the arrangement appears to look like body segments.

Stage-12: After one day of release from clod storage at 15°C, the embryo appears slightly longer than stage XI. The head and caudal lobes are longer and appearance of segments is slightly clear.

Stage-13: After 2 days of release at 1-5°C, the embryo appears longer than stage XII. Mesodermal segments are clearly seen and depression in head lobe starts to appear.

Stage-14: After 2.5 days of release at 15°C, the embryo becomes slender and 18 segments can be clearly seen.

Stage-15: After 2.5 to 3 days of release at 15°C, the embryo is in its longest stage and occupies ¾ of the circumference of the egg. Depression in the head is clearly observed. It is actually the stage most suitable for double refrigeration.

Stage-16: After 3.5 to 4 days of release at 15°C, the embryo can be characterized by appearance of neural groove and appearance of body segments. This stage is not suitable for double refrigeration. At this stage, the eggs should be brought at room temperature for incubation.

The effective preservation in terms of number of days at stage 15°C is shown in Table 6.4.

Hibernation schedule

In tropical countries, natural temperature available is not conducive for preservation of bivoltine silkworm eggs. Further in tropical conditions where climate is favourable

Table 6.4: Effective cold storage duration of diapause eggs (Source: Mizuno)

Embryonic stage	*Temperature of cold storage (°C)*			
	- 2.5	0	+2.5	+5
Stage -1 1	170 days	150 days	150 days	120 days
Stage -12	120	120	70	70
Stage -13	70	70	70	70
Stage -14	70	100	90	40
Stage -15	60	60	100	30
Stage -16	60	60	80	30
Stage -17	30	30	30	30

for commercial silkworm rearing throughout the year, bivoltine male component is required for the production of multivoltine × bivoltine hybrids. However, it is not possible to rear bivoltine throughout the year to raise the seed cocoons. Therefore, bivoltine eggs are produced in favourable season and are released periodically as and when required. For this purpose, eggs are cold stored in cold storages, which are designed to have facilities for maintaining different temperatures throughout the year with humidity of 70-80%. Different hibernation schedules for various periods are in vogue to meet the seed supply programme throughout the year.

(a) Schedule of cold storage for 4 months

Bivoltine female moths allowed to lay eggs in oviposition room at 25°C and 70-80% humidity are examined next day for disease freeness. Healthy eggs are washed in 2% formalin solution for 10-15 minutes, and then washed in running water to remove excess of formalin. These eggs are then shade dried and transferred to cold storages, where they are preserves at 25°C for 10 days. These eggs are transferred at 20°C for 2 days; 15°C for 2 days; 10°C for 3 days, 5°C for 50 days and 2.5°C for 50 days. They are then released from cold storages and are subjected to 15°C for 6 hours and incubated at 25°C and 70-80% humidity (Table 6.5).

Table 6.5: Four months hibernation schedule

Preservation temperature (°C)	25	20	15	10	5	2.5	15	25
Preservation Duration (days)	10	2	2	3	50	50	6hr	Incubation till hatching

(b) Schedule of cold storage for 6 months

Female moths are allowed to lay eggs in oviposition room where a temperature of 25°C and humidity of 70-80% is maintained. Most of the eggs are laid in dusk. Next day moths are examined for disease freeness and healthy eggs are washed in 2% formalin solution for 10-15 minutes. Then these eggs are washed in running water to remove excess formalin. The eggs are dried in shade and kept at 25°C and 70-80% humidity for 20 days. The eggs are then transferred to cold storage. At cold storage, the eggs are kept at 20°C for 15 days; 15°C for 10 days; 10°C for 10 days; 5°C for 50 days and 2.5°C for 60 days. The eggs are then transferred to 15°C for 1 day and later released for incubation at 25°C and 70-80% humidity (Table 6.6).

Table 6.6: Six months hibernation schedule

Preservation temperature (°C))	25	20	15	10	5	2.5	15	25
Preservation duration (days)	20	15	10	10	50	60	1 day	Incubation till hatching

(c) Schedule of cold storage for 10 months

Two-step refrigeration is followed for preservation of eggs for long duration of 10 months. Female moths are allowed to lay eggs in oviposition room where a temperature of 25°C and humidity of 70-80% is maintained. They are washed in 2% formalin for 10-15 minutes and then transferred in running water to remove excess of formalin. These eggs are dried in shade and then to cold storage where they are preserved at 25°C for 50 days: 20°C for 40 days; 15°C for 25 days; 10°C for 25 days; 5°C for 60 days and 2.5°C for 55 days. These eggs preserved at 2.5°C for 55 days are released for intermediate care at 15°C for 3-4 days and then cold stored again at 2.5°C for 30-40 days. They are released for incubation at 25°C and 70-80% humidity after completion of specific period of cold storage (Table 6.7).

Table 6.7: Eight to ten months hibernation schedule

Preservation temperature (°C)	25	20	15	10	5	2.5	5	15	2.5	5	15	25
Preservation duration (days)	50	40	25	25	60	55	1	3-4	30-40	1	1	Incubation till hatching

Cold storage of acid treated eggs

Silkworm eggs, which are acid treated by the general method at 46°C of pretreated HCl of 1.075 specific gravity, can be cold stored for 10-20 days only. It is better to avoid cold storage after acid treatment. However, if it is inevitable, the eggs preserved for 12 hrs at 25°C following acid treatment are transferred to 15°C for 6 hrs. They are then transferred to 5°C up to 20 days. Cold storage duration should be short as far as possible but in no circumstances it should be beyond 20 days. The optimum time for cold storage of acid treated eggs is when the embryos have developed appendages. If cold storage is delayed, it leads to death of embryos resulting in poor hatching. If cold storage of acid treated eggs are done after 48 hrs of acid treatment, the preservation duration must be less than 10 days.

Acid treatment of eggs after cold storage

In order to postpone hatching over a period not as long as regular hibernation or not so early as by acid treatment, a technique of chilling the eggs and acid treatment in combination is followed (Table 6.8).

If the eggs are acid treated within an hour of release from cold storage, the sudden change in temperature will adversely affect the eggs leading to poor hatchability. At

Table 6.8: Schedule of hatching at different periods

Duration of preservation**	Type of preservation	Procedure
10-30 days	Cold storage of acid treated eggs	Acid treatment after 20 hrs of oviposition→15°C for 6 hrs→5°C up to 20 days.
40-50 days	Short term chilling	30-35 hrs at 25°C after oviposition→15°C for 6 hrs→chilled at 5°C for 30-40 days→release and acid treated.
50-60 days	Long term chilling	
	(i) 40-50 days chilling	40-50 hrs at 20°C after oviposition→15°C for 6 hrs→chilled at 5°C for 40-50 days→released and acid treated.
	(ii) 60-70 days chilling	40-50 hrs at 25°C after oviposition→15°C for 6 hrs→chilled at 5°C for 40 days→transferred to 2.5°C for 20-30 days→released and acid treated.

** Incubation period included

the same time, if the eggs are acid treated after 3 hours of release from cold storage, the desired result is not obtained as hatching is affected. Therefore, the eggs after being released from cold storage must be subjected to acid treatment within 1-3 hours. For the treatment, hydrochloric acid having specific gravity of 1.100 at 15°C preheated to a temperature of 48°C is used. Duration of acid treatment is usually 5-6 minutes but is variable according to the silkworm races.

(a) Short-term chilling and acid treatment

Eggs laid at 25°C and 70-80% humidity preserved for 30-35 hrs after ovipositions are transferred at 15°C for 6 hrs. By this time, the eggs turn into reddish brown colour. These eggs are then cold stored at 5°C and 70-80% humidity for 30-40 days. They are released from cold storage after completion of scheduled duration and kept at room temperature (25°C) for 1-3 hrs before performing acid treatment at 48°C for 5-6 minutes by dipping in preheated HCl solution of 1.100 specific gravity. This is known as short-term chilling.

(b) **Long-term chilling and acid treatment**

(i) **40-50 days chilling:** The eggs laid at 25°C and 70-80% humidity are preserved in the same condition for 40-50 hrs. By this time, the colour of eggs changes to reddish brown and embryos have reached the spoon shape stage. These eggs are stored at 15°C for 6 hrs and then transferred to cold storage at 5°C for 40-50 days. These eggs after completion of specific duration are released from cold storage and kept at 25°C for1-3 hrs. These eggs are subjected to acid treatment at 48°C for 5 minutes in HCl solution of 1.100 specific gravity.

(ii) **60-70 days chilling**: In case the hatching is to be delayed beyond 60 days, the eggs within 40-50 hrs after oviposition preserved at 25°C and 70-80% humidity are transferred to cold storage at 5°C for 40 days. Later these eggs are transferred and subjected to 2.5°C for 20-30 days and then brought back to room temperature (25°C) and treated with HCl solution of 1.100 specific gravity at 15°C preheated to 48°C for 5-6 minutes. This is known as long term chilling.

Tips during preservation of eggs

- Aestivation of eggs at 25°C temperature and 70-80% Relative Humidity (RH) for required duration is necessary to establish diapause.
- Diapause eggs should pass through moderately low temperature (20°C, 15°C and 10°C) before the start of cold storage at 5°C or 2.5°C to avoid cold injury/shock to the eggs.
- While releasing the cold storage eggs for incubation, they must pass through intermediate

temperature of 15°C to reduce high temperature injury.

- To terminate diapause effectively, it is necessary to cold store the eggs at 5°C for 50-60 days.
- For longer duration of cold storage (double refrigeration) at 2.5°C, it is necessary to provide intermediate care at 15°C for 3 days in order to prolong hibernation schedules.
- Exposure of hibernating eggs to 15°C for 3 days after release from cold storage not only avoids a sharp change in temperature but also prepares the younger embryos to develop uniformly in order to obtain single-day hatching in hibernating eggs of bivoltine.
- Since termination of diapause needs oxygen from the time of onset of termination, it is necessary to provide sufficient space in the cold storage for developing embryos.
- Compactness during preservation in cold storages leads to irregular hatching and poor quality of crop.

Damage of silkworm eggs during preservation

(i) **Dead blue-eggs:** The eggs during incubation develop up to blue stage and then die due to cumulative effect of various conditions prevailing during mounting, preservation of pupae, artificial hatching and incubation. In this case, larvae develop completely inside the egg but it does not have the capacity to break the eggshell and as a result dies inside the eggshell. Changes in the temperature during cold storage, duration and temperature prevailing during intermediate care, duration and temperature of water during washing, degree of stimulation through water or acid treatment, effect of chemicals besides abnormal conditions during incubation and handling are responsible for eggs to die at blue stage.

(ii) **Dead coloured-eggs:** Usually refers to the eggs, which are unfertilized and red in colour. Due to improper method of preservation and cold storage, the viability of eggs is lost even before the pigmentation stage and the eggs die. These types of eggs are also caused due to improper handling of eggs, improper washing of eggs, rapid activation, insufficient diapause, poor variety of breeds, improper acid treatment besides due to affect of pests and chemicals.

(iii) **White fluffy-eggs:** These types of eggs are usually caused when they are transferred from high temperature to low temperature without passing through intermediate temperature. These types of eggs are also caused due to too much drying after washing or acid treatment soon after transportation. If the effect is very mild, the development proceed up to revolving stage of eggs and sometimes larvae hatches out from the eggshells and shows normal larval development.

(iv) **Unfertilized eggs:** Unfertilized eggs are caused due to unfavourable environmental conditions after mounting, improper handling of moths during mating and egg laying. Unfertilized eggs are observed in large numbers among the eggs laid at the end of oviposition as compared to the eggs laid at the beginning of oviposition. Acid treatment for longer period also causes mortality of eggs, which appears to be unfertilized. Unfertilized eggs do not form any colour and if these eggs are pressed, they do not rupture but makes sound.

(v) **Abnormal hatching:** In a laying, though eggs appear like diapausing eggs hatch within few days after oviposition i.e. during aestivation period of diapausing eggs. This is caused due to improper management during pupal preservation especially when the temperature is not maintained properly.

(vi) **Abnormal larvae:** Abnormal larvae are caused due to improper acid treatment and cold storage of eggs. Though it is considered to be a genetic disorder it also occurs due to abnormal temperatures and influence of Hcl solution.

Besides above abnormalities, irregular hatching and mortality of infant larvae, light yellow coloured eggs etc are also occurring during preparation and preservation of eggs.

Table 6.9: Developmental events during preservation of silkworm eggs of bivoltine breeds

Sl. No.	*Tempt. (°C)*	*Stage of embryo*	*Physiomorphological status of eggs*
1	25	Pre-diapause stage	
		Stage 1 (2 hrs)	Fertilization
		Stage 2(10hrs)	Cleavage
		Stage 3 (10-20 hrs)	Blastoderm formation
		Stage 4 (20-24 hrs)	Germ band formation; optimum age for HCl treatment; maximum oxygen consumption
		Stage 5 (24-30 hrs)	Cephalic lobe formation; primitive groove appearance; pigmentation in serosal cells
		Stage 6 (30-40 hrs)	Spoon shaped embryo; formation of ectoderm and mesoderm; segmentation of mesoderm
		Stage 7 (40-72 hrs) (Chilling stage)	Appearance of 18 segments; respiration switch over from aerobic to anaerobic; pentose phosphate pathway with glycolysis operates to convert glycogen into polyols; steep decline in oxygen consumption
		Diapause stages Stages 8 (14 days) (Diapause stage-1)	Yolk cell migration; embryo surrounded by yolk cells; mitotic division stops on 4th day; continued steep decline in glycogen content
		Stage 9 (60 days) (Diapause stage 2)	Wider central region lacking yolk cells; rate of respiration comes down to 2-5%, arrest of water loss

2	20, 15, 10	Stage 9 (continues)	Total arrest of water loss; eggs are under anaerobic respiration; rate of metabolism is diminished.
3	5	Hibernating stage Stage 10 and 11	Cryoprotection of embryo by sorbitol and glycerol; 60 days onwards starts declining in the levels of sorbitol by the activation of NAD-sorbitol dehydrogenase for the resynthesis of glycogen (a sign of termination of diapause); starts oxygen consumption (aerobic respiration)
4	2.5, 1.0, 0, -2.5	Stage 11 (continues)	Low rate of metabolism to save energy; no embryonic growth. It means releasing of eggs for synchronization and incubation
5	-10, -15, -20	Stage 11 (continues)	Super cooling of eggs, silkworm eggs can survive by avoiding freezing and adopting super cooling
6	15	Intermediate care Stage 11, 12 and 13	Post diapause development; aerobic respiration increases, embryonic growth by elongation of embryo and not by increasing the number of cells by mitotic division
		Stage 14	Critical stage I
		Stage 15 (3-4 days)	Critical stage II (fit for double refrigeration)
7	2.5	Stage 15 (double refrigeration) (30-40 days)	
8	25	Incubation stage (organogenesis–stage 16)	16 hrs light & 8 hrs dark/day to maintain bivoltine characters; starts losing 1-2% of water per day. Hence maintain 75±5% RH to avoid desiccation; with in 0.5 hr after shifting from 15°C to 25°C the neural groove appears; starts gradual increase in oxygen consumption

(contd...)

Table 6.9: (Contd...)

		Stage 17 (1.5 to 2 days)	Appendages formation in thoracic region. From this stage onwards 400-500 lux light with 100 cm distance is optimum
		Stage 18 (2.5 to 3 days) Stage 19	4 pairs of abdominal buds are seen from 3 to 6 abdominal segments Shortening of embryo
		Stage 20 (3 to 4 days)	Further development of appendages, head and thorax distinguishable, it is better to transport the eggs before attaining the blastokinesis stage
		Stage 21 (A, B and C) (4.5 to 5 days) Stage 22 (5 days)	Early, middle and late blastokinesis, completion of dorsal closure Complete embryonic reversal
		Stage 23 (6 days)	(blastokinesis is completed)
		Stage 24	Steep rise in oxygen consumption and CO_2 release
		Stage 25	Setae formation
9	25	Stage 26 (8 days) (head pigmentation – I)	Up to 0.5% CO2 in air tolerable, beyond this causes uneven development, irregular and delayed hatching.
		Stage 27 (head pigmentation – II)	Sensitive to high CO_2 level and low humidity.
		Stage 28 (9 days) (early body pigmentation)	Dark colouration helps in obtaining the synchronized hatching stage.
		Stage 29 (10 days) (late body pigmentation)	Sensitive to low RH and high CO_2 level, hence many eggs die in this stage.
		Stage 30 (10-11 days)	Hatching of young larvae within 2-3 hrs after exposing to light

EMBRYONIC DEVELOPMENT

The structure of egg is the determiner of the pattern of development. The first detailed study on the development (embryogenesis) of silkworm, *Bombyx mori* egg was carried out by Toyama. Since then embryological studies were confined especially in solving the practical problems, such as identification of suitable stages for refrigeration of early embryos and the initiation, continuation and termination of diapause in order to develop an effective system for long-term cold storage of silkworm eggs. Takami (1969) was apparently the first who published a review on the embryogenesis of the silkworm, *Bombyx mori*.

I. Structure of Egg

Shape, Size and Colour

Takami (1946) reported that eggs of the silkworm (*Bombyx mori*) belong to non-regulative type. It is short, spheroid, slightly attenuated at the anterior end where the micropyle is situated and laterally flattened. The shape of egg is entirely dependent on the shape of chorion, which is formed in maternal body. Hence, the egg shape is inherited pseudo-maternally. Though the size and weight of eggs vary from breed to breed, voltinism to voltinism and even season to season but it is approximately 1.30 mm long, 1.00 mm wide and 0.6 mm thick (Miya, 1984) having 0.5 mg weight and about 1.075 specific gravity. Among the eggs of a moth, the once which are being laid first are heavier than those laid later. The eggs weight changes due to environmental conditions and even the eggs of same genotype have weight variations due to differences in the rearing conditions.

Except few exceptions (white and red eggs), the eggs (*Bombyx mori*) are usually brownish yellow in colour. Generally deep coloured eggs are common in Japanese races, while eggs of Chinese races are commonly light in colour. Usually, the chorion is colourless and semitransparent and hence the yolk colour is easily observable through shell in newly laid eggs. Yolk is normally light yellow in colour but in some genotypes, it is dark yellow. The colour of yolk is entirely dependent on the maternal genotype, having a close relation to the haemolymph colour and cocoon colour of the mother moth (Tazima, 1964).

The colour of egg is also due to the colour of serosal cells. The pigment present in serosal cells is attributed to one of the amino acids-tryptophane. The pigment is formed in a series of steps in a sequence: tryptophane→ oxytryptophane→formylkynurenine→kynurenine→ 3-hydroxykynurenine→chromogen→chrome (pigment). In this series of reaction, certain enzymes participate. The eggs in which pigment is not formed indicate absence of enzymes resulting in white eggs. The eggs receive gluey substance of moth on the underside during deposition to adhere to the substratum/egg card. The gluey substance is being secreted from the sebific gland or accessory gland, opening at the vestibulum.

Eggshell (Chorion)

A new generation begins at the moment of fertilization of an oocyte by an appropriate sperm. After fertilization, a series of well-defined structural and biochemical changes occur within the oocyte leading to genesis of offspring (Margaritis, 1985). For these processes to occur successfully, the egg has to be enclosed in such an entity as to permit embryogenesis to proceed safely. The major role played in this direction is by an oocyte covering, which is commonly referred to as eggshell. The function of eggshell is:

- To allow and facilitate sperm entry into the egg for fertilization which will lead to genesis of offspring.
- To provide elasticity for easy oviposition.
- To protect oocyte from unfavourable environmental conditions such as temperature fluctuations, humidity, dryness (Yamashita and Hasegawa, 1985).
- To ensure adequate oxygen supply for all biochemical reactions occurring within the

developing embryos and at the same time getting rid off carbon-dioxide.

- To facilitate hatching at the end of embryogenesis.

The eggshell is very complex, multilayered, multiregional, supra-molecular structure. There are three major layers in any insect shell: the vitelline membrane, the endocrine and the exocrine. The exterior layer is thin, with rough web-like sulci and stripes, the second layer is much thicker than exterior, with a structure of stripes and gramules, the inner layer is very thin with a construction of multipores. Eggshell is made mainly of chorionin, which is composed of scleroprotein and some sacchriode and lipoid. The major amino acids composed of scleroprotein are presented in Table 6.10. The eggshell is produced by mesodermal follicular epithelial cells, which are the parts of follicle. Each follicle is a unit within the paired ovary. In *Bombyx mori,* ovary is polytrophic meroistic type. The number of ovarioles in each ovary is four and looks like a coiled spring of beads containing eggs. Each ovariole contains approximately 50-60 follicles at various stages of oogenesis. Eggshell formation is a gradual process involving certain cellular activities. Such activities have been recognized ad analyzed morphologically and biochemically in *Antheraea polyphemus* and *Bombyx mori.*

Choron synthesis starts with the formation of 'trabecular layer' on the outer side of vitelline membrane by the release of micro particles from follicular epithelium. Several layers of he helicoidally arranged fibrillar lamellae cover the trabecular layer. The outer regionof egg contains unique 'osmiophilic' layer with 15-20 lamelae and very narrow micropyle. Rough surface endoplasmic reticule and golgi bodies increase greatly in number at the later stage of inner layer formation and are dispersed throughout the cytoplasm of follicle cells. The middle layer of chorion is formed by secretary granules, which are recognized in Golgi regions. The middle layer of chorion consists of numerous fibrous elements that are seemed to be transformed from the secretory granules. Degenerative changes take place remarkably in the components of follicle cells, after the formation of choron.

Table 6.10: Amino acid content in the chorionin of *Bombyx mori* eggs

Amino acids	*Outer layer*	*Middle layer*	*Inner layer*
Glycine	36.8	35.0	18.2
Alanine	8.5	3.1	8.3
Serine	3.2	4.5	6.7
Tyrosine	8.1	1.5	2.2
Valine	6.1	5.1	6.0
Asparagine	4.0	4.9	9.6
Gutamic acid	3.7	3.5	11.6
Threonine	3.3	2.0	5.1
Lysine	0.1	0.4	2.5
Phenylalanine	1.9	1.2	0.15
Isoleucine	3.3	2.1	3.8
Arginine	2.3	3.2	3.5
Leucine	6.4	1.4	7.0
Proline	4.3	2.3	10.1
Histidine	0.4	0.0	1.1
Methionine	0.0	0.4	1.1
Cysteine	5.8	29.6	0.5
Tryptophan	1.8	0.8	0.7

Micropyle and Vitêlline membrane

The surface of micropyler region shows a petal-like pattern, with the opening of micropyler canals at its centre. The micropyler canals are normally 3-4 in number but in some cases 6-8 canals have also been observed. Each micropyler canal can be divided into two parts—a tube penetrating the chorion and a protrusion connecting the tube to the vitelline membrane. The former is designated as 'ectomicropyle' and the latter 'endomicropyle'. In addition to micropyle, there are about 5000-10000 tiny pores around the egg surface. These pores permit air entry to meet the requirement of oxygen during embryonic development.

Beneath the chorion is very thin vitelline membrane enclosing the serosa and semi-liquid fluid (yolk), which fills the eggs. The vitelline membrane is secreted uniformly and its formation starts after the degeneration of nurse cells i.e. at the time when oocyte occupies almost the entire egg chamber. The vitelline membrane is composed of an electron dense outer layer and an inner layer containing abundant irregularly shaped electron dense granules of various size.

II. Development of egg (Embryogenesis)

Different developmental stages of mulberry silkworm eggs (stage 1-30) were shown in Table 6.9.

Fertilization

The fertilization is a life-saving event, which saves sperm and ovum from certain death, with the union of the two gametes acting as an evolutionary springboard to launch a new individual into the future. When male and female moth of *Bombyx mori* copulate, ejaculation occurs and innumerable spermatozoa enter into the bursa copulatrix of female moth's reproductive organ. Through ductus seminalis, ductus tortuosus and receptaculum seminis, these sperms reache the lower part of ovipositor and wait for an egg coming down to ovarian tube. Just before the egg is being laid, the spermatozoa enter into it through the micropyle.

Two layers—the vilelline membrane and the chorion—surround the mature egg of the silkworm. The chorion consists two groups of cells—the outer layer and the inner layer. The inner layer and the inner portion of outer layer are mechanically soft and pliable, while the outer portion of outer layer is mechanically rigid. The morphological feature of the chorion that allows penetration of sperm is micropyler apparatus, situated at the anterior end of the egg. Further, the morphological organization of chorionic layer is extremely modified in the region of micropyle. The first maturation (reduction) division begins just before oviposition and terminates 5-6 minutes after the eggs are being laid. Thus, the nuclei in the egg, which have been just oviposited, are in anaphase stage of first reduction division. The female nucleus is diveded into two, of which one is being eliminated under the vite line membrane (the first polar body). the remaining one again divides into two, one of which is again being eliminated (second polar body). This second maturation division takes place in about next 20 minutes, releasing the second polar body. This whole process of reduction division takes approximately 90-100 minutes from oviposition.

As soon as reduction division is completed only one nucleus will be seen in the egg, which becomes a female pronucleus. During the interval when all these changes take place in egg nucleus, the sperm sheds its tail. The central body of sperm divides into two and the anterior part swells into spherical body called male pronucleus. The female and male pronuclei unite to form the zygote. This process is known as syngamy, which is being completed within 2 hours of deposition of egg (stage 1). Thus after fertilization, the zygote restores the original chromosome number of the organism (2n = 56). Though the number of supermatozoa entering the egg may be several, only one of them penetrates into an ovum and fertilizes the female pronucleus and the rest degenerate and are absorbed.

Cleavage and Blastoderm formation

As in most insects, the silkworm egg also undergoes superficial cleavage. The content of eggs consists of two parts—the protoplasm and the endoplasm. Protoplasm forms a reticulum that pervades the substance of egg and forms a bounding layer beneath the vitelline membrane. This is termed as periplasm, which is free from yolk spheres. The endoplasm (yolk), which occupies the central part of the egg is contained within the protoplasmic reticulum. The zygote nucleus forms many nuclei by synchronous mitotic divisions, which is being reported 10 times approximately within 10 hours of oviposition (stage 2). Afterwards, luminous circle of microtubules appear around the cleavage nuclei. Takesue et al, (1980) suggested that these microtubules are responsible for the movement of cleavage nuclei towards the egg surface.

These dividing nuclei surrounded by protoplasm will be transformed into cells. Subsequently, greater number of these cleavage cells migrates towards the periphery of the egg, merge in the periplasm and form a layer directly beneath the vitelline membrane called blastoderm. Some of the cleavage nuclei do not move to the periphery but persists and form yolk cells or vitellophages. These vitellophages have the function of supplying nutrients to the embryo. The nuclei projecting into the periplasm are then pinched off from the yolk system and approximately 10-20 hours of oviposition, uniform blastoderm appears (stage 3).

Germ band and Amnion formation

The cells, which form the blastoderm, are alike. About 20 hrs of oviposition, part of blastodermal cell divides asynchronously several times and become thicker and cuboidal in appearance on the ventral side. These cells change gradually from cuboidal to cylindrical shape and then become distinguishable from the other part called germ band or germinal cord (stage 4). The yolk membrane forms enfolding during the late germ band stage. Afterwards, folk system is divided into many mases, each enclosng one or severalnuclei and yolk organelles. This process is known as yolk segmentation.

Parallel to the major axis of the germ band, envelop-like structure appears from both sides and partly covers the germ band. These are amniotic folds. Amniotic fold consists of two layers (inner and outer), grows inwards, towards each other, and finally reaches the centre of the germ band. The outer layer of the fold extends from all the sides and meets to form the serosa, which covers entire surface of the egg. The inner layer of the folds meets and unites in the thick portion of the blastoderm to form amnion. The cavity formed by the two amniotic folds in which germ band lies are known as amniotic cavity. The thick portion of the blastoderm covered by amnion develops into embryo.

Organogenesis

A long and narrow depression (primitive grove) in the middle on the ventral side of the germ band is formed (stage 5). The primitive groove invaginates deeper and deeper and the tips of invaginations are brought together covering the groove. After completion of covering, the groove cannot be seen externally except leaving a small aperture (blastopore) on the head. Beneath this primitive groove, a group of spherical cells are found, which leads to the formation of mesoderm or endomesoderm.

The ventral plate, which is an elliptic disc at the end of 24 hrs of oviposition, changes into spoon-shape at the end of 35 hrs and become enlarged (stage 6). Afterwards, the germ band sinks into yolk and by divisions of yolk cells, primary yolk cells are formed which later lead to the formation of secondary yolk cells. The anterior end of spoon (swollen part at the head region) is called 'procephalic' or 'protocephalic' lobe and that at the tail end is 'caudal lobe'. At this stage, mesoderm becomes morphologically distinguishable from the ectoderm.

At the end of approximately 2 days of oviposition, neural groove appears in embryos (stage 16, non-diapause). Appendages development in gnathal and thoracic regions starts at the very next stage (stage 17). After three days of oviposition, abdominal limb buds are formed from third to sixth abdominal segments (stage 18). Paired gonad analages also appear at the same time. Next stage of development indicates beginning of embryo shortening (stage 19), invagination of spiracles and silk glands besides formation of strand like gonad anlages. After four days of oviposition, the head and thorax become differentiated (stage 20), with the grouping of gnathal appendages.

The anterior six segments of embryo fuse together to form the head. During fusion, two segments disappear thus leaving four in the head region. Thoracic appendages develop into three segmented legs. In the abdominal region, except the five pairs of appendages, which persist later in the larva, remaining disappears during the course of development. Last three segments of the abdomen fuse together to form single segment and thus leaving abdomen with only nine segments. Blastokinesis begins at this stage. Actually, blastokinesis is the characteristic of all those insects whose eggs are rich in yolk and the germ band is invaginated therein. Blastokinesis occurs 4-5 days after oviposition. The embryo starts to move around as it seeks its correct position in the egg (stage 21A, B & C). For instance the embryo, which was in the supine position with its abdomen facing outer of the egg turns round, so that its abdomen faces the inner side. This whole process is called blastokinesis. The anterior and posterior ectodermal invaginations (stomodaeum and proctodaeum) forms the fore intestine and hind intestine respectively. During this stage, the embryo, which was located on the ventral side of the egg, moves towards the dorsal side.

After blastokinesis, histogenesis proceeds actively and continues till the larva hatches. The first embryonic moult takes place just after blastokinesis followed by second moult immediately, after which the larval cuticle is secreted (stage 24). After revolution, various organs are gradually formed and eggs hatch in about 5 days later. The number of embryonic segment in *B. mori* is reported to be 18. Of these, four anterior segments form the head, three segments form the thorax and the other eleven segments form the abdomen.

Mesoderm cells, form four pairs of appendages on the head region and three pairs on the thoracic region. Besides these seven pairs of appendages, the mesodermic cells also form one pair of appendage on each of the eleven abdominal segments. Of these eleven pairs of appendages on the abdominal region, only 3rd, 4th, 5th, 6th and 11th abdominal segments appendages develop further and remaining six pairs disappear during the course of development (stage 18).

While antenna, skin, mouth parts, thoracic leg, abdominal leg, caudal leg, silk gland and other dermo-glands besides fore and hind intestine, nervous system, trachea, sense organs, malphigian tube and external genetalia are formed from ectodermal cells, internal genetalia, muscles, dorsal vessels, sub-esophageal gland, corpuscles, pericardial cells, fat tissues originate from mesoderm. In diapausing embryos, cell division is arrested and embryogenesis ceases immediately after formation of the cephalic lobe and segmentation of mesoderm (stage 7). Yolk cells and yolk granules change their shape and properties as a part of diapause process. THe most striking feature of the diapausing eggs is the dark colouration of serosal cells due to the formation of ommochrome pigment. When diapause is terminated (stage 15), embryogenesis resumes and follows the pattern as in non-diapause eggs. At stage 6, the development rate in diapausing eggs becomes slower than in non-diapausing eggs. Hence, stage 8-15 is absent in non-diapausing eggs and all other stages of development in both the cases are similar. Further, in diapausing eggs, stage of development from 16 onwards is delayed approximately one day in comparison to non-diapausing eggs.

Respiration through the eggshell

Respiration is a fundamental biological phenomenon necessary for the maintenance of biochemical reaction, which are the characteristic of the living system. The gas exchange process is passive and is based upon diffusion governed by coefficient and relative partical pressure of oxygen on ethire side of the eggshell. Respiratory canals are funnel-shaped tubes, which become narrower as they enter inward. These respiratory canals are aeropyles and are responsible for gas exchange process during embryogenesis. These aeropyles are tiny holes transversing relatively thick chrion and conducting the ambient air directly to the trabecular layer and from there to the occyte. These aeropyles function during embryogenesis in gas exchange as per 'Bernoulli Velocity Gradients Theory'. The aeropyles are distributed in large numbers over the entire surface of the egg except around the micrpyle.

Structurally, aeropyle openings are somehow elevated or surrounded by crowns. These respiratory devices conduct the ambient air to the internal trabecular layer for both storage and immediate consumption. Oxygen moves within the trabecuar layer and cross the innerlayers (endochrion and vitelline membrane) and reaches the developing oocyte. The inner membranes are structurally porous, so that the oxygen can pass through, where the metabolic processes are taking place. Moreover, if the ambient environment is poor in oxygen, having a partial pressure lower than that within the embryo; it may prove fatal for the development. Carbon dioxide is driven easily from inside, since its partial pressure in the environment is virtually zero.

Since the oxygen and carbon dioxide molecules are bigger than the water molecules; it was not possible for biological systems to evolve a kind of membrane, which would be permeable only to oxygen and carbon dioxide, but not to water. hence, the loss in water content during embryogenesis cannot be ruled out.

Number of workers has described the phenomenon of gradual loss in weight of fertilized eggs during the course of their embryonic development. Therefore, the weight of silkworm eggs is not a constant factor during the course of development. The maximum loss in weight of eggs has been reported on the day of hatching. The loss in weight of eggs in the course of embryogenesis is partly due to the exhalation of carbon dioxide and partly due to the loss in moisture content (Mathur and Singh, 1990). The difference in egg weight is also due to energy loss during embryogenesis.

7

DIAPAUSE AND HATCHING

DIAPAUSE

The nature of diapause in mulberry silkworm, *Bombyx mori* is primarily determined by genetic characters and endocrinological mechanisms, mediated by environmental factors such as temperature and photoperiod and is almost maternal. Hibernating potency besides nucleic acid and carbohydrate metabolism is also equally responsible for induction, initiation, maintenance and termination of diapause. Since mulberry silkworm enter diapause as embryo, the duration of egg life depends on the duration of embryonic diapause which represents a syndrome of physiological and biochemical events.

Embryonic diapause in *Bombyx mori* induced by active secretion of sub-esophageal ganglion is attributed to the metabolic adjustment, which serves to bring about a new physiological state. Metabolic conversion of trehalose to glycogen at induction, glycogen to sorbitol at initiation and sorbitol to glycogen at termination of diapause is correlated and in each metabolic shift, a key enzyme becomes active in response to hormonal and environmental stimulation.

Colouration or pigmentation of insects is mainly due to melanin, pterine, pigments, ommochrome and carotenoid. In some insects, colouration is closely correlated with diapause and colour pattern is sometimes used as an index to distinguish diapause from non-diapause. Among these pigments, ommochrome is well documented in relation to embryonic diapause. Diapause development is under the control of endocrinological system mediated by environmental conditions such as temperature, photoperiod, humidity etc. Hence, diapause is characterized by an active mechanism for adaptation to the adverse seasons.

Diapause can occur at embryonic *(Bombyx mori, Aedes aegypti)*, larval *(Cydia pomonella, Gilpinia polytoma)*, pupal *(Antheraea mylitta, Hyalophora cecropia)* or adult *(Eurydema* sp., *Leptinotarsa decemlineata)* reproductive stages of life cycle and the stages are characteristically fixed in each species (Table 7.1).

Table 7.1: Diapause nature in different insect species

Nature of diapause	*Example*
Embryonic diapause	*Bombyx mori, Melanoplus differntialis, Aedes* aegypti, Aeschna mixta
Larval diapause	*Cydia pomonella, Anax* sp., *Epistrophe bifasiata, Gilpinia polytoma, Cephus cinctus, Lucilia caesar*
Pupal diapause	*Antheraea pemyi, Hyalophora cecropia, Antheraea mylitta, Philosamia cynthia, Saturnia pavonia, Mimas tiliae*
Adult diapause	*Eurydema* sp., *Pterostichus* sp., *Leptinotarsa decemlineata, Musca autumnalis*

(a) Nature of diapause

Genetic characters primarily determine the nature of diapause in the silkworm *(Bombyx mori)*. The insects having only one generation in a year (univoltine), embryonic diapause occurs in all generations regardless of environmental conditions, is known as 'obligatory diapause', while those having two or more generations in a year (bivoltine or polyvoltine), diapause is expressed in next generation when the mother receives specific stimuli from environment is termed 'facultative diapause'. The univoltine forms lay only hibernating (diapausing) eggs, which are also called 'Kurodane eggs', and multivoltine forms lay only non-hibernating eggs which are known as 'Nemadane eggs', while the behaviour of bivoltine are intermediate. Bivoltine silkworm breeds lay non-hibernating eggs during first generation and hibernating eggs in the next generation, which hatches out in the following spring and thus producing only two generations in a year. Practically, univoltine and bivoltine silkworm breeds produce superior cocoons to those of multivoltines in both quality and quantity. Generally, silkworms programmed to lay diapause eggs are superior to those that of non-diapause eggs. The silkworm eggs of diapauses type are pigmented (dark brown) due to presence of ommochrome formed in serosa cells, while non-diapause eggs are light yellow/white due to lack of this pigment. Tryptophane metabolism in insects has been studied extensively and the pathway from tryptophane to ommochrome has been reviewed in detail by Linzen (1974). In general, three major metabolites directly involved in the biosynthesis of the pigments are formyl-kynurenine, kynurenine and 3-hydroxy kynurenine. The corresponding enzymes responsible for their production are kynurenine-formamidase, kynureninase and kynurenine-3 hydroxylase. Ommochrome is synthesized in developing ovaries and other tissues such as fat body during tryptophane metabolism as shown below:

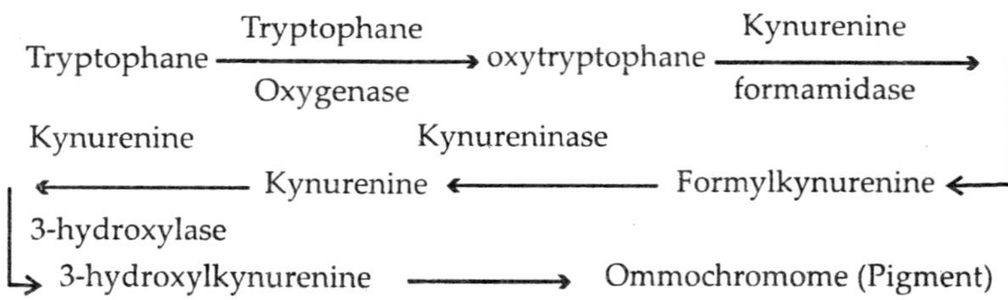

(b) Hibernating potency value

Nagatomo assumed a series of three sex-linked alleles, Hs, Hs2 and hs and three pairs of autosomal genes H1h1, H2h2 and H3h3 responsible for the hibernation and reported different kinds of voltinism in relation to 'Hibernating potency value' (H.V.) (Table 7.2). The eggs with 0-1 HV value always lay non-hibernating eggs (multivoltine), while those with 11-12 HV value will lay only hibernating eggs (univoltine). Bivoltine silkworm breeds have HV value in between 5-7. The silkworm eggs with HV value of 2-4 are intermediate between multivoltine and bivoltine and lays some non-hibernating eggs at high

Incubation temperature Contrary to this, the silkworm eggs with HV value of 8-10 are intermediate between bivoltine and univoltine and lay both hibernating and nonhibernating eggs at low temperature incubation.

Table 7.2: Relationship between hibernating potency value and voltinism in silkworm (Bombyx mori) (Source: Nagatomo, 1953)

Hibernating Potency value	*Voltivoltism*	*Characteristics*
0-1	*Multivoltine*	*Always lay non-hibernating Eggs*
2-4	*Intermediate between Multi and bivoltine Temperature*	*Lay some non-hibernating eggs at high incubation*
5-7	*Bivoltine*	*Lay non-hibernating eggs at Low temperature and Hibernating eggs at high Temperature of incubation*
8-10	*Intermediate Between bivoltine and univoltine*	*Lay both hibernating and non-hibernating eggs at low incubation temperature*
10-12	*Univoltine*	*Always lay hibernating eggs*

(c) Change of diapauses nature

The silkworm (Bombyx mori) diapauses determination is almost maternal, That is, temperature and photoperiod are most efficient at the embryonic stage of previous generation (Table 7.3 and Table 7.6) and only supplemental in the post- embryonic stage. The sensitive embryonic stage begin just after blastokinesis. Incubation of eggs of bivoltine breeds at high temperature results in the induction of diapauses eggs. Incubation as low as 15ºC causes production of non-diapause eggs in the next generation, whereas diapauses eggs are induced by incubation at 25ºC. When eggs are incubated at intermediate temperature of 20ºC, the development fate remains undetermined in the embryos. High temperature at younger larval stage and low temperature at late larval stage act to induce diapauses eggs (Tazima, 1978). Photoperiod is one of the principal physical factors regulating diapause. In B. *mori,* egg diapause is regulated by photoperiod as well as temperature during embryonic stage of the female and is completely independent of photoperiod during post-embryonic development. Thus, photoperiod becomes effective in regulation to development only when eggs are incubated at an intermediate temperature. In these eggs, long photoperiod causes induction of diapause and short photoperiod non-arrested state of development (Table 7.1).

In silkworm, injection of Uranyl nitrate, Quabain and 5'-AMP into females destined to lay diapause eggs caused them to lay non-diapausing eggs. Converse was demonstrated by injection of KCl and Quabain into pupae of non-diapause type. However, despite extensive studies, the mechanism of action of these chemicals remains unknown.

Table 7.3: Effects of temperature and photoperiod on egg diapause in *Bombyx mori* (bivoltine breeds)

Temperature and photoperiod during incubation		*Temperature °C Developmental stage*		*Resulting moths laying diapause and non-diapause eggs*
		I – II	*IV-pupal*	
25°C	Light	25 or 20	25	Diapause
	Dark	25 or 20	25	Diapause
20°C	Light	25 or 20	25 or 20	Diapause
	Dark	20	25	Diapause << Nondiapause
		25	25	Diapause < Nondiapause
		25	20	Diapause >> Nondiapause
15°C	Light	20	25	Diapause < Nondiapause
		25	25	Diapause > Nondiapause
		25	20	Diapause >> Nondiapause
	Dark	25 or 20	25 or 20	Nondiapause

Note: Light - 16 hours light and 8 hours dark
Dark - 16 hours dark and 8 hours light

(d) Termination of diapause

Exposure of silkworm diapause eggs to oxygen is one of the artificial methods of termination of diapause. The exposure of diapause-destined eggs to oxygen gas can prevent the expression of diapause and eggs resumed embryonic development while under an oxygen-deficient environment non-diapause eggs ceased their development. Oxygen is also indispensable for diapause development during chilling of diapause eggs (Ando, 1974). However, mechanism involved in terminating the egg diapause by exposure to oxygen is still not known. Diapause in silkworm eggs can be terminated to obtain effective hatchability by means of:

I. Cold storage-chilling (hibernation schedule)

II. Hydrochlorisation (hot or cold acid treatment)

III. Cold storage and hydrochlorisation (chilling and treatment)

The application of these methods depends on the programme of hatching desired. Chilling is one of the effective methods of terminating, diapause. Exposure of diapausing silkworm eggs to a temperature as low as 5°C over 60 days completely terminates diapause and embryogenesis resumes when these eggs are transferred at 25°C. Optimum temperature to break the embryonic diapause is in between 5 to 7.5°C. The required chilling duration to break the diapause depends on the time gap the eggs have been kept for aestivation at 25°C after oviposition. Various comprehensive hibernation schedules for preservation of bivoltine eggs for different durations to get the desired hatching at appropriate time have already been recommended and some of them are in-vogue to meet the demand of seed supply throughout the year.

HCl treatment (hydrochlorisation) of silkworm diapause eggs has been the method of choice for blocking the diapause both at commercial and basic research laboratory level. There are two methods of HCI treatment. In the first method 20-24 hrs old oviposited eggs are soaked in HCI solution (specific gravity: 1.075 at 15°C) at 46.1°C for 5 minutes. This avoids the eggs to enter into diapause and hence when incubated at 25°C, larvae hatches in 10-11 days after treatment. In the second method 20-24 hrs old oviposited

Eggs are soaked in HCI solution (specific gravity 1.10 at 10 C) at room temperature for 60 to 90 minute, Sometimes, to block the diapauses for longer period in order to get hatching at desired time, chilling followed by acid treatment is also used. In this method, 48 hrs old eggs are first chilled at 5 C for more than 30 days and then soaked in HCI solution (specific gravity 1.10 at 15 C) at 48 C for 5 minute. This treatment causes diapauses eggs to hatch within two months after oviposition.

However, it is still an open question how hydrochlorisation block diapauses. Park and yoshitake (1970) suggested that HCI infiltrated into eggs impedes the embryonic protein synthesis system I yolk cells, which results in resumption of embryogenesis. Further, HCI treatment is reported to stimulate the activity of specific esterase isozyme and RNA synthetic activity in treated diapauses eggs. Activity of 'esterase A' increases dramatically within 30 minutes of HCI treatment. The esterase attains maximum activity before the eggs are competent to develop, and thus 'esterase A' is prerequisite for resumption of development.

(c) Hormonal control of diapauses

Of the endocrine system, sub-esophageal (SG) has been understood to play very vital role in the induction of diapauses. It is generally accepted that egg diapauses in silkworm is induced by an active principle secreted from a pair of large neurosecretory cells located in SG and. This active principal is known as Diapause Hormone' (DH). Two forms of DH (DH-A and DH-B) have been identified which are neuropeptides having molecular weight of 2,000-3,000 and consist of 12-14 amino acids. The DH-A molecules contains 14 amino acids and two amino sugars, while DH-B contains the same amino acids but no amino sugars (Table 7.4). THIs reveals that amino sugar component of DH-A is apparently not essential for hormonal activity.

There are several differences between diapauses and non-diapause eggs after oviposition. Diapause eggs showed high accumulation of 3-hydroxykynurenin, glycogen and ecdysteroids with reduced accumulation of cyclic guanosine monophosphate (GMP). Among these, 3-hydroxykynurenine and glycogen exhibit dramatic changes on the commencement of diapause, where 3-hydroxykynurenine is oxidized to ommochrome, resulting in the dark colouration of the diapause eggs and glycogen is mainly converted into sorbitol, which acts as an anti-freeze for the diapause embryo. DH also exerts an inhibitory effect on 'esterase 'A', an' enzyme essential for mobilizing the yolk needed for completion of embryogenesis. Molecular analysis of DH action has demonstrated that DH directly induces trehalase gene expression in developing embryos, which eventually brings about hyperglycogenism in mature eggs, leading to sorbitol production at the onset of diapause. DH function is conceived to be the initial and essential reaction leading to the diapause-associated metabolism in silkworm eggs.

Table 7.4: Amino acid composition of Diapause Hormone -A (DH-A) and Diapause Hormone -B (DH-B) (after Yamashita and Hasegawa, 1985)

Amino acid	*Diapause Hormone-A*	*Diapause Hormone-B*
Lysine	0.3	1.2
Arginine	0.8	1.0
Aspartic acid	1.3	1.3
Threonine	1.0	0.9
Serine	1.0	1.5
Gtutamic acid	2.1	2.2
Proline	3.0	2.4
Glycine	2.1	2.1
Alanine	2.2	2.1
Valine	1.7	1.0
Isoleucine	1.9	1.2
Leucine	3.0	3.0
Tyrosine	0.9	0.7
Phenylalanine	0.9	0.8
Tryptophane	-	1.0
Glucosamine	0.9	
Galactosamine	0.9	

Values represent mole ratios

Table 7.5: Relationship between the conditions of incubation, rearing, mounting and diapausing character of resultant egg in bivoltine silkworm races (Source: Tazima, 1978)

Developmental stage	*Environmental conditions*	*Effect*	*Remarks*
During incubation	Temperature		
	High	Diapausing	Whole eggs at 25°C or above
	Low	Nondiapausing	Whole eggs at 15°C or above
	Humidity		
	Humid Dry	Diapausing Nondiapausing	Humidity affects the voltinism only when the incubation temperature is at 15-25°C
	Light	Diapausing	Light (18 hrs or more a day). Photoperiod affects only when incubation at 15-25°C
	Dark	Nondiapausing	In case of 12 hrs darkness a day
Early larva	Temperature		
	High Low	Diapausing Nondiapausing	Only when incubation temperature was at 15-25°C
Late larva	Temperature		
	High Low	Nondiapausing Diapausing	Only when incubation temperature was at 15-25°C
Mountaining and later	Temperature High	Nondiapausing	Only when incubation temperature was at 15-25°C
	Low	Diapausing	

II. Metabolic changes during embryonic diapause

Since the first detailed study on the development of silkworm *(Bombyx mori)* eggs, embryological studies were confined especially in solving the practical problems such as identification of suitable stages for refrigeration of early embryos and the initiation, continuation and termination of diapause in order to develop an effective system for long-term cold storage of silkworm eggs. In these studies, morphological changes of embryos were used to assess their long-term survival. Moreover, the tolerance of eggs to cold storage varies with the stage of embryonic development besides genotypes because of adaptation phenomenon, metabolic changes and also genetic variations etc and hence relatively recent studies on silkworm eggs become more concern with physiology, biochemistry and metabolic activity associated with termination of embryonic diapause for effective handling.

(a) Biochemical composition of silkworm egg

Newly laid eggs of silkworm are composed of protein (~ 10%), lipids (~ 8.5%), glycogen (~ 2.5%), chorion (~ 18%) and water (~ 60%). More than 95% of the total protein is yolk protein: vitellin (~ 40%), 30 KD protein (~ 35%) and egg-specific protein (ESP) (~ 20%). These proteins are quite different from each other in their physiochemical and biological properties. Each protein exhibits a unique profile of degradation during embryogenesis, viz.,

- Egg-specific protein is utilized early and completely disappeared by the time of hatching.
- Vitellin begins to decrease at later stage of embryogenesis and some of it remains unutilized in hatched larvae. Thus, vitellin metabolism appears to be independent of the diapause phenomenon in *B. mori* eggs.
- 30 kD proteins are less utilized during embryogenesis.

ESP is degraded during embryogenesis by a called hydrolysis catalyzed by trypsin like seryl protease and alters the carboxyl site of Lys^{114} and $Argenine^{210}$ of ESP. The developmental increase in activity is due to increase at transcription of mRNA for this enzyme protein. Therefore, the utilization of ESP is a programmed event correlated with embryogenesis.

The second major component of egg is lipid (~ 8.5%), which is composed of triglycerols (~ 80%) and phospholipids (~ 20%). Other constituents such as free fatty acids, mono and triglycerides are usually present in small quantities. Most of the metabolic energy (approximately 70% of the total energy) is derived from the oxidation of triglycerol. The oxidation of lipids is advantageous for embryogenesis of terrestrial cleidoic eggs because large amount of metabolic water (1.07 g/g lipid) is released. Phospholipids are distributed as major component of yolk and used for formation of embryonic cells. Lipid is the major component consumed during diapause and the lipid concentration is higher in diapausing silkworm eggs than in non-diapausing eggs. Diapausing insects accumulate high level of glycerol and sorbitol led to the recognition that diapause is achieved by unique metabolic route that is not needed for non-diapausing eggs.

Glycogen in silkworm eggs undergoes dramatic changes during diapause. In the diapause eggs, the following reversible reaction occurs with the initiation and termination of diapause -

Glycogen ⟷ Sorbitol + Glycerin

With the initiation of diapause, the above reaction is right oriented while during termination, it is left oriented. The experiment with 14^{C} glycine showed that sorbitol is totally derived from glycogen, while glycerin is produced only when glycogen content reached the lowest level. About the mechanism of reversible reaction, following steps exists:

(i) Glucose + NADPH ⟷ Sorbitol + $NADP^{+}$

(ii) Glucose-6-p/fructose-6-p + NADPH ⟷ Sorbitol-6-p + $NADP^{+}$

(iii) Glyceraldehydes + NADPH ⟷ Glycerin + $NADP^{+}$

(v) 2-OH acetone-p + NADH ⟷ 2-p glycerin + NAD^+

(b) Nucleic acid metabolism

In the silkworm eggs, diapause is decided during the maturation process of the egg in the ovary of pupal body. Therefore, there is a close relationship between diapause occurrence and metabolism of egg cells. In insects, nucleic acid is not only related to the expression of genes but also influence protein synthesis, cell division, growth and development. In univoltine genotypes, sub-esophageal ganglion if removed at early pupal stage, the female will lay non-diapausing eggs, while normal female laid diapause eggs. If the mature eggs inside the ovariole of above two groups taken out, it is found that DNA content of diapause eggs is 25.29% lower than that of non-diapause eggs and RNA content of diapause mature eggs is 25.48% less but the DNA/RNA ratio of these two groups were the same (Table 7.6). Hence, it is inferred that DNA content of mitochondria of diapause eggs is probably lower than non-diapause eggs.

Table 7.6: Relationship between diapause and metabolism in mature eggs of the silkworm, *Bombyx mori*

Characters	*Nature of eggs*	
	Non-diapause	*Diapause*
DNA (µg/mg)	0.87	0.65
	(100)	(74.71)
RNA (µg/mg)	18.84	14.04
	(100)	(74.52)
Glycogen (%)	1.60	1.87
	(100)	(116.88)
Lipids (%)	26.5	27.5
	(100)	(103.77)
Oxygen	26.82	13.64
Consumption ($mm^3/g/h$)	(100)	(50.19)

RNA plays a major role in protein metabolism and embryo morphogenesis. It is reported that mRNA carrying out the early morphogenesis information is synthesized during the egg formation process and is deposited in the cytoplasm of egg before fertilization. The entrance of sperm activates the egg and the mRNA in latent condition is activated first. During the pre-diapause stage, the DNA content in both non-diapause and diapause eggs are used very rapidly. But 48 hours after oviposition, the DNA metabolism of these two types of eggs are quite different (Table 7.7). The DNA content of diapause eggs keeps constant after 48 hours of oviposition is perhaps the biochemical pre-condition for stoppage of embryo morphogenesis and initiation of embryonic diapause. On contrary, the DNA content of non-diapause eggs continues to increase rapidly. In non-diapause eggs within 24 hours of oviposition, with the increase of DNA content, RNA content decreases. After 72 hours of oviposition large amount of RNA is synthesized and accumulated in the non-diapausing eggs. This is closely related to the synthesis of protein during embryonic development. On the contrary, in diapause eggs within three days of oviposition, the RNA content keeps constant though large quantity of DNA is synthesized and accumulated. Within 24 hours of oviposition the RNA/DNA ratio in both the types of eggs (diapause and non-diapause) increases rapidly but after 48 hours they reach the same level. Later the DNA/RNA ratio of non-diapause eggs increase rapidly.

Table 7.7: Nucleic acid metabolism during early embryonic development of diapause and non-diapause eggs in *Bombyx mori*

Embryo development	**24*	**48*	***12*	***120*
DNA (μg/mg)				
Non-diapause	1.37	1.67	1.86	12.25
Diapause	1.00	1.49	1.54	1.58
RNA (μg/mg)				
Non-diapause	15.84	15.98	15.54	17.76
Diapause	14.27	14.33	14.00	13.58
DNA/RNA				
Non-diapause	0.086	0.104	0.120	0.127
Diapause	0.071	0.103	0.110	0.117

Pre-diapaused period ** Diapaused period

(c) Carbohydrate metabolism

Carbohydrate metabolism is the main pathway of biochemical regulation of diapause in the silkworm. It is proved that induction, initiation, maintenance and termination of diapause are related to carbohydrate metabolism. Amount of glycogen accumulated in diapause eggs is 1.7 times higher than in non-diapause eggs. More than 90% of carbohydrate accumulated in the silkworm diapause eggs is glycogen. The concentration of glycerin varies with genotype besides seasons from 32-40 mg/g egg. Glycogen accumulated in the silkworm egg is from the glycogen stored in the fat body during pupal stage, which is converted into trehalose and is released into haemolymph and then absorbed by developing oocyte. The trehalase localizes in plasma membrane of vitellogenic follicles where haemolymph trehalose is hydrolyses into glucose to be taken up by oocytes. The glucose is immediately used to synthesize glycogen as a storage reserve, by which hyperglycogenia is induced in diapause eggs. Consequently, DH provides the metabolic state preparatory to diapause initiation. It has been demonstrated that enzyme involved in trehalose synthesis include trehalase, hexokinase, phosphoglucomutase, UDP-glucose-pyrophosphatase and glycogen synthetase. Of this trehalase is a membrane bound restriction enzyme existing on the surface of oocytes and follicle cells. The amount of trehalose in the pupal body fluid entering the ovary and the amount of glycogen synthesized in the egg is related to the trehalase activity. Thus, the increase of glycogen content in diapauses eggs depends on the increase of trehalase activity. At the initiation of diapause, the stored glycogen is converted into sorbitol by the activation of phosphorylase 'b' to 'a' under anaerobic condition and thus during the whole diapause stage, the glycogen content in the silkworm eggs keeps at a very low level but the sorbitol content keeps at a very high level. The pathway of glycogen to sorbitol is coupled to pentose phosphate pathway, through the supply of reducing power (NADPH). In these eggs, activity of glucose-6-phoaphate (G-6-P) dehydrogenase is about twice higher than that of phosphofructokinase and G-6-P amounts equivalent to about 10% of the accumulated sorbitol are oxidized through pentose-phosphate pathway. The other fraction of G-6-P is eventually metabolized to glycerol. After the termination of diapause, sorbitol is again converted into glucose and the key enzyme involved in the activity is NAD-sorbitol dehydrogenase, which plays a significant regulatory role in the metabolic cycle.

Accumulation of huge quantity of sorbitol in the diapausing eggs is generally regarded as a protecting agent of eggs from cold injury in winter. One of the remarkable differences between diapause and non-diapause eggs within few days of oviposition is that glycogen rapidly disappears in the diapausing eggs but remains at its initial level in the non-diapause eggs. The utilization of sorbitol is controlled by 'Nicotinamide Adenine Dinucleotide-Sorbitol Dehydrogenase' (NAD-SDH). Yaginuma *et al.* (1990) reported that incubation of diapause eggs at 25°C does not induce the activity of NAD-SDH until 90 days. Moreover, the activity appears at very low level between 90-160 days. Similarly, chilling at 5°C for less than 30 days does not induce activity but 40 days period of chilling effectively stimulates activity. In contrast, 0.5°C never induces activity even with an exposure exceeding 250 days. Utilization of sorbitol in diapause eggs thus appears to be controlled by NAD-SDH activity through mediation of temperature. In non-diapause eggs, the sorbitol content increased on 2nd day of oviposition and then decreased rapidly.

(d) Sorbitol production

There is a significant biochemical difference at the time of oviposition between eggs destined to become diapause and non-diapause. The eggs developed in the presence of diapause hormone accumulate large quantity of glycogen. When oogenesis proceeded in the absence of diapause hormone, the laid eggs become non-diapause with less accumulation of glycogen and during embryogenesis, conversion of glycogen to sorbitol does not occur. Sorbitol is an ideal metabolite to assess the diapausing state of silkworm eggs. In diapause eggs, the initiation of sorbitol synthesis is correlated with the time when embryogenesis progressively slows down. Conversion of glycogen to sorbitol at this stage is monitored by the enzyme 'glycogen phosphorylase-a activity. Conversion of glycogen phosphorylase-'b' to 'a' is being reported absent in non-diapause eggs under normal conditions.

Glycogen phosphorylase-b kinase responsible for conversion of 'b' to 'a' form is identified in silkworm eggs and is reported to have some similarities in kinetic properties to that in other insect tissues. There is no difference in their activity between diapause and non-diapause eggs. When newly laid non-diapause eggs are exposed to low temperatures, sorbitol is accumulated and the extent of accumulation is closely dependent on the temperatures of exposure. In this case, glycogen is also used as an initial substrate for the formation of sorbitol. Thus, in non-diapause eggs, sorbitol production seems to be a biochemical adaptation against low temperature stress.

In diapause eggs, sorbitol began to decrease after continuous chilling for at least two months or by treatment with HCI on one month chilled eggs. The more advanced fall in sorbitol took place in eggs chilled for longer period. In all cases, sorbitol is stoichimometrically reconverted to glycogen. Thus, the conversion of sorbitol to glycogen is a specific sign signalling the breakdown of diapause in silkworm eggs. In the metabolic pathway from sorbitol to glycogen, NAD-sorbitol dehydrogenase, which catalyses the reaction from sorbitol to fructose is noticed to be the key enzyme. This activity is not being detected in eggs unchilled or chilled for less than two months and abruptly appears in eggs chilled for more than two months. The duration of diapause may be determined by analyzing the amount of oxygen required to prevent the decrease of sorbitol content in the eggs, which indicates that conversion of sorbitol to glycogen upon termination of diapause is closely related to the respiratory system via-GP cycle. Diapause termination is also closely related to the oxygen consumption during diapause period and that the activity of NAD-SDH enzyme is associated with the oxygen required for the termination of diapause. It is established that supply of oxygen to diapause eggs affects the maintenance of diapause period and when eggs are kept under anaerobic condition, the conversion of sorbitol to glycogen is delayed leading to delayed diapause termination.

(e) Sorbitol utilization

Diapausing silkworm eggs chilled at 5°C for at least three months when transferred to 25°C, the eggs resumed embryogenesis and hatches within two weeks. Soaking the pre-chilled diapausing eggs into hot solution can also bring about hatching. In these eggs, sorbitol content began to decrease after continuous chilling for at least two months or by treatment with HCl on one month chilled eggs. Greater fall in sorbitol content took place in eggs chilled for longer periods. Conversion of sorbitol to glycogen does not take place if eggs are kept continuously at 25°C even for more than six months. After diapause, all sorbitot in the eggs is converted into glycogen. During embryogenesis, the main carbohydrate consumed is glycogen. The glycogen-sorbitol-glycogen metabolic process is roughly the same as the process of diapause onset, maintenance and termination. In other words, the change of carbohydrate metabolism of the silkworm eggs is a close relative to the phenomenon of diapause. The sequence of major physiological events occurring in eggs of silkworm until the establishment of diapause is as:

(i) One day after oviposition

- ➢ Optimum age for acid treatment to block diapause initiation; beginning of ommochrome formation in serosal cells.
- ➢ Beginning of glycogen decrease and maximum glycogen consumption.

(ii) Two days after oviposition

- ➢ Steep decline in oxygen consumption.
- ➢ Abrupt increase of glycogen phosphorylase-a activity.

- Decline in affinity of lysosomes in embryonic cells to acridine orange with supra vital staining; the affinity is lost during diapause.
- Arrest of increase in DMA content.

(iii) Three days after oviposition

- Arrest of nucleic acid synthetic activity in nuclei of embryonic cells and gradual decrease in yolk cells in-vitro.

(iv) Four days after oviposition

- Arrest of mitotic activity in embryo.
- Continued steep decline in glycogen content and gradual accumulation of sorbitol and glycerol respectively.

(f) Changes in amino acid pool

Significant changes in some free amino acids occurred during the initiation and termination of diapause. In particular, a sudden large increase in alanine content (about 50μ mol/g eggs) occurred at the initiation of diapause (Suzuki *et al.*, 1984; Osanai and Yonezawa, 1986). Then alanine declines gradually with the increase of glutamate and especially proline. Content of proline that is always low during the initiation and maintenance of diapause, increased suddenly during the termination period indicating the conversion of alanine to glutamate and proline in diapausing eggs. In diapausing insects, a high concentration of free amino acids as well as of polyols and sugars serves to decrease the super cooling point (Somme, 1982). The super cooling point of *Bombyx mori* eggs is lower during diapause and hibernation (Suzuki *et al.*, 1983), and the increase of total amino acids and the accumulation of alanine or proline might be responsible for this effect. Proline serves as an energy source for later stages of embryonic life (Osanai and Yonezawa, 1986).

ARTIFICIAL HATCHING

Based on the number of generations in a year, silkworm eggs are classified as univoltine—the eggs of which hatch once a year, bivoltine—the eggs of which hatch twice a year and polyvoltine—the eggs of which hatch several times a year and thus resulting into one, two and many generations in a year respectively. These eggs are classified as diapausing and non-diapausing eggs. Bivoltine and univoltine enters into diapause within 40-50 hrs of egg laying at 25°C. The eggs when laid are yellow in colour. Gradually they change into light brown and then to purple brown. Under normal conditions, these diapausing silkworm eggs remain in diapause for a year after being laid and will not hatch until either given artificial stimulation or subjected to cold storage for a sufficient period. The mother moth in univoltine/ bivoltine forms releases a hibernating substance. This diapausing/hibernating substance, when released, arrests development of embryos and thus embryos will not develop even under optimum environmental conditions. However, after eggs are laid, if they are subjected to an artificial treatment at an appropriate age, stage and time, stimulate further growth without allowing them to enter into diapause. This 'artificial method of stimulating hatching is known as artificial hatching'.

Characteristics of multivoltine and bivoltine silkworm seed

Multivoltine	*Bivoltine*
Eggs are non-pigmented and non-hibernating	Eggs are pigmented and hibernating
Eggs hatch within 10-12 days of oviposition	Eggs do not hatch naturally after 10 days of oviposition
Acid treatment is not required to stimulate hatching	Acid treatment is required to stimulate hatching
Flat card/sheet egg method is applied for egg production	Eggs are mostly produced by loose egg production method
Sexes are separated at moth stage for production of hybrid	Sexes are separated at pupal stage for production of hybrid
Eggs cannot be preserved for more than 20 days at 5°C	Eggs can be preserved up to 6-10 months under different ibernation schedule

1. Methods of artificial hatching

There are several methods of artificial hatching that can be broadly classified into:

A. Physical methods

(i) Low temperature stimulation (chilling)

(ii) Hot water treatment

(iii) Stimulation by friction

(iv) Electrical stimulation

(v) Stimulation by exposing to sunshine

(vi) Stimulation by high atmospheric pressure

(vii) Artificial over wintering

(viii) Stimulation by ultraviolet/supersonic treatment

B. Chemical methods

(i) Hydrochloric acid treatment

(ii) Nitric acid treatment

(iii) Sulphuric acid treatment

(iv) Enzyme treatment

(v) Ozone treatment

(vi) Sodium chloride solution treatment

(vii) Per chloride treatment

Tanaka (1964) stated that Verson was apparently the first discovered artificial hatching by electrical stimulation. Later Araki and Miura succeeded in using a high voltage electrical source and stated that negative electrical discharge is more effective than positive electrical discharge. With the discovery of this method large electrical hatching machines using negative electrical discharge by intermittent direct current of 25000-50000 volts were fabricated. Terni and others discovered friction method. In this method eggs laid on cards when brushed strongly for 5-6 minutes by a hard brush, 40-50% eggs laid will hatch as quoted by Tanaka (1964).

Kui and Van reported that when hibernating eggs are dipped into hot water at 51-56°C for 3-15 seconds about 10 hrs after egg laying, results in 90% hatching. Gowda *et al.* (1998) stated that eggs treated with hot water at 55°C for 8 seconds duration resulted in good hatchability. They observed large number of dead eggs with the increase in temperature or duration of treatment. Ishii reported that when eggs were soaked in 3% hydrogen peroxide at 40-47°C for 7-10 minutes on the second day of egg laying. 100 percentage of them hatched. Rollet reported exposing of eggs to high atmospheric pressure.

Moreover, the artificial hatching method should have high and uniform hatching rate, simple equipments, easy to handle besides high work efficiency and economical in use. Taking into consideration of these facts, immersion of eggs in hydrochloric acid solution has been established most economical and safe, to obtain higher hatchability. This technique is now being widely practised for the treatment of bivoltine eggs.

2. Appliances for acid treatment

(i) Acid treatment bath

(ii) Specific gravity meter

(iii) Measuring cylinder (500-1000 ml capacity)

(iv) Clock (A stopwatch with second's hand)

(v) Acid frame and acid container (for loose eggs)

(vi) Water tank for removal of acid

(vii) Drying apparatus

If acid treatment bath is not available, then following apparatus will also be required:

(i) Hydrochloric acid container

(ii) Heater

(iii) Thermometer

3. Preparation of hydrochloric acid solution

(a) Hydrochloric acid

There are pure and industrial varieties of hydrochloric acid (HCl). The saturated solution of pure hydrochloric acid is colourless, transparent, dissolves easily in water, and vaporizes immediately into a thick white 'og when it comes in contact with air. It is strong stimulant, corrosive and at 15°C contains 42.09% hydrogen chloride. The specific gravity of pure hydrochloric acid is 1.212. However, it is better to use pure form of HCl solution for acid treatment but it is quite expensive. Industrial HCl is light brown or yellow in colour. It contains 30% hydrogen chloride and has specific gravity of 1.180. It is suggested to use always commercial grade chemically pure hydrochloric acid with 1.15 to 1.18 specific gravity and 30% hydrogen chloride. Commercial grade acid used must be free from impurities like mercury, nitrates and fluorides etc.

There is positive correlation between specific gravity and concentration of HCl. In other words, if specific gravity increases, the concentration of HCl solution increases and vice-versa. The specific gravity of HCl solution also varies with the temperature of the acid and there is negative correlation between the two. In other words, if the temperature of HCl solution is higher, the specific gravity will be lower (Table 7.8).

Table 7.8: Relationship between temperature and specific gravity of hydrochloric acid

Temperature (°C)	*Specific gravity*
15	1 .0750
20	1 .0732
23	1 .0722
25	1.0715
27	1.0710
29	1 .0708
30	1 .0697
31	1 .0694
34	1 .0683
40	1 .0663
46	1 .0642
50	1 .0624

From 15°C, when temperature increases or decreases, the co-efficient of specific gravity of HCl acid solution varies as follows:

Relationship between specific gravity and co-efficient of variation

Range of specific gravity	*Variation of co-efficient of specific gravity*
1.065-1.075	0.0003
1.080-1.100	0.0004
1.105-1.120	0.0005

Approximate specific gravity of HCl solution can be estimated with the help of temperature and variable co-efficient.

(b) *Concentration of hydrochloric acid*

There are two methods of diluting the original solution of HCI to obtain the desired concentration for acid treatment. These are:

(i) **Dilution based on concentration:** While preparing the solution of desired concentration by adding water to the stock solution, the amount of water to be added can be calculated on the basis of the following formula:

$$A = \frac{B-C}{C}$$

Where,

A = Quantity of water to be added

B = Concentration of stock solution

C = Concentration of desired solution

For example, by using the stock solution of 38% concentration of industrial HCl, 2% concentrated solution of desired strength can be prepared in the following way:

$$A = \frac{B-C}{C} = \frac{38-2}{2} = 18$$

Ratio, 18:1

Therefore, eighteen parts/liters of water should be added to one part/liter of stock solution to prepare 2% concentrated hydrochloric solution.

(ii) **Dilution based on specific gravity:** When preparing solution of HCl acid of desired gravity on the basis of specific gravity, the quantity of stock solution to be used can be estimated by the following formula:

$$A = \frac{B-1}{C-1} \times 100$$

Where,

A = Quantity of stock solution required

B = Desired specific gravity

C = Specific gravity of stock solution

For example, in order to prepare the acid solution of 1.075 specific gravity by using the stock solution of 1.18 specific gravity of HCl, the quantity of stock solution to be used will be:

$$A = \frac{B-1}{C-1} \times 100, \text{ i.e. } A = \frac{1.075-1}{1.180-1} \times 100 = 41.66$$

Therefore, to prepare 100 liters of HCl solution of 1.075 specific gravity, 41.66 liters of stock solution of specific gravity 1.180 and 58.34 liters of water will be required. When the acid gets turbid or once in three days or after treating 5 kgs of eggs, filter the acid and reuse. Every time before the treatment, the specific gravity should be measured to ensure to make it to the desired level.

4. **Artificial hatching by acid treatment**

Artificial hatching is usually carried out before the appearance of hibernating characters to block the hibernating tendency and stimulate the embryos for development instead of allowing them to enter into diapause. There are two methods of acid treatment:

- Hot acid treatment (common acid treatment)
- Cold acid treatment (room temperature treatment)

However, in these two types of acid treatment, the concentration and temperature of HCl acid, the specific gravity of acid and duration of acid treatment may vary but in principle both the methods are one and the same and is being carried out with the same purpose.

A. Hot acid treatment

(a) **Time of acid treatment:** Acid treatment is to be conducted at the appropriate age and stage of development of silkworm eggs. The best time considered is between the fusion of amnionic fold and formation of embryo, which is in between 16-30 hrs of egg laying at 25°C. For safer point of view, the eggs between the age groups of 20-24 hrs are ideal for acid treatment. Therefore, if time of egg laying is taken as 20 hrs (8 P.M. night) (by the time when most of the eggs are laid), then the acid treatment should be conducted between 16-20 hrs the following day. However, if temperature at the time of egg laying and preservation is high, acid treatment should be conducted slightly ahead and a little later if preservation temperature is low. Since the rate of embryonic development differs according to the preservation temperature of eggs after egg laying, the time of acid treatment is decided on the basis of time apse and egg preservation temperature. Temperature range between 27-30°C does not have any harmful effect on egg development; moreover, preservation temperature above 30°C after egg laying is harmful and should be avoided in order to achieve higher hatchability and healthy larvae.

(b) **Concentration of HCl acid solution:** The concentration of HCl solution for hot acid treatment should be 15% with 1.075 specific gravity.

(c) **Temperature of HCl solution:** HCl acid heated up to 46°C (115°C) is used for hot acid treatment of silkworm eggs. The temperature of the solution should not vary ± 0.5°C.

(d) **Duration of acid treatment:** The 5 minutes' duration of treatment has been considered adequate with HCI acid solution heated up to 46°C having 1.075 specific gravity. Acid should be heated indirectly. Temperature of acid should be checked from time to time during treatment. Shake the eggs gently and frequently during the treatment for uniform exposure of all eggs to acid solution. After washing, if water removal is incomplete in loose eggs, the HCl acid used for acid treatment becomes slightly diluted and hence after dipping, the temperature decreases consequently. Therefore, eggs should be dried properly before acid treatment. While for Chinese (oval cocoon) silkworm eggs, five minutes' duration of dipping of eggs in hot HCl solution is adequate to stimulate embryonic development, the same is five and half minutes in case of Japanese (constricted cocoon) silkworm races. In case of hybrids, the duration of acid treatment is same as that of the mother variety.

B. Cold acid treatment

It is also known as 'room temperature acid treatment' because hydrochloric acid used for the purpose is not preheated. In this case, concentration of acid is higher and duration of treatment is longer in comparison to hot acid treatment. But this method has certain advantages viz.,

- Simple and can be adopted without involving any special equipment.
- Conducted at room temperature and hence heating of acid is not required.
- It is safer than hot acid treatment, though it takes longer duration.
- Eggs do not drop off the egg card.
- Unfertilized eggs crumple during treatment and hence can be identified very easily.

- It is more economical.
- As risk factor involved in this method is very minimum, it can be handled even by unskilled person.
- As no electricity for heating of acid is required, it can be practised at all the places and at all the times.

(a) **Time of treatment:** Optimum time for cold acid treatment of bivoltine eggs is 15-20 hrs after egg laying preserved at 25°C.

(b) **Concentration of hydrochloric acid and duration of treatment:** At room temperature (25°C), the optimum concentration of HCl acid solution in the range of 21-22% with specific gravity of 1.108-1.110 is comparatively safe and dependable. If the specific gravity decreases below 1.10, the duration of treatment should be increased. Duration of treatment is decided according to the room temperature. If temperature of acid is lower than 25°C, the duration of treatment should be more. The duration of acid treatment at different temperature with acid concentration of 21% (1.108 specific gravity) is detailed in Table 7.9.

Table 7.9: Acid treatment duration at room temperature (Source: Narasimhanna, 1988)

Oviposition time	*Duration of treatment (minutes)* *Temperature of solution*		
	24°C	*27°C*	*29°C*
10 hrs	60-70	40-70	40
15 hrs	60-80	60-80	40-50
20 hrs	60-100	60-80	40-50
25 hrs	60-100	60-80	40-50

Removal of acid and drying: Soon after acid treatment, the eggs are washed in running water to remove all traces of acid from silkworm eggs. It is necessary to avoid irregular and poor hatching. Water temperature while washing eggs treated with HCl should be maintained within 15-30°C and water should continuously be stirred to remove hydrochloric acid as soon as possible. Blue litmus paper may be used to determine whether the acid is completely removed or not. After washing thoroughly, the eggs should be dried in well-ventilated room.

Cold storage of acid treated eggs: Silkworm eggs, which are acid, treated (hot or cold acid) for artificial hatching if incubated will normally develop and hatch in about 10 days. However, if due to some unavoidable circumstances, the hatching is to be delayed, the treated eggs are cold stored at 2.5°C up to 20 days without any harmful affect. If it is necessary to postpone the acid treatment itself, then eggs between the age groups of 20-24 hrs are first cold stored at 5°C for a week prior to acid treatment. In such cases, it is important that humidity during cold storage should be maintained at the optimum level of 75-80%.

Acid treatment after cold storage: This method can be applied in case hatching is required after 40 days of egg laying. In this method, 40-50 hrs old eggs on becoming dark brown after deposition at 25°C are cold stored at 5°C, for 35-70 days. Before subjecting the eggs for preservation, it is necessary to take following points into consideration:

- The preservation temperature after oviposition.
- Time or hours of cold storage.
- Time of acid treatment.
- Time specified for acid treatment should be followed strictly; otherwise it may lead to decrease in hatching.

The eggs are to be released from the cold storage to 24 ± 1°C through intermediate temperature of 15°C (2-3 hrs) on the desired day in between 35-70 days and are treated with acid to facilitate embryonic development. At this stage, cold storage inhibits diapause activity of eggs on the one hand and promotes hatching activity on the other. If cold storage period is shorter than 35 days, the hatching is affected considerably. Therefore, minimum period of cold storage of eggs at 5°C is more than 35 days in order to obtain better hatchability. On the contrary, if eggs are cold stored for more than 90 days, they can hatch without acid treatment. The eggs, which are cold stored for more than 90 days, should not be acid treated, as it is harmful and will result in many dead eggs. Eggs after taken out from the cold storage are kept at room temperature for 1-2 hrs before dipping into hot or cold acid solution for acid treatment in order to stimulate artificial hatching. After acid treatment, eggs are washed properly in water and shade dried.

In this method, it is necessary that eggs must pass through intermediate temperature of about 15°C for 18 hrs at the time of removing them out of the cold storage or keeping them into cold storage from room temperature in order to avoid the sudden change of the environmental conditions. Though the duration of immersing of eggs into acid in both the types i.e. acid treatment shortly after egg laying and that of cold storage is generally same, however, race dependency cannot be ignored.

Assessment of acid treatment: Results of acid treatment can be assessed as indicated below:

Age of eggs	*Properly treated eggs*	*In-sufficiently treated eggs*	*Excessively treated eggs*
24 hrs after treatement	Colour of eggs turns to pale or light brown, Colour change is slow, Appearance of slight depression on the upper surface of chorion	Depression formation is not seen and eggs resemble to hibernated eggs	No colour change Depression is very clear and deep
2-3 days later	Clear formation of depression on the 2nd day and will be larger on the 3rd	Very slow formation of depression. Even on 3rd day the depression is not seen	Appearance of dead eggs with brownish colour

Care during acid treatment

- Thermometer, hygrometer and timer should be perfect.

- Purchase HCl from a reliable source only and check specific gravity (1.15 to 1.18) and colour of the acid (pale yellow).
- Only plastic material should be used in treatment room.
- Ensure proper ventilation in the treatment room.
- For personnel safety, it is suggested to wear protective glasses and apron.
- Check the water temperature while washing in running water. Too cold or too hot water should not be used.

INCUBATION

Quality silkworm seed is the basic requirement of the sericulture industry. The crop performance and silk productivity are directly related to the quality of seed. It is very difficult to define the term 'Quality of silkworm seed' but for all practical purposes, the quality silkworm seed can be considered as eggs produced from good cocoons under optimal environmental conditions. Quality can deteriorate due to improper handling during its processing, preservation, hibernation, acid treatment, chilling, incubation, transportation etc. Incubation is one of the most important techniques in seed handling. Incubation is an acclaimed important step to obtain uniform hatching, normal growth of larvae, quality of cocoon crop and quality of cocoons. Therefore, the term incubation can be defined as preservation of silkworm eggs under optimum environmental conditions of temperature (25 ± 2°C), RH (75 ± 5%) and photoperiod (16 L: 8 D) during embryonic development, so as to suit the silkworm eggs to develop normally to provide uniform and maximum hatchability on the expected day. The term incubation is used especially to those eggs, which are naturally active or artificially activated eggs and not to those eggs, which are kept under aestivation.

Purpose of incubation: Incubation aims at:

(a) To promote proper development ensuring that eggs of different varieties should hatch on the designated date.

(b) To enforce uniform hatching to produce healthy larvae.

(c) To maintain the voltinisrn of the race.

(d) To stabilize the hibernating characters of the bivoltine eggs.

(e) To maintain uniform larval growth for successful cocoon crop.

Types of incubation: Incubation is of three types:

(a) **Interruption incubation:** In the interruption method, the temperature at the beginning of incubation is kept at 15-18°C and after one or two days the incubation is allowed for four days at 22-23°C up to blastokinesis stage. At the final stage of incubation, the temperature is maintained at 25°C until hatching.

(b) **Progressive incubation:** In the progressive incubation method, the temperature in the beginning is maintained at lower level and thereafter it is kept constant around 25°C until hatching.

(c) **Kyuri incubation:** This method is not in practice now a days as the technique of artificial hatching method is well practised. However, in this method the temperature in the beginning is maintained at 20-23°C and during the development of embryo when thoracic appendages appear or just before the blastokinesis, the temperature is brought down to 15°C. This condition is continued until just before hatching. At the time of hatching once again, the temperature is increased to 24-25°C. This incubation method is adopted when it is necessary to obtain non-diapause eggs.

Devices for silkworm egg incubation: Incubation can be practised by adopting the following techniques:

(i) **Room incubation:** In places where cold storages are available, exclusive incubation rooms are constructed. These rooms have provision of

maintaining optimum temperature and humidity conditions besides having the provision of regulating the photoperiod. Incubation rooms should not be overcrowded with silkworm eggs as it increases the carbon-dioxide content.

(ii) **Mud pot incubation:** Mud pot incubation is ideal for individual farmers. Mud pots are filled with water at the bottom and covered with wet muslin cloth. The pot is placed over wet sand. The layings are hanged inside the pot with the help of a rod.

(iii) **Double walled incubation chamber:** This method of incubation is suitable for individual grainages. The temperature and humidity can be maintained to near optimum conditions by this method. This method of incubation is suitable during summer months.

(iv) **Tray incubation:** The layings can be incubated in tray by providing paraffin paper and wet foam pads. During favourable seasons, the silkworm egg sheets are spread in the rearing trays for incubation. The rooms should be heated with the help of electric heater up to the required temperature. Boiling water in wide mouthed vessel on charcoal stove can increase humidity. This helps in increasing temperature and humidity both.

(v) **Incubation in incubator:** Incubators with light facility can also be used for incubation of silkworm eggs. The temperature in incubator is set to the required level and humidity is maintained by keeping a tray of water inside the incubator preferably at the bottom.

Factors related to incubation: The main factors related to incubation are disinfections, transportation, temperature, relative humidity, photoperiod, aeration and black boxing.

(a) **Disinfection:** Rooms and equipments where incubation has to be carried out should be

thoroughly disinfected prior to commencement of incubation. Silkworm eggs should be surface sterilized with 2% formalin for 10-15 minutes before and after cold storage of eggs.

(b) **Transportation:** Irregularities in hatching and subsequent crop losses can also be attributed to improper transportation methods. Extreme environmental conditions such as high temperature coupled with low humidity and oxygen deficiency during the course of transportation are harmful. Therefore, care should be taken to provide optimum incubation conditions during transportation. It is advisable to transport silkworm eggs during early developmental stages at the time when temperature fluctuation is less i.e. during morning or evening time specially by keeping them in transportation boxes fabricated for the purpose.

(c) **Temperature:** Temperature is one of the most important factors that play a vital role during incubation. Although the embryonic development takes place between 10-30°C their development is not uniform leading to irregular hatching over a period of time. The optimum temperature of 25 ± 2°C is ideal for incubation at which the embryonic growth is normal. Any fluctuation from the optimum during incubation affects the development of embryos. Temperature above 30°C is highly deleterious as hatching is significantly affected and at 33°C, hatching is almost negligible.

(d) **Humidity:** Humidity is an important factor, which directly affects the physiology of silkworm eggs. The humidity range of 70-80% is ideal for maintaining the normal development of silkworm eggs. Humidity less than 60% results in loss of water from silkworm eggs and humidity of 90% and above leads to retention of physiological wastewater resulting in poisoning of embryos. Humidity in combination with temperature has

very strong effect on the developmental physiology of eggs. Though a temperature of 25 ± 2°C is ideal for incubation but if humidity is as low as 30 ± 5%, the ideal temperature itself becomes dangerous for the development of eggs. It not only affects hatching but also retards growth and prolongs the incubation period. Low humidity during pinhead and blue egg stage makes the gluey substance that covers the eggs rather hard as cement and the larvae find it difficult to bite the eggshell and eventually fail to hatch. A combination of high temperature and low humidity results in desiccation and majority of eggs fail to hatch.

(e) **Photoperiod:** Photoperiod has a direct effect on voltinism in the bivoltine. Bivoltine silkworm eggs should be incubated at 16 hrs lights and 8 hrs dark to maintain the diapausing nature in the ensuing generation. The intensity of light should be 0.1 watt or above. In case of low temperature incubation, the eggs are kept in darkness throughout the day or the light conditions per day should not exceed 12 hrs. If eggs are allowed to remain under light conditions throughout the day, the hatching will not be uniform. In order to obtain maximum hatching within a short period, the eggs in eye spot stage are kept in darkness and on the day of hatching, they are suddenly brought out to bright light conditions.

(f) **Aeration:** Since the eggs undergoing incubation respire vigorously, the room should be airy, so that there is no hindrance to free respiration. Aeration from the middle of the incubation plays very important role. Good ventilation provides good circulation of air, which helps in driving out poisonous gases produced due to metabolic activity of silkworm eggs. It is established that carbon dioxide level above 0.3% is deleterious and kills the developing eggs. Therefore, incubation

room should be properly ventilated or aerated.

Table 7.10: Temperature and humidity during incubation of eggs

Type of eggs	*Temperature*	*Duration*	*Humidity*
Acid treated eggs	24-26°C	Up to hatching	75 ± 5%
Hibernated eggs	15°C	3 days	75 ± 5%
	24-26°C	Up to hatching	

(g) **Black boxing:** Black boxing technique provides synchronized hatching in a short period. The eggs, which are not black boxed, hatch irregularly over a period of time. In order to obtain synchronized hatching in a short period, photoperiod is manipulated during the later stage of egg development especially at the time when egg development reaches to pinhead stage (head pigmentation stage), the eggs are subjected for complete darkness known as 'scotophase' and exposed to light after 48 hrs. This procedure is based on the fact that faster egg development takes place in the light up to head pigmentation stage and darkness enhances uniform development from pinhead stage up to onset of hatching. This technique of providing complete darkness to developing embryos from pinhead stage to the onset of hatching is known as 'black boxing technique'. It has twin advantages:

- To force late maturing or lagging embryos to accelerate their development and join their developed counterparts.
- The insects being photosensitive in nature, darkness inhibits hatching process largely. This inhibition is intricately related to the 'biological clock' operating in the nervous system.

Methods of black boxing: The methods of black boxing are:

(a) **Dark room method:** The entire room where silkworm eggs are incubated can be made dark by switching off the lights when eggs reached the head pigmentation stage and exposed to light only after 48 hrs.

(b) **Incubator method:** The layings are incubated in total darkness in incubators when they reach head pigmentation stage.

(c) **Black cloth method:** The layings kept in trays for incubation are covered with double-layered black cloth when developing embryos reaches head pigmentation stage and exposed to light after 48 hrs.

(d) **Wooden box method:** A wooden box painted on inner side with black paint can be effectively used for incubation. Eggs after reaching to head pigmentation stage are kept in these boxes and exposed to light after 48 hrs.

(e) **Black paper method:** The layings are kept in black paper cover, which are sealed by using clips to avoid entry of light. The clips are opened and eggs are exposed to light on the expected day of hatching.

Stage of black boxing: Silkworm eggs should be black boxed when majority of eggs (80%) has reached the head pigmentation stage. Black boxing of eggs at body pigmentation stage (blue egg stage) is not ideal, as light stimulus would have already been perceived by the brain cells of embryos, as a result hatching will be initiated inside the black box itself (Rao *et al.*, 1998). The head pigmentation stage is identified by a small black dot in the eggs near the micropylar end. The black spot appears mostly on the 7th day in multivoltine breeds and on the 8th day in bivoltine breeds under optimum incubation conditions.

Light exposure to stimulate hatching: A photoperiod of 16 hrs light and 8 hrs darkness during incubation up to pinhead stage and then shifting to darkness and later sudden exposure to bright illumination enable uniform hatching. Hatching occurs within 2-3 hrs after exposure to light. The layings from the dark phase are exposed to bright light at about 6 A.M. In the absence of electricity, the layings can be brought under natural light. A relative humidity of 70% is ideal at the time of hatching.

Effect of incubation environment on voltinism: The major environmental factors affecting voltinism are:

(i) **Temperature:** Temperature during incubation has greatest influence on voltinism. In other words, temperature during incubation plays an important role in determining that whether bivoltine silkworms will lay hibernating or non-hibernating eggs. When bivoltine eggs are incubated at a temperature of 25°C or above, the resulting moths will lay hibernating eggs, and when incubated at a low temperature of 15°C, they will lay non-hibernating eggs regardless of environmental conditions during larval and pupal stages. An intermediate temperature of 20°C during incubation will result in production of mixture of hibernating and non-hibernating eggs (Table 7.11).

Table 7.11: Influence of temperature during incubation on various stages of development of bivoltine silkworm

Incubation stage	*Grown larval stage*	*Mounting/ pupal stage*	*Voltinism of eggs laid*
High tempt. (Above 25°C)	High tempt. (Above 25°C)	High tempt. (Above 25°C)	Hibernating
	Low tempt. (18°C)	Low tempt. (20°C)	Non-hibernating
Low tempt. (15°C)	High tempt. (Above 25°C)	High tempt. (Above 28°C)	Non-hibernating
	Low tempt. (18°°C)	Low tempt. (20°C)	Non-hibernating
Intermediate tempt. (Above 20°C)	High tempt. (Above 25°C)	High tempt. (Above 28°C)	Mostly Non-hibernating
	Low tempt. (18°C)	Low tempt. (20°C)	Mostly Non-hibernating

(ii) **Light:** Light during incubation also influences voltinism but the effect is not evident if temperature is above 25°C or below 15°C. At the intermediate temperature, if long photoperiod is provided to the developing embryos, the resulting moths will lay higher rate of hibernating eggs. On the contrast, the short photoperiod induces more non-hibernating eggs. It is established that the influence of light is next to temperature.

(iii) **Humidity:** The influence of humidity on voltinism is next to light. Humidity does not affect voltinism if incubation temperature is above 25°C or below 15°C. At intermediate incubation temperature, high humidity is favourable for inducing more hibernating eggs, while low humidity favours non-hibernating eggs. Temperature, light and humidity affect the voltinism of silkworms at the stage between when embryo begins to form the thoracic legs and when the head begins to be pigmented. The basic requirement for the bivoltine to lay hibernating eggs is a temperature above 25°C. If eggs are incubated at a temperature below 15°C and kept in dark and dry condition, most of the bivoltine races may produce non-hibernating eggs in the resulting moths.

8

SEED CROP REARING

REARING OF PARENT SILKWORMS

Rearing of parent silkworm is known as seed crop rearing and it is meant for producing parent silkworm eggs. The rearing of seed crop is different from the commercial rearing of silkworms. The objective of seed crop rearing is to produce healthy silkworm seed, which is free from all the diseases in general and from pebrine infection in particular on the one hand, and to produce larger quantities of eggs that will yield excellent results in the next generation on the other. Many factors contribute to the success of silkworm rearing and quality of cocoon crops. Apart from the rearing techniques, mulberry quality and quantity, management, silkworm races, egg handling, larval protection from diseases and pests, preparation of rearing etc have significant impact on crop success.

Brushing: The process of transferring the freshly hatched larvae to the rearing bed provided with mulberry leaves is called brushing. A suitable time for brushing the newly hatched larvae is about 10.00 hours as most of the larvae hatch by 8.00 to 9.00 hours and develop good appetites within one to two hours of hatching. In order to obtain uniform hatching, developing eggs at blue stage are kept in black boxes on the day prior to hatching. Next morning, eggs are exposed to defused light, so that the larvae hatch uniformly in response to phototropic stimulus. By this method, more than 90% hatching can be achieved in short period of one to two hours. Newly hatched larvae are black and hairy and look like black ants.

Methods of brushing: The method of brushing in practice is briefly described below:

(a) **Eggs on cards:** The cards with newly hatched larvae are placed in the rearing tray and tender leaves cut into small size (0.5 cm^2) are sprinkled over the egg card. The hatched larvae crawl onto the tender leaves and starts feeding. After 1 to 2 hours, the cards are removed, the bed is uniformly prepared and first feeding of mulberry leaves is given.

(b) **Loose eggs:** Loose eggs are kept at the bottom of a container covered with mosquito net cloth of 3 mm mesh. After hatching of eggs, tender leaves chopped into small size (0.5 cm^2) are spread over the net. When the larvae have crawled over the leaves, the net with larvae and leaves is transferred to the rearing trays in such a way that they spread uniformly on it. Sometimes, the freshly hatched larvae are brushed with a feather from the egg card directly on the rearing trays. This method is not recommended for brushing as it may cause injury to the freshly hatched larvae. After brushing, the egg cards should be retained for inspection of pebrine pathogen and calculation of fecundity and hatching per cent.

Time of brushing of larvae: Black boxed silkworm eggs are exposed to light in the morning at 6 AM and by 8 to 9 AM all those eggs that are expected to hatch complete their hatching. Those eggs that do not hatch in the morning of first day are covered with thin paper and kept in incubator. After one or two hours of hatching, the newly hatched larvae get an appetite and begin to crawl about. This is the time for brushing. If the larvae are not brushed at this stage, they will get tired, hungry, weak and susceptible to diseases later. If the season is warm and dry, it is safe to transfer them to the rearing beds a little earlier.

Determination of brushing date: Brushing date is determined on the basis of mulberry budding, availability of leaf and suitability of the season. Incubation is initiated 10 to 12 days prior to the date of brushing. Generally, incubation period varies with silkworm breeds, incubation methods and stage of embryonic development. Normally, hibernated eggs take 11 to 14 days and non-hibernated eggs 10 to 12 days for hatching from initiation of incubation.

Determination of rearing scale: Rearing scale is determined on the availability of labour, mulberry leaf productivity, space of rearing house, rearing tools, facilities etc. As sericulture is subsidiary occupation, rearing scale is generally determined on the basis of availability of family labour and mulberry leaf but if it is large scale or an exclusive farming, rearing scheme is chalked out based on employment and other factors as indicated.

Harvesting of leaf: For rearing young age silkworms, the best time for harvesting mulberry leaf is either early in the morning or in the evening. As different quality of leaf is required for different instars, a systematic leaf harvest is followed as indicated below:

- For the first instar: 4th and 5th leaf below the most slithering leaf.
- For the second instar: 5th to 7th leaf below the most slithering leaf.
- For the third instar: 7th and 8th leaf below the most slithering leaf.

During bright sunlight leaf plucking as far as possible should be avoided because in the daytime, a rise of air temperature causes evaporation from leaves and therefore harvested leaves are liable to wilting during storing. The mulberry garden should be set up near to the rearing place to avoid long transportation time, which makes leaves liable to wilting. If mulberry plantation is nearby, fresh leaves can be given to the silkworms. The harvested leaves should be packed loosely and transported rapidly to keep their freshness as much as possible.

Preservation of fresh leaves: The storage duration of fresh mulberry leaves should not be beyond 24 hours.

The leaves must be stored at a place where the lowest evaporation takes place. The freshly harvested succulent leaves undergo rapid changes following harvest. The loss of moisture particularly is very rapid during hot dry seasons and this affects the palatability of leaves for silkworms. If temperature is high, leaves wither fast and thus become nutritively poorer. To prevent withering of leaves, attempts are made to maintain the relative humidity in the storage room to its required optimum level. Leaves are preserved loose under a wet gunny cloth which could be kept sufficiently wet all the time by sprinkling water on it repeatedly at convenient intervals. The larvae that are fed with such water treated leaves during preservation should be adequately spaced so that there may be proper ventilation in the rearing beds. Care should also be taken to see that directly wet leaves carrying water droplets over them are strictly avoided as this would lead to diseases. If any droplets are found on the leaves, they should be wiped out before being given for feeding to the silkworms.

In rainy season, however, the situation exits quite opposite to that exits in summer. The humidity is generally high and hence problem is not of leaf moisture preservation but that of removing excess moisture present in the leaf. The leaves harvested in the rainy season should be spread out thinly on the floor to driven out excess moisture present on the surface of the leaf before feeding to the silkworms. Sprinkling of water for preservation of leaf is not necessary during this season.

Rearing of young silkworms

A. ***Characteristics of young silkworms***

(a) Young silkworms, particularly those in the first instar, have a high growth rate. During the first instar, body weight increases by 10 to 15 times, whereas in the other instars the weight increases by 5 to 6 times only. Similarly, per unit body weight the amount of food supplied, oxygen intake and evaporation are largest in the first instar.

(b) Young silkworms have stronger resistance against high temperature and humidity than grown silkworms. Therefore, rearing them slightly at high temperature and humidity results in higher silk productivity.

(c) Young silkworms are less resistant to pathogenic microorganism than grown silkworms and therefore rearing of young silkworms under more hygienic conditions has great impact on the stabilization of cocoon crop.

(d) Young silkworms are strong against dirty air but weak against carbonic acid gas, ammonia, muscardine etc. If the concentration of carbon dioxide gas in rearing room or in rearing box exceeds *2%*, the growth of silkworms is retarded. If temperature rises to 30°C or higher, viral diseases may be liable to occur.

(e) In newly born larvae, water content is very low but increases rapidly up to second instars when feeding starts. Silkworm requires high water content in mulberry leaves to supply the needed water requirement in their body.

B. *Mulberry leaves for rearing*

It is desirable to provide mulberry leaves suited to various phases of growth during the young larval stage. Each age of silkworm larvae could conveniently be divided into seven stages viz., first feeding stage, sparse eating stage, moderate eating stage, active eating stage, pre-moulting stage, last feeding stage and moulting stage. Larvae have good appetite at the first feeding stage and comparatively little appetite at the sparse eating and moderate eating stage. They eat the most at the active eating stage. Therefore, quantity of leaf should be regulated according to the feeding patterns.

Mulberry leaves to be fed to young silkworms must have high moisture value. Feeding of leaves having a poor nutritive value reduces the resistance of young silkworms against diseases. The standard leaf positions suitable for rearing of various young stages of silkworms are:

- Newly hatched larvae: 3rd and 4th yellowish green leaves from the top.
- First instar: 4th and 5th tender leaves from the tip below the leaves exposed to maximum light i.e. top most full blown leaves which are light green.
- Second instar: 5th to 7th leaves from the top turning to dark green.
- Third instar: 7th and 8th leaves from the top, which are dark green in colour.

The nutrient composition in mulberry leaves differs according to the age. Younger the leaf, higher the protein content and lower the carbohydrate content (Table 8.1). The maximum light exposed leaves are those, which are yellow-green and have extremely shiny surface or luster. It is desirable to provide most suitable leaves close to the standard to the larvae but if these leaves differ in maturity to some extent, they can be mixed and provided. To obtain leaves suited for young silkworm rearing, it is advisable to establish a special mulberry field for young silkworms i.e. chawki garden and to ensure its proper management.

Table 8.1: Nutrient composition in mulberry leaves (%)

Position of leaves from the top	*Water content*	*Dry matter*	*Protein*	*Composition of dry matter*			
				Carbohydrates	*Oil*	*Fiber*	*Ash*
1	81.75	18.25	35.06	8.34	2.42	9.61	9.53
5	77.25	22.75	28.75	20.34	2.10	9.78	8.61
10	72.96	27.02	24.24	24.86	3.45	10.08	9.39
15	73.19	26.81	23.06	21.53	4.30	10.36	10.97
20	74.24	25.76	19.88	19.53	4.67	10.60	13.37
25	75.75	24.25	21.81	18.93	4.97	10.82	15.06

Rearing environment: Climatic conditions including temperature, humidity, air circulation, gases and light affect the growth and development of silkworm resulting in influencing productivity and quality of silk, it is necessary to regulate maximum productivity of good quality cocoons. These factors show a significant interaction and their effect on the physiology of larvae varies depending upon combination of factors, developmental stage, nutritive status of feed etc.

(i) **Temperature:** Among the various environmental factors that influence the cocoon crops, the most important is temperature followed by humidity. Since silkworms are cold-blooded animals, temperature has a direct effect on the growth, development and physiological activity, in nutrient absorption, digestion, blood circulation, respiration etc. With the increase in temperature, the larval growth and development is accelerated resulting in decrease in larval duration, while at low temperature growth and development is slow leading to prolonged larval period. Generally the temperature range for normal growth is 18-30°C, but the optimum temperature range for rearing of young age larvae of bivoltine parental strain is 26-28°C for 1st and 2nd instars and 24-26°C for 3rd instar. In case of multivoltine strains slightly higher rearing temperature than that required for bivoltine is necessary. The room temperature is generally low during winter and high during summer months and therefore suitable measures should be adopted to regulate it to the optimum level.

(ii) **Humidity:** Humidity also plays an important role in the silkworm rearing. It has mostly indirect effect on growth and development. Indirectly, humidity influences silkworm physiology through withering of leaves and sanitation of rearing beds. Under too dry conditions, the leaves wither very fast and become unsuitable for feed, resulting in retarded growth of larvae. Retarded growth of young age larvae makes them weak and easily susceptible to diseases and other adverse conditions.

Ordinarily high relative humidity during rearing of young age silkworm larvae results in lesser loss of silkworm larvae than low relative humidity. During late age silkworm rearing, low humidity reduces their loss. However, during moult and throughout the moulting phase, the humidity should invariably be maintained slightly lower than in the rearing period. Humidity during rearing phase of 1st, 2nd and 3rd instar should be maintained at 85%, 85% and 80% respectively. For regulating humidity in the rearing bed, paraffin paper and wet foam pads or paper bands are used. If humidity is too low, sprinkling of water on the floor may be found useful to increase it.

(iii) **Ventilation:** Silkworms like any other animal require fresh air for their various physiological activities. The freshness of air can be determined by its CO_2 contents. Due to respiration, carbonic acid gas is released in the rearing bed and rearing room. Although atmospheric CO_2 content is generally 0.03 -0.04% in the rearing room but it can increase due to firewood, coal, smoke of fuel, carbon dioxide produced due to fermentation of leaves on rearing beds, respiration of mulberry leaves, carbon mono-oxide, ammonia and sulphur dioxide etc. and these gases are injurious to growth, development and health of silkworm larvae. When built up of these poisonous gases reaches beyond the tolerance limit of silkworm larvae, they start to show the symptoms of sluggishness and even stop to feed. Young silkworm larvae are more susceptible to the poisonous gases and hence artificial circulation of air is extremely useful in bringing down the temperature and humidity besides removing the poisonous gases from the rearing room. Carbon dioxide content exceeding 1% in rearing room is reported to be bad for silkworm and the relation between concentration of CO_2 in a rearing room and mortality of silkworm is linear (Suzuki *et al.*, 1962).

(iv) **Light:** Light constantly influences the physiology of silkworm. Silkworms are photosensitive and

generally have a tendency to crawl towards the dim light. Larvae of silkworm do not prefer either strong light or complete darkness but usually light phase in contrast to the dark phase activates the larvae preferring light within the range of 15-30 lux. Rearing in either complete darkness or in bright light leads to irregularity in growth and moulting. Light phase usually makes larval duration longer than the dark phase. Photo phase for rearing of silkworms should be 16 hours light per day followed by a Scot phase of 8 hours. It is advisable to rear silkworms in dim light during the daytime and in the dark during at night for healthy growth of larvae. Rearing of silkworms in continuous light delayed growth considerably leading to appearance of pentamoulters and reduced larval and cocoon weights.

Methods of chawki rearing: Different methods are in practice for rearing of early stages of silkworm. In all methods, importance is given to correct temperature, humidity and photoperiod for vigorous and healthy growth of larvae. Mostly, three methods are in practice for rearing of young silkworms –

(a) Paraffin paper method

(b) Box rearing method

(c) Hot chamber rearing method

(a) Paraffin paper rearing method: This method is also known as covered rearing method. In this method, paraffin paper is used at the bottom as well as on the top of rearing trays to cover it. The objective of covering rearing trays with paraffin paper is to ensure optimum humidity in the bed and to keep mulberry leaves fresh for a longer period to ensure full nourishment and uniform development. Feeding is mostly given two to three times a day. The paraffin paper used for rearing of young silkworms should be of superior quality with melting point of above 55°C. Superior quality paraffin paper could be used repeatedly which will result in lowering of rearing costs.

During the first two instars, the rearing bed should be covered at both the top and the bottom, with the four sides wrapped. The top covering should be removed at moulting stage to dry rearing bed. Before covering the bed with paraffin paper at the top of rearing bed, wet foam pads on all four sides of rearing bed are placed to maintain required humidity. The top paraffin paper must be removed at least 20 minutes prior to feeding in order to provide adequate aeration and to dispel accumulated toxic gases. At the time of moulting, a thin film of lime powder sprinkled over the bed helps to keep the bed dry. But if humidity is high or in places which are humid, there is danger of muscardine and therefore a thin layer of muscardine powder may be spread over the bed to protect the silkworm against diseases at the time of hatching, at each moult and in middle of each stage.

(b) **Box rearing method:** Boxes or trays made up of wood or plastic are used for box rearing. The boxes may be with lid or without lids. Silkworms are reared in the boxes with a cover in which wet foam pads are placed around the rearing bed to provide high humidity. The frequency of feeding is 2-3 times a day. The cover should be removed 30 minutes before each feeding and also during moulting in order to regulate humidity. While using this method care must be taken to disinfect the silkworms by sprinkling anti-muscardine powder because due to high humidity in the rearing beds, the larvae are subject to muscardine disease. Wooden boxes of uniform size and 10-15 cm deep are used for this type of rearing. Normally, 5-8 boxes are piled one over the other for rearing.

(c) **Hot chamber rearing method:** This method is widely adopted by Chinese sericulturists for young age silkworm rearing. With this method, over 30% labour and about 25-35% leaves could be saved. This method has the advantage in maintaining uniform temperature, moisture, and freshness of leaves, high leaf utilization ratio, less frequency of feeding, uniform and fast larval development. Owing to the high humidity and high temperature existing in it, the hot chamber should be thoroughly sterilized before rearing.

Moulting and mounting care: Under optimum rearing conditions, the 1st instar larvae takes three to three and half days to settle for 1st moult and two to two and half days for 2nd moult. Moulting duration is mostly 20-24 hrs. When the worms start settling for moulting, the top paraffin paper and wet foam pads are removed in order to provide low humidity. When all the larvae settle for moult, slaked lime is dusted @ 4-5 g/ sq. ft. During moulting, the bed is spread to reduce its thickness and to allow the left over leaves and bed for drying. Feeding is resumed when more than 95% of the larvae are out of moult. Before feeding the larvae, bed disinfectants are dusted over the larvae and feeding is provided half an hour later. Tender leaves are given to freshly moulted larvae.

Transportation of chawki worms: Chawki worms should be transported from the chawki rearing centers to the rearing site when they are in the 2nd moult or 2 feeds after the 2nd moult during cool hours particularly in the evening. The larvae are packed in wax paper and transported. However, transportation to long distances should be avoided. As soon as it reaches to the rearing site, the wax paper should be opened; larvae are spread in the tray kept on rearing stand for the rearing of the larvae.

Chopping of leaves: While supplying mulberry leaves for feeding to young age silkworms, it is necessary to chop and provide them in the recommended sizes and quantities. While rearing the young age silkworms, the size of chopped leaves is increased as the larvae develop. The common size is 0.5 to 1.0 cm^2 for the 1st instar, 1.5-2.5 cm^2 for the 2nd instar and 3.0-4.0 cm^2 for the 3rd instar (Table 8.2). However, when the larvae are out of each moult, the first feeding is again given with slightly reduced size chopped leaves. Mulberry leaves are chopped with chopping knife on a thick wooden board. The wooden board is mostly one meter in length and 2 feet in width. However, in case of large scale rearing, the use of chopping machine is recommended.

Table 8.2: Standard chart for chawki silkworm rearing (100 Dfls or 40,000 larvae)

Factors	*1st instar*	*2nd instar*
Temperature (°C)	27-28	26 – 27
Humidity (%)		
Rearing	85-90	85 – 90
Moulting	75-80	75 – 80
Feeds per day (No.)	4	4
Quantity of leaf (kg)		
Multivoltine	2.5	10
Bivoltine	2.5-3.0	13 – 14
Leaf size (cm^2)	0.5-1.0	1.5-2.5
Bed area (m^2)		
Multivoltine	0.30-1.25	1.25-3.5
Bivoltine	0.36-1.35	1 .35-4.0
Bed cleaning	1	2
Bed disinfectant (gm)	60	120
Larval period (days)	3.0-3.5	2.5-3.0
Moulting period (hrs)	20	20-24

Rearing of late age silkworms

The method of rearing of advanced stage larvae is different from that of young silkworms. Unlike the young silkworm larvae, the advanced stage larvae withstand high temperature and humidity. They normally thrive well under comparatively lower temperature and humidity than those for young larvae. The growth of advanced stage larvae is fast and the consumption of mulberry leaf is very high. The temperature should be around 24°C during 4th instars and between 22-23°C during 5th instars. Since the environmental conditions vary with the rearing season, suitable modification in the rearing method is necessary. For example, under high humidity conditions as in rainy season, more ventilation and greater spacing should be resorted to, and all care should be taken to avoid overfeeding to the larvae. During winter season, the rearing room should be warmed by some means to the optimum level. However, during summer and autumn season rearing, it is necessary to bring down the temperature and if there is high humidity, arrangement should be made to maintain it to the required level. Larvae should be provided with sufficient quantity of mulberry leaf during this active feeding stage. For late age silkworms, more mature leaves, which contain less of moisture and more protein content, should be used. Attention should be focused on proper preservation of leaf, as health of larvae depends very much on the quality and quantity of leaf consumed. If leaf is not sufficiently fresh, its edible quantity is reduced and worms tend to undergo starvation inspite of the presence of leaf in the rearing bed. It is advisable to give fairly a large quantity of leaf as feed during night.

Characteristics of grown silkworms

Grown silkworm differ from young silkworms in many aspects:

(a) Grown silkworms are weak to high temperature, high humidity, poor ventilation and other metrological environments.

(b) The digested and ingested amount of mulberry leaves increases and they eat even over mature and somewhat less water content leaves. However, their digestion ratios are lower than those for young silkworms.

(c) They are resistant to poor quality of leaves, deficiency in feeding dosages and other nutritional deficiencies.

(d) Their resistance to chemical is strong. Because of their characteristics, the environment and rearing techniques applicable to 4th and 5th instars differ greatly from those of young silkworms.

Method of rearing of late age silkworms

For rearing the advanced age larvae, three methods of rearing are commonly in use. They are:

(a) Shelf rearing method

(b) Floor rearing method

(c) Shoot rearing method

(a) Shelf rearing method

Rearing of silkworms in rearing trays arranged one over the other in tiers on rearing stand is called shelf rearing. Generally, rearing stands are arranged in rows parallel to the wall with adequate space in the center for removing the trays and attending the cleaning of rearing beds and feeding to the silkworms. The trays are pulled out to provide the feed and then kept back. Each rearing stand can accommodate up to 10 rearing trays. This method has been followed for a very long time and in terms of optimum use of available space, it is very profitable and economical. In India, sericulture farmers use round bamboo trays of 1.2 – 1.4 meter in diameter for rearing of late age silkworms. Under this system of rearing, mulberry leaves are picked individually and fed to the silkworms. Usually 4 feedings are given in a day and nets are used to clean the bed once in a day. Mostly for cleaning, it is advisable to spread the cleaning net in the tray before feeding in the morning. Leaves are broadcasted over the net and larvae from below the net crawl on it. After, 3-4 hours, when almost all the larvae crawl on the leaf from below the net, it is removed and the refuse below the net is rejected. The net along with the larvae is again spread over the tray. Shelf rearing has the advantage of accommodating more silkworm larvae in a limited area than any other method.

(b) Shoot rearing method

In this method, the silkworms are reared on big branches in one or two tiers. The shoots are harvested from the fields and are fed to the silkworms straightaway. The mulberry shoot rearing method is of various types viz., flat surface, slop, mixed, vertical slop, Fuji-type, Kamaboko type etc. Out of these methods, flat surface method is most popular. The rearing sheets are usually one meter wide and have any convenient length accommodating to the length of rearing house. In shoot rearing method, the number of feeds provided to the silkworms is 2 or 3 per day. The mulberry leaves should be uniformly distributed on the rearing bed so that each and every larva has equal access to the leaves. For this, the branches should not be too much bend, leaves should not be too dense and also the size of leaves should be medium.

As whole shoots are supplied for every feed, larvae kept moving upwards consuming the mulberry leaves. In this method, there is better aeration and therefore, it is possible to have 50% more larvae per unit area of rearing sheet as compared to shelf or floor rearing method. Bed cleaning is performed once in 4th instars and also only once in 5th instars. During 4th instars, the rearing bed is often covered with plastic sheet in order to prevent excessive wilting of mulberry leaves. Just prior to ripening of larvae, they should be provided with whole leaves instead of shoots as otherwise; it will have an adverse effect on their subsequent rearing as well as mounting on cocoon frames. When the larvae are in moulting phase, the rearing bed should be kept dry by spreading lime or brunt husk over.

To clean the bed, ropes of convenient lengths are spread parallel to each other lengthwise on the bed and after 2 or 3 feeds, when all the worms have crawled on the new branches, the bed held by ropes is rolled into loose bundles. After cleaning the beds, the rolled up branches and worms are transferred back on to the rearing beds and spread out again.

The shoot rearing saves on labour cost up to 70% compared to leaf feeding method, which constitute a major expenditure in silkworm rearing at the 4th and 5th instars. The amount of leaves required is reduced approximately by 25% in 4th instars and 10% in 5th instars. Worms and leaves do not come in contact with litter, hence chances of secondary contamination is reduced. This method ensures better aeration in the bed with better cocoon and ERR. As handling of silkworm is minimized, better hygienic conditions can be maintained which reduces chances of contamination and spreading of disease.

(c) Floor rearing method

The floor rearing of silkworm is carried out on fixed rearing seats. The rearing seats arranged in 2 or 3 tiers as in shoot rearing method to accommodate as many silkworm larvae as possible. The rearing seat measures 1-1.5 meter in width and 5-7 meter in length or according to the convenient length of the rearing house. There should be sufficient space between two tiers to provide feeding to the larvae and for cleaning to the bed. This space is mostly kept in between 0.6-0.8 meter. The rearing seat is usually made of wood or bamboo strips. The larvae are fed with the leaves or branches cut into small pieces of 15 cm. The number of feeds provided per day is three or four. Bed cleaning is carried out with the help of rearing/cleaning nets in the same way as in the case of shelf rearing. Moreover, the bed cleaning is less frequent in floor rearing in comparison to shelf rearing. Bed cleaning is carried out twice during 4th instars and 3 times during 5th instars. During 4th instars, the rearing bed is covered with plastic sheet/wax paper to save mulberry leaves from drying. If there is too much humidity, the wax paper is removed. In order to reduce humidity in the rearing bed, lime powder is spread on it.

Leaf preservation

Leaf preservation is an important step in tropical sericulture. It is better to supply fresh mulberry leaves to the developing larvae. However, considering the economy of labour and periodic deterioration of weather conditions, it is necessary to harvest and store enough quantity of mulberry leaf, which can be utilized subsequently for feeding. However, if the conditions during the preservation of mulberry leaf are not proper, the quality of leaf will deteriorate resulting in unstable cocoon crop.

During winter and spring season, the prevailing temperature and humidity conditions and normal moisture content of leaf mostly do not call for special method of leaf preservation because temperature is cool and humidity is high but at the same time, it is advisable not to preserve the mulberry leaf for a very long period. During rainy season, however, water content in the mulberry leaf is very high and if the same is supplied for feeding, it may lead to spread of various diseases. Therefore, the plucked leaves are first spread on the floor for some time (3-6 hrs) and then preserved in leaf bins or under slightly wetted cloth or gunny.

During summer season, when the temperature is high and humidity is low, withering of leaf takes place very fast. To prevent withering of leaves, attempts are often made to increase and maintain humidity of the rearing room as well as of leaf preservation room. For this purpose, freshly harvested leaves are preserved in leaf chambers of any convenient size (3' × 5' × 3') lined with gunny cloth and covered with slightly wetted gunny cloth. In case of shoot harvest, they are made to stand erect on the floor and covered with wet cloth or gunny. In summer season, the cloth or gunny cover should be sprinkled or sprayed with water to keep them wet all the time.

Mulberry storage room should be clean and completely disinfected. Significance of such type of leaf preservation leads to gain in weight and good health of larvae resulting in stable cocoon crop. However, it is advisable as a general practice to pluck or harvest leaf twice in the day, once in the morning and again in the evening during the cooler hours. First harvest of morning leaf should be given for 2nd and 3rd feeding of the day and 2nd harvest of evening should be given as night feed and also the next day morning feed. In order to save the mulberry leaves from wilting during storage, they are periodically shuffled. When mulberry shoots are stored, they are tied into loose bundles and kept erect/vertically on the floor. Tender leaves meant for young silkworms can be preserved in boxes, baskets or pots covered with wet clean cloths.

Temperature and humidity control

The growth of silkworms will be delayed if the temperature and humidity are too low and accelerated if it is high leading to poor cocoon crop. Therefore, it is important to keep optimum rearing temperature and humidity for normal growth and development. Requirement of temperature and humidity for optimum growth of 4th and 5th instars is furnished below (Table 8.3).

Table 8.3: Standard rearing chart for late age rearing of 100 Dfls (40000 larvae)

Instars	*Temperature (°C)*	*Humidity (%)*	*Quality of feed*	*Frequency of feed*	*Spacing / 100 Dfls (Sq. ft)*		*Quantity of Feeding (kg / 100 Dfls)*	
					BV	*MV*	*BV*	*MV*
4th	25 – 26	70-75	Medium	4	115 – 225	100 – 200	195	160
5th	24 – 25	70-75	Medium or coarse	4	225 550	200 400	1120	960

Table 8.4: Standard quantity of bed disinfectant for 100 Dfls

Stage of larvae	*Vijetha (gm)*	*RKO (gm)*	*Resham Jyothi (gm)*
Out of 1^{sl} moult (before resumption)	50	60	35
Out of 2nd moult (before resumption)	150	120	105
Out of 3rd moult (before resumption)	600	580	300
Out of 4th moult (before resumption)	1250	960	840
4th day of 5th instar (after bed cleaning)	2000	1540	2160
Total quantity (gm)	4050	3260	3440

Areas of low temperature and humidity: The rearing house will have to be heated artificially and proper ventilation through windows must be provided. It is useful to place a metal container filled with water over the heater or stove to raise both temperature and humidity to the desired level.

Areas of high temperature and dryness: The open corridors shed provide suitable climatic regulation in the rearing house. To increase the humidity and reduce the temperature, following practices may be useful -

- Open the doors and windows of the rearing rooms and hang a moist cloth to provide humid air circulation in the room.
- Sprinkle water on the floor of the rearing room. Spraying of water on the roof reduces temperature and increases humidity.
- If daytime temperature is too high, doors and windows should be closed.
- Electric fan should be used to ventilate the room as and when required.
- In the evening doors and windows should be opened to allow cool air to circulate.

Areas of high temperature and humidity: To protect the rearing house from direct sunlight, trees should be planted around the shed of rearing house. Good circulation of air will help to reduce the temperature to a considerable extent.

Maintenance of hygiene during silkworm rearing

- Avoid borrowing of rearing appliances.
- Do not use rearing equipments without disinfections.
- Avoid overlapping rearing.
- Maintain personnel and rearing hygiene.
- Restrict the entry of persons into the rearing house.
- Silkworm eggs should be disinfected with 2% formalin before head pigmentation stage.
- Any person entering the rearing house must disinfect foot and hand before entering.
- A foot mat soaked in 2% bleaching powder be placed at the entrance and person entering the rearing house should step on to this.

- Wash hands in 2% bleaching powder in 0.3% slaked lime solution.
- Replace the disinfectant every day.
- Diseased/unequal or diseased suspected larvae must be picked from the rearing tray and disposed into 5% in slaked lime in basin. Basin must be covered with lid.
- Diseased larvae should be picked by forks or sticks. If it is picked by hand, disinfect the hand by washing in 2% bleaching powder in 0.3% slaked lime solution.
- Perform bed cleaning using bed-cleaning net and these nets should be disinfected every day after use by dipping in 2% formalin solution for 10 minutes.
- Bed refuse should be collected on vinyl sheet and transferred into manure pit. Vinyl sheet must be disinfected every day by dipping in 2% bleaching powder in 0.3% slaked lime solution.
- Silkworms should always be reared on rearing sheet paper (newspaper).
- Wipe the floor after bed cleaning with 2% bleaching powder in 0.3% slaked lime solution.
- Dust the bed disinfectant as per schedule, quantity and precautions. Feed the larvae after 30 minutes of bed disinfections.
- Mulberry leaf should not be stored in house, instead store in a separate room.
- Provide recommended spacing, sufficient ventilation, good quality and quantity of mulberry leaf for and growth of
- Spray bleaching powder in mounting place.
- Avoid injury to silkworms while rearing and mounting.
- Pick diseased larvae from the mountages and them 2% bleaching in 0. in a basin.

SEX SEPARATION/DISCRIMINATION

Utilization of hybrid vigour in silkworm started as early as 1900 when Toyama first introduced F1 hybrids in Japan. Since then by the virtue of advantages of the better growth, greater vigour, better productivity, higher resistance to diseases and unfavourable climatic conditions besides stable cocoon crop and increased vigour over the parental strains, hybrids are extensively utilized by all the silk producing countries. Now, almost all the silkworms raised in India for commercial cocoon production are from the hybrids. To produce the F1 hybrids of the silkworm and for inter-bed/inter-line mating, it is inevitable to separate male and female sexes of pure breeds before emergence and or copulation. Sex separation is carried out for:

I. Preparation of hybrids

II. Synchronizing the emergence of male and female moths

III. Cocoon assessment, inter-bed/inter-line mating etc. in breeding programme and basic seed productions.

IV. Undertake feed index, host preferences and other gender related studies.

Methods of sex separation

Various techniques are available in silkworm to separate sexes in the egg stage (sex-limited egg colour), larval (imaginal buds for sexual organs and sex limited larval markings), cocoon (cocoon colour), and pupal (morphological features, size and weight) stage besides distinct developmental trends in male and female larvae and sex separation at pupal stage by means of electric capacity measurement. The method of automatic sex discrimination by single cocoon scaling is reported from China. The system appears to be very accurate under laboratory conditions as 97% of sex discrimination is possible just by adopting 'Bayes' linear discrimination function built by the cocoon weight and shell weight. Moreover, the result is not very encouraging at commercial scale. Sex separation (sexing) in silkworm is primarily carried out by morphological features as detailed in Table 8.5.

Table 8.9: Distinguishing characters between male and female silkworm

MALE - MOTH	**FEMALE-MOTH**
Usually smaller in size	Comparatively bigger in size
More active	Sluggish (less active)
Antennae bigger	Comparatively smaller
Abdomen narrow and small	Abdomen broad and large
Posterior end tapering	Posterior end blunt (arc like structure)
Caudal end with a pair of hook (Harps) like claspers	Caudal end with a knob like projection covered with sensory hairs
PUPA	
Cuticle is slightly darker in colour	Cuticle is lighter in colour
Smaller in size	Comparatively bigger in size
Abdomen narrow and small	Abdomen broad and large
Posterior end tapering	Posterior end blunt
Presence of dot like marking in the center of ninth abdominal segment on the ventral side	Presence of a longitudinal slit 'X' marking on the ventral side of 8th abdominal segment extending from anterior to posterior margin of the segment
Lighter in weight	Heavier in weight
LARVA	
Presence of a tiny milky white follicular structure called Harold's gland in the center line of the ventral side of the junction of 8th and 9th abdominal segments. As the larvae grow, the spot merges with the skin colour.	Presence of small round spot on the ventral side of both the left and the 8th and 9th abdominal segments called Ishiwata's gland. These spots slowly fade out with growth and finally disappear
COCOON	
Volume: Smaller; Weight: Lighter	Volume: Larger; Weight: Heavier
Shell ratio: Higher	Shell ratio: lower

In India incidentally, none of the authorized parental silkworm breeds viz., KA, NB18, NB4D2, CA2, CC1, CSR2, CSR4, CSR5, CSR18. CSR19, SH6, SF19 (bivoltine), Nistari, Pure Mysore, MY1, RD1, P2D1, BL23, BL24 (multivoltine) are having sex limited markings on their larval body, thus making the job of sex separation apparently impossible during larval stage.

Sex discrimination of larvae

The most popular method available for sex separation is based on imaginal buds for sexual organs in pupa and larva besides on sex limited markings. Tazima (1978) reported the best time for discriminating between two sexes in the early fifth instar just after two feedings of fourth moult based on Ishiwata and Harold's imaginary glands. Separation of thousands of larvae in this short stipulated period of time is quite difficult on large commercial scale. However, sex discrimination by sexual gland requires skilled technique and has to be conducted by expert workers. Moreover, this method is not very efficient and leads to error, thus has not become a popular practice.

Sex discrimination of pupae

Though the separation of male and female pupae by identification of pupal marking is quite easy, other factors such as cutting of cocoons, enormous engagement of labourers to cut large quantity of cocoons in commercial grainages, the damage caused to pupae while cutting the cocoons, damage by dermestid beetle on the naked pupae and due to handling makes this method too laborious and cumbersome besides this practice requires cutting of all the available cocoons leading to considerable loss in quantity of silk of both the parents. Again the mistake committed in the identification of the sexes cannot be ruled out. So, after emergence undesirable sexes not required for hybrid preparation must be picked. The result due to all these problems is that practically no sex separation is usually carried before emergence in the grainages. In this processes again considerable quantum of laying produced are selfed seed rather than hybrid and also pierced cocoons fetch very less or negligible return.

Sex separation at pupal stage on the basis of weight differences by means of brine/salt assortment is also available but here again cutting open of all cocoons, pupa and shell separation, soaking the pupa in salt solution and removing it from the container etc requires additional labour besides wasting of huge quantity of either sexes not required for hybrid/seed preparation and hence this practice has not attracted the attention of breeders and grainures. Kataoka *et al.* (1973) stated that the sex separation at pupal stage is possible by measuring the change in the electric capacity but it varies with the pupal growth besides the value of the electric capacity. It somewhat also varied according to distance between two plates of the test capacitor and size of the cocoons tested, rather large values were reported in small size cocoons measured in narrow distance.

Sex discrimination of seed cocoons

Ming (1989) observed that when moths emerged from their uncut cocoons, the average rate of egg production can be approximately 20% higher than when cocoons are cut opened because the risk of injury due to handling of pupae is reduced. Since female cocoons are generally heavier than the males of the same race, use can be made of these differences to separate the female cocoons from the male by cocoon weight differences.

The separation of sexes based on cocoon weight differences in male and female has the following advantages:

- The unwanted component (male in case of multivoltine and females in case of bivoltine) of seed can be disposed of for raw silk production.
- Selfing can be prevented which otherwise may lead to deterioration in the quality of hybrid seed.
- Number of trays to be attended reduced by 35-45% and thus increases the efficiency of skilled workers.
- The potency of bivoltine male moth is protected otherwise would mate with females and ejaculate once by the time they are picked up.
- Emission of moth scales (dust), a health hazard in commercial grainages, is reduced significantly as the male component of one of the parents is eliminated.

- There is no need of cocoon cutting.
- As the pupae are inside the intact cocoons, the risk of preservation of pupae in the naked form is eliminated and thus mortality during preservation is reduced considerably.
- 35-45% unwanted components (male or female) is disposed of leading to reduction in the accumulation of pierced cocoons.
- There is immediate realization of sale proceeds from the cocoons sold for reeling.

Before employing sexing based on cocoon weight differences, few samples of cocoons are taken at random from the same batch of the seed cocoons. The weight of criterion cocoon is determined based on the ranges of the weight between male and female cocoons. This is used as differentiation weight for sex separation of seed cocoons. Cocoons that are heavier than the criterion weight belong to the female group and those lighter to the male. Cocoons of the same weight as the criterion cocoons belong to the mixed group of both sexes.

The correct evaluation of criterion cocoon has considerable effect on the work as a whole. The criterion weight must maintain a rate of sexing of 90% or higher. At the same time, the sexing rate of mixed group should be controlled to 10% or less. If this requirement is not met, the sex separation by cocoon weight differences will be of no significance. Studies conducted indicated that there is inherent error exiting in the population, which vary in accordance to the crop status and season. The inherent error is primarily due to overlapping of cocoon weight of males and females. The error could be reduced to a considerable limit, if separate cut-off points are determined for males and females besides introducing an intermediate range, wherein the cocoons are required to be physically verified.

For determining the cut-off points, cocoons are taken at random from the sample, cut opened, sexed, recorded weight individually with the help of electronic digital monopan balance, values are arranged in ascending or descending order, and cut-off points are decided. There are usually three systems to determine the cut-off points:

(a) By percentile frequency and subjective analysis, the frequency table could be constructed. Based on higher percentile value cut-off points for male are determined in contrast to female cut-off points which are determined based on initial percentile value. In this way two cut-off points, one for males and other for females with three distinct groups viz., above percentile value-male, below percentile value-female and intermediate percentile value-mixed group (male and female) are formed. This intermediate group can be sex separated manually. This one is the most efficient method of sex determination based on cocoon weight differences.

(b) By calculating mean of both the sexes in the population to determine the cut-off points. In this method, only one cut-off point is determined and the values above the mean are considered as female while below as male. This is not very efficient method because chances of error are more due to single cut-off point and inherent error.

(c) By addition or subtraction of ¼ populations Standard Deviation (S.D.) the cut-off points are decided in the percentile procedure. If only males are required for hybrid preparation ¼ population SD is subtracted from the population mean, in contrast to the addition of % ¼ population SD if only females are required for the purpose. By adopting this method, error can be reduced considerably and can be brought below 7%.

By using the single digital balance, the efficiency is much higher as it does not take much time to display the weight. Whereas in sensitive balance with 10 mg accuracy i.e. two digit balance, it takes time to display the correct weight and thus affect, the speed of weighment of cocoons.

A skilled worker can sex separate about 10,000 -12,000 bivoltine and 6,000-8,000 multivoltine cocoons in an eight hours shift.

By adopting the procedure 50% cocoons of multivoltine (male cocoons) and 50% cocoons of bivoltine (female cocoons) can be saved while preparing MV × BV hybrid combination. These intact cocoons could be sent to reeling for commercial silk production fetching higher return to the grainure.

Sex separation at larval and cocoon stages is the best proposition due to the following advantages -

- Cocoon cutting is avoided thereby reducing the labour significantly. Damage to pupa during cocoon cutting is also avoided.
- Pupa inside the shell is protected well otherwise, emergence percentage is affected and moths lose vigour if soiled due to urination.
- When only one of the parents is utilized for hybridization, as in cross breed egg production, the unwanted component could be more appropriately used for reeling.

COCOON FORMATION

Of the many contributing factors responsible for the production of quality cocoons, rearing and mounting environment, type of mountages used, rearing season and racial characteristic of the breed/hybrid plays a major role.

Physiological characteristics of mature silkworm

The characteristics of mature or ripe silkworm appear by the end of the last instars of normally developed silkworm. When silkworm ripens, it stops feeding and looks for a suitable place to spin cocoons. The characteristic of approximately mature silkworms is:

- The water content in the larval body decreases from 85% to about 75% and excessive water is excreted together with its faeces.
- Silkworm loses its appetite and finally stops eating.

- The worm appears translucent first in the thoracic region, which later develops towards the abdomen.
- Generally, a mature silkworm shows negative geotropism i.e. crawl upward along the wall or rearing bed/stand.
- Mature larvae crawl here and there to find suitable site for cocooning.
- Mature silkworm larvae show aphotropism.

Silk gland is the source of silk. Silk gland is transformed labial gland having three distinct and functional parts-the posterior, the middle and the anterior with 500, 250 and 300 gland cells respectively at each side with approximately 2000 gland cells altogether. It increases 1.6×10^5 fold from hatching to full grown larvae without any cell division. During the growth of larvae, it increases 20, 6, 5 and 40 folds in different instars larvae and finally accounts for 40% of the larval body weight. Posterior part secretes silk substance known as 'fibroin', while the middle part serves as reservoir for receiving the fibroin from the posterior silk gland. It also secretes around the fibroin, a natural gummy substance known as 'sericin'. These substances when coming into contact with air harden into silk filament. Posterior end of the gland is closed while fore end joins together to a common excretory duct opening into the spinneret. The filament is composed of:

Fibroin	: 72-81%
Sericin	: 19-28%
Fat and Wax	: 0.5-1%
Colouring matter and Ash	: 1-1.4%

The pH of fibroin is 2.1-2.5, having a chemical formula of $C_{15} H_{26} N_5 O_6$, while sericin has a pH of 3.8-4.2 with a chemical formula of $C_{15} H_{25} N_5 O_6$,

Cocoon formation

Silkworm cocooning process may be divided into four stages as shown in the following page:

- Mature silkworm that appears translucent raises its head and crawls here and there to find a suitable cocooning site. It first spins some silk waves into the mounting to form a framework of a cocoon and then continues to spin to form a cocoon net. Irregular and loose silk is spun to thicken the cocoon net and gradually cocoon frame is formed.
- The worms body bends towards its back, its abdominal legs are fixed on the internal wall of the cocoon cavity, its head swings left and right to spin silk.
- Secretion of large quantity of silk makes the silkworm shrink remarkably. The swinging of its head slows down and finally loses the rhythm of swinging. As a result, a thin layer of pupal covering is formed. Finally, towards the upper end of the cocoon, larva secretes the last silk material forming a loose and soft cocoon top. Thus, the cocooning process is completed and the larva becomes ready for pupation.

Environmental conditions

The spinning silkworms are very sensitive to physical disturbances like temperature, humidity, air current and photoperiod. During mounting, optimum temperature and humidity must be 23-25°C and 60-70% respectively. Care must be taken to avert the temperature, rising above 28°C or humidity increasing to more than 90%, because such temperature and humidity are detrimental to quality of cocoon. Since temperature and humidity exert the greatest influence on the cocoon quality during the initial 50 hrs after mounting, attention must be paid to control the microclimatic conditions during the first 50 hrs of spinning.

The worms should be mounted in the chandrikes or mountages at the time of proper maturity to harvest uniform cocoons. If environmental conditions during spinning are not optimum, it will lead to a neatness defects of raw silk also. Neatness declines remarkably if mounting is performed at high temperature exceeding 28°C at a humidity of more than 90%. Reelability is the most important property of cocoons for raw silk production and is vulnerable to change due to mounting conditions. If temperature and humidity in the mounting rooms are 28°C and 94% respectively, reelability sometimes drops as low as 20% lower than the value attainable with the mounting room temperature held at 25°C and Relative Humidity of 70%. Therefore, adequate care must be taken about the temperature and humidity during mounting. Too high temperature makes worms hurriedly build cocoons, so that double cocoon increases and the cocoons thus produced have loose cocoon shell and inferior quality. Too low temperature slows down the speed of cocooning and pupation. The cocoons are often short, thin or perforated at both ends and lose its normal colour, texture and luster. Non-cocooning silkworms will also increase.

Air current has an indirect effect on the quality of cocoons. Its function is to dispel the high moisture in the mounting room and introduce the dry air from outside. It can also lower the temperature in the mounting room. In the beginning of mounting, strong wind is to be avoided to make the worms to find suitable cocooning site as quickly as possible. After 24 hrs of mounting, when most of the worms have built thin cocoon shell, an air current with 0.5-1.0 m/sec should be provided to dispel the high moisture to improve cocoon quality. Ripe worms are very sensitive to light. They evade the strong light over 100 lux, but shows phototaxis to about 13 lux.

Mounting materials

Type of mountages and mounting material used for spinning of cocoons play a vital role in the production of quality cocoons. An analysis of crop data of silkworm clearly indicates that among the many factors that contribute for a good yield, mounting material used for spinning of cocoons play an important role. Even if silkworm crop is healthy, wrong mounting methods, spinning conditions, mounting density and bad types of mountages can result in inferior quality of cocoons. Moreover, the aim of mounting material is to provide much cocooning space to ripe worms with reduced labour. Following points, therefore, must be taken into consideration while selecting a cocooning frame -

- Cocooning space should be more.
- Easy handling and light in weight.
- Ridges and furrows should be firm and uniformly distributed.
- Surface should be rough to get grip for larvae while spinning.
- Mountages should be cheap, sturdy and durable.
- Labour for mounting and harvesting of cocoons should be minimum so as to save labour and raise working efficiency.
- Better aeration between ridges and furrows for reduction of humidity during spinning to improve the reelability.
- Should be easy for thorough disinfection and convenient for storage.
- Mountages should be convenient to conduct the operation of mounting.
- Should be non-corrosive and non-biodegradable.
- Better if suitable for self-mounting.
- Should have certain hygroscopicity.

Different types of mountages used for mounting purposes are:

- Straw mountages
- Grass mountages
- Plastic mountages
- Pine-shoot let mountages
- Mustard hay mountages
- Plastic bottle brush mountages
- Square-frame mountages

- Centipede-like mountages
- Rotary mountages
- Bamboo strip mountages

Of these, plastic mountages, bamboo strip mountages and rotary mountages are mostly in use in different sericultural tracts of the country. The type of mountages used may affect the cocoon quality. The structure of mountages directly affects the spinning and cocooning of silkworm. The microclimate in the mountages also affects the cocoon quality in general and its reelability in particular.

Mounting time

Mounting time also has an influence on the production of quality cocoons. Both mountings too early and too late have adverse effects. Too early mounting often results in light cocoon weight, low cocoon-shell ratio, more spotted cocoons, etc. It also increases the number of wandering silkworms in mountages besides non-cocooning silkworms.

Mounting methods

(i) **Hand picking method:** Fully matured silkworms are picked up one by one with hand and collected in a hand tray. After picking, these larvae are transferred onto the mountages for cocooning.

(ii) **Shaking-off method:** When only few silkworms are found mature, they are mounted by picking. When half of the larvae become mature, mulberry branches or the net for the grown silkworms are spread on the rearing bed. After most of the larvae have crawled onto them, transfer and shake the larvae off the branches or nets in the hand tray. From here, the larvae are then gently spread onto mountages. Shoot rearing method is more suitable for this type of mounting wherein shake the larvae off the shoots directly.

(iii) **Natural mounting method:** Since the mature silkworm larvae have the habit of moving upward,

mountages be directly placed on rearing bed. The larvae automatically crawl onto the mountages. This is considered a labour saving method in many countries.

Causes of non-spinning silkworms

(i) **Caused by chemicals:** Traces of chemicals when comes in contact with larvae during rearing makes the central nervous system of silkworm paralyze and affects its normal spinning, resulting non-spinning silkworms. This case is more serious when such contact is during the later stage of 4th instar.

(ii) **Caused by diseases:** Silkworm diseases like Grassarie, Flacharie, Muscardine and Pebrine etc also cause non-spinning of silkworms.

(iii) **Physiological causes:** The non-spinning/ cocooning silkworms may be caused by overgrown silk glands which suppresses the tracheae at the border of head and thorax of the larvae or by in-coordination between the spinning movement and dehydration of liquid sericin which affects the liquid silk to become silk wave or by the abnormal distribution of tracheae on the posterior silk gland, which hinders the gland and normal activity of breath or sometimes it may be caused by malformation of silk gland cells in the middle or posterior part of the gland.

(iv) **Unfavourable environment:** Unfavourable environment during rearing viz., too high rearing temperature or too tender leaves makes imbalance in the endocrine system resulting in the abnormal development of silk gland. Harmful gases during rearing also cause non-cocooning of silkworms. High temperature and high humidity during mounting affects respiratory rate of mature silkworm larvae leading to physiological abnormality and paralyzed nerves, whereas, low temperature during mounting may prolong the

cocooning period and in these both cases induce non-cocooning silkworms.

(v) **Improper handling:** Improper handling during mounting sometimes injure the silkworms body wall or silk gland etc and makes the larvae unable to form cocoon.

Defective cocoons

Defective cocoons are broadly classified into the following categories:

Immature cocoons: Immature cocoons are those, where the pupal formation is incomplete. This occurs usually when cocoons are harvested prematurely. Therefore, to avoid occurrence of immature cocoons, harvesting should be performed when pupa appears dark brown in colour, slightly shrunken in size with glistering eyes.

Rusty cocoons: In some cases, intestinal fluid of matured larvae during spinning in mountages falls on already-formed cocoons. Such cocoons produce rustling sound when shaken individually, indicating sticking of dead papa to the sides of the shell. Such putrefying pupae stain the shell and make it unfit for grainage or reeling.

Black stained cocoons: Due to putrification of pupae, black stains appears on the outside of cocoons and thus spoiling them and making them unfit both for seed cocoons and commercial reeling. Such cocoons must promptly be removed from the healthy lot to avoid spoiling of it.

Spotted cocoons: Improper storage of cocoons under bad ventilation and damp condition causes development of a fungus belonging to the family Aspergillaceae on the shell leading to brownish or yellow spot on the cocoons, deteriorating its quality

Weak-end cocoons: Weak-end cocoons are formed due to unfavourable environmental conditions during spinning besides due to use of improper mountages. Weak-end cocoons are invariably formed in multivoltine breeds.

Malformed cocoons: Overcrowding at the time of spinning and use of bad mountages lead to malformed cocoons. These cocoons are abnormal in shape, scaffold-pressed or cocoons having non-uniform texture of cocoon shell rendering them unfit for seed production as well as for commercial reeling.

Calcified cocoons: In these types of cocoons, pupae are destroyed due to attack of fungus called *Botrytis bassina.*

Loose-knit/fragile cocoons: Loosely built with open space between layers constituting the shell form knit/fragile cocoons.

Undersized cocoons: These cocoons are below normal in size with thin cocoon shell and very low cocoon-shell ratio. These cocoons should not be used in seed production.

Mutes cocoons: Pupa becomes dead and sticks to the shell inside the cocoon and hence does not make any sound when shaken. Decaying pupa sometimes releases putrefying body fluid, which stains the cocoon-shell.

Double cocoons: One pupa per cocoon is a regular/universal phenomenon in silk insects. The metamorphosis of two larvae and rarely three, into pupa, in one and the same cocoon is referred as double cocoon formation. The double cocoons are also called jointed cocoons/combined cocoons or associated cocoons. Various factors are responsible for the formation of double cocoons, but crowding during spinning plays a major role. These double cocoons are abnormally shaped and thick-shelled cocoons. As it is not as genetic character, these types of cocoons can be used in seed production.

9

HYBRID VIGOUR AND CORRELATION OF CHARACTERS

HYBRID VIGOUR

In the field of biological sciences it is well known that hybrids become very strong, a fact mentioned by Darwin in his book *'Origin of Species'* in 1859. Mendel in 1865 showed that grass blades of hybrids are very tall and that they grow rapidly. In America, based on the studies of Schall in 1908 and East in 1909, it was possible to prepare excellent hybrids of maize.

The term heterosis derived from the Greek word 'Heteros' and 'Osis' (heteros = different; osis = conditions) was coined by Shull in 1914 (as quoted by Shull, 1948) to describe the superiority of cross breeds. This phenomenon was first studied by Koetreuter in 1763 (East and Hayes, 1912) and termed it hybrid vigour relative to their parents irrespective of the cause. Dobzhansky refers this to luxuriance and stated that both heterosis and hybrid vigour are synonymous and referred to increased growth. Genetically, heterosis is the function of a hybrid over the parents resulted from crossing of unlike individuals differing in their one or more parameters. The pioneering works of Toyama (1906), a Japanese silkworm-breeding expert, on hybridization and use of F1 hybrids for commercial rearing made an epoch in the history of sericulture. The hybrids, which were the crosses of Japanese and Chinese origin, became so popular with the farmers there that by 1919 over 90% of eggs produced were of hybrid origin, reaching 100% by 1928.

Characteristics of F1 hybrids of silkworm

- Usually stronger compared with parent variety.
- Greater vigour, faster growth, development, productivity and can withstand unfavourable environmental conditions.
- Better reproductive capacity.
- Resistance to diseases and suitable for artificial diet.
- Uniform cocoon; better cocoon weight, shell weight, shell ratio and cocoon yield.
- Better adoptability expressed in the form of stable cocoon crop.
- Uniform hatching, moulting and spinning.
- Comparatively shorter larval duration than that of parents or the mid-parental value.
- Better filament length and raw silk yield.
- Thicker filament with reduced renditta.

Classification of heterosis: The various types of heterosis have been reviewed by Nittler (1978) and can be classified as follows -

(a) **Individual heterosis:** Improvement in performance, vigour etc in an individual (relative to the mean of its parents) that is not attributable to either maternal, paternal or sex-linkage effects.

(b) **Maternal heterosis:** Refers to heterosis in a population attributable to using crossbred instead of purebred.

(c) **Paternal heterosis:** Refers to any advantage in using crossbred verses purebred on the performance of progeny.

Chandrasekharaiah (1994) classified heterosis in silkworm as balanced, mutational and pseudo heterosis.

(i) **Balanced heterosis:** The heterosis resulting from hybridization is referred to as balanced or true heterosis.

(ii) **Mutational heterosis:** The heterosis resulted from creation of mutation is known as mutational heterosis.

(iii) **Pseudoheterosis or false heterosis:** The heterosis resulting from more favourable environmental conditions is referred to as pseudo-heterosis or false heterosis.

Sarkar (1998) stated that according to Mackey heterosis might be classified:

(i) **Based on direction**

(a) Positive heterosis (+) (Beneficial)

(b) Negative heterosis (-) (Non-beneficial)

(ii) **Based on function**

(a) Luxuriant heterosis

(b) Adaptive heterosis

(c) Selective heterosis

(d) Reproductive heterosis

Theoretical basis of heterosis: The several theories have been proposed to explain the manifestation of heterosis, which are reviewed by Bowman (1958). The theories are:

(a) **The dominance theory:** The dominance theory postulates that the parental lines are homozygous dominant for different favourable loci. This theory is proposed on the basis of the superiority of dominant alleles over the recessive alleles. The dominance theory states that inbreeding in a particular line produces homogygosity for some recessive genes and when crosses are made between such inbred lines the recessive genes of one line get masked by the dominant genes of the other line producing heterotic effect in F1 (Reddy and Raju, 1998). In such instances, it is the presence of dominant genes that produces heterosis rather than heterozygotic loci.

(b) **Over-dominance theory**: The over-dominance theory postulates that the heterozygote is superior to homozygote. Various versions of this include 'enheterosis theory' (super dominance or over-dominance at the chromosomal level) and the 'physiological balance theory, (Randal, 1953). Mostly, the theory of dominance and over-dominance leads to the same expectations. In both the cases, gain on out-breeding and loss (decrease) of vigour on inbreeding is established. Dominance theory is based on the homozygous dominant alleles for different characters present in the parental lines while non-dominance theory is postulated on the basis of effect of allelic differences in heterozygote.

(c) **The epistasis theory:** It includes all types of inter locus interactions. Sheridan (1980) stated that epistatic theory is either 'F1 epistasis' or 'parental epistasis'. However, contribution of epistasis to heterosis in cross breeds has generally been considered negligible (Falconer, 1981). Hayman and Mather (1955) reported generalized formulae for various types of genetic interactions including dominance modifications, dominant epistasis, recessive epistasis, duplicate genes, recessive suppressor and complementary genes. They further stated that heterosis is derivations of either complementary or duplicate gene interactions.

(d) **Heterozygous combination theory:** Shull and East in the past independently hypothesized that heterozygous conditions were better than any dominant conditions in the hybrids.

(e) **Biochemical theory:** Biochemical basis for heterosis accords with the assumption that the primary heterotic effect is concerned with growth substances such as regulatory proteins and hormones, the predominant activity of which is registered in the early part of the developmental

cycle of the silkworm. Greater metabolic efficiency in mitochondria of the heterotic hybrid was observed while no such changes occurred in those not exhibiting heterosis.

Initial arguments about the mechanism of heterotic effect supported the dominant gene hypothesis. There were single genes that responded in a way resembling heterosis. But there were several objections to the theory:

- Amassing all favourable alleles could possibly develop a completely homozygous superior line.
- If dominance was the major contributor to heterosis, the F2 frequency distribution should be skewed and be reflected in the binomial of (3/4 + 1/4) n. However, the linkage between favourable and unfavourable genes would tend to reduce or eliminate such skewedness.
- Single gene loci could show an over dominance effect from dominance in breeding trials have not been very successful. Current thinking has arrived at a blend of both theories. There is no doubt that for some loci, dominance is the major interaction contributing to the heterosis. However, as an explanation of the heterosis mechanism, there are enough inconsistencies to consider other alternatives.

Before starting hybridization studies it is imperative for breeders to adopt following strategies to obtain better heterosis leading to fruitful and desired results -

(a) Collection of endemic and exotic genotypes of both multivoltine and bivoltine silkworm.

(b) Evaluation and documentation of the collected genotypes and studies on their genotypic and phenotypic stability.

(c) Clustering/grouping of genotypes morphologically and genetically both through diallel analysis besides study on region, season and environmental stability.

Yokoyama (1957) while reviewing the literature on hybridization studies in silkworm from 1927 to 1957 by previous workers stated that it is economical for the farmers to rear F1 hybrids. In India utilization of hybrid vigour started during 1920s. However, this did not contribute to the rapid progress in productivity. After few years, the male parental strain involved in the hybrid viz., C. Nichi became polyvoltine (Reddy and Raju, 1997). During 1940 attempts were made to improve the indigenous multivoltine races viz., Nistari and Chotopolu by hybridization with a few Italian races and Nismo, Ichhot and Iton were evolved from the hybrid population which were reported to be better than Nistari (Ghosh, 1949; Datta, 1984). Cross-breeding of silkworm races, which differed in voltinism and quantitative characters, were initiated during 1960s by utilizing polyvoltine Pure Mysore and exotic bivoltine races such as J112, C108, J122 × C122, J124, Sanish, Azarbaizan and NN6D. Even though these hybrids were found superior the goal of achieving increased productivity could not be fully realized.

In India, first systematic hybridization following the diallel crossing method was reported by Krishnaswamy *et al.* (1964) involving 5 genetically pure multivoltine races. Since then various crossing systems like diallel, line × tester, three-way crosses and double crosses were attempted by various workers for the utilization of hybrid vigour at commercial level (Narasimhanna *et al.* 1976; Sengupta *et al.* 1974). Almost all the economic traits expressed hybrid vigour in the hybrids exhibiting superiority over inbred lines. The characters viz., fecundity, larval weight, single cocoon and shell weight, cocoon-shell ratio, cocoon yield/100 Dfls, ERR by number and weight are found to improve substantially in F1 hybrids. In addition, reduced mortality in F1 hybrids, less renditta, better filament length adds to the advantage to the silk reeling industry. The heterosis varies from season to season, crosses to crosses, characters to characters, and sexes to sexes besides voltinism to voltinism. If the parental genotypes possess high value for the characters, the degree of heterosis will be less for that particular trait in the hybrid. Heterosis is calculated over check parent value (CPV), mid-parent value (MPV) or better parent value (BPV) by using following formulae:

(i) Heterosis over CPV = $\frac{F1 - CPV}{CPV} \times 100$

(ii) Heterosis over MPV = $\frac{F1 - CPV}{MPV} \times 100$

(iii) Heterosis over BPV = $\frac{F1 - BPV}{BPV} \times 100$

If the value for a particular trait is high in F1, the calculated heterosis will be positive but if F1 value is less then the heterosis will be negative and negative heterosis should not be exploited except for larval duration and renditta as short larval duration and less renditta are the beneficial characters.

Hybrid vigour in different crossing systems

Hybrid vigour is at its best in F1 hybrid which decreases gradually as F1 > F2 > F3 > F4 > F5 so on and the phenomenon of hybrid vigour disappears in about 14 generations in silkworm. Silkworm strains can be crossed in different manners viz.,

(a) Single cross [A × B]

(b) Three-way cross [(A × B) × C]

(c) Double cross [(A × B) × (C × D)]

The quantitative characters in silkworm are highly variable and have a greater economic value. F1 (single cross) hybrids are most commonly used for commercial cocoon production because they represent high heterosis for most of the economic characters (Harada, 1961). It has also been reported that F1 hybrids are less variable than parental lines, three-way and double crosses (Watanabe, 1960, 1961). Variability in cocoon shape has been used in identification of uniform strains and hybrids (Mano, 1994).

In the study of heterosis in the silkworm, many characters have been found to have a relationship with the qualitative and quantitative aspects of silk yield (Ohi *et al.*, 1970). However, the characters in hybrids showing high manifestation of heterosis are:

- Shorter feeding duration and better larval weight.
- Lower rate of mortality and better Effective Rate of Rearing (ERR).
- Higher cocoon weight.
- Heavier shell weight.
- Longer filament length.
- Better pupation rate and raw silk percentage.

The earlier results of Osawa and Harada showed the following values of hybrid vigour for different characters considering the mid-parent value as 100 (Table 9.1).

Table 9.1: Heterosis for different characters in silkworm

Characters	*Heterosis %*
Feeding duration	97
Larval mortality	56
Silk filament size	103
Shell weight	124
Egg number	123

However, the level of heterosis recorded for different strains by different workers is not consistent. Subba Rao and Sahai (1990) using 30 Bivoltine × 30 Bivoltine hybrids reported highest manifestation of heterosis for cocoon yield (14.25%) which is a function of both survival rate and cocoon weight (Table 9.2). While conducting studies on 10 multi × 10 multivoltine, Singh and Rao (1996) reported highest heterosis for cocoon yield/100 Dfls that differs from season to season with highest value in unfavourable season (Table 9.3)

Nagaraju (1990) reported that highest heterosis for survival rate in multivoltine × bivoltine crosses. Studies made by various workers reported that the degree of

Table 9.2: Heterosis for different characters in *Bombyx mori* (mean of 30 Bi × 30 Bi hybrids) (Source: Subba Rao and Sahai, 1990)

Characters	*Heterosis %*
Cocoon yield	14.25
Cocoon weight	3.89
Shell weight	3.29
Denier	3.08
Larval duration	2.58
Survival rate	0.87

Table 9.3: Heterosis for different characters in *Bombyx mori* (mean of 10 multi × 10 multivoltine hybrids) (source: Singh and Rao, 1996)

Characters	*Heterosis (%)*	
	Favourable	*Unfavourable*
E.R.R. (Number)	10.39	23.84
ERR weight	40.49	69.59
Single cocoon weight	25.54	50.43
Single shell weight	32.22	60.91
Cocoon-shell ratio	2.70	14.25
Yield/1 00 Dfls	73.37	119.83

heterosis varies steeply for different characters. Such wide differences in the manifestation of heterosis suggest that the parental strains involved in the hybrids differ in their genetic make-up as reflected in their sharp differences in origin, voltinism and quantitative traits such as larval duration, single cocoon weight, single shell weight, filament length etc. (Yokoyama, 1957; Chang *et al.*, 1981; Gamo and Hirabayashi, 1983; Sathenahalli *et al.*, 1989). It is established that heterosis becomes lesser with the increase in mid-parental value. In other words, when the quantitative characters of the parents are improved through selection excessively, they become more homogeneous for genetic components; consequently the heterosis tends to become smaller as found for weight of cocoon and length of silk filament.

Heterosis in three-way crosses: In India, exploitation of using three-way crosses of the silkworm was demonstrated by many workers. Most of the studies (Hirobe, 1985; Udupa and Gowda, 1988) showed that three-way and double cross hybrids are inferior to single hybrids. Nagaraju (1990) also obtained similar results for three-way cross hybrids of (multi × multi) × Bi and multi × (Bi × Bi). Such a difference between hybrids of single, three-way and double crosses was interpreted considering the fact that one of the parents involved in three-way and both the parents in double cross hybrids are actually F1 individuals (Nagaraju *et al.*, 1996). Furthermore, the population produced by three-way or double cross hybrids is a mixture of genotypes, all of which could in principle have been produced by single crosses but differs from single cross hybrids in the following three ways (Falconer, 1981):

- If the superiority of single cross is due to epistatic interactions, some of its superiority is lost in three-way and double crosses.
- There is genetic variation within the crosses and consequent loss of phenotypic uniformity.
- The variance between crosses is reduced and the best three-way and double-cross hybrids are consequently not as good as the best single cross hybrids.

However, Krishnaswamy (1987) clearly demonstrated that three-way cross cocoons result in improved reelability, reduced renditta, lower size deviation and improved tenacity compared to those of the conventional single hybrid cocoons. During hot and humid season, when rearing of bivoltine F1 hybrid is unsuccessful at field level and indigenous races give very low and poor quality yield, three-way crosses can play as an intermediary technology for commercial use. Three-way crosses showed highest heterosis for yield/100 Dfls followed by cocoon shell weight during unfavourable season (Table 9.4). It is also established that heterosis for different characters is higher during unfavourable seasons compared to favourable season and MPV over BPV (Table 9.4) in the combinations tried by many workers.

Table 9.4: Heterosis of different characters in three-way crosses (mean of 4 three-way cross involving multivoltine as female and bivoltine F1 hybrids as male parent) (source: Das *et al.*, 1997)

Characters	*June-July*	*Oct-Nov*	*Dec-Jan*
Larval period	–6.52	–8.33	–4.62
Survival %	33.39	12.13	3.97
Single cocoon wt	27.18	19.66	19.18
Single shell wt	44.96	28.41	22.07
Filament length	39.70	18.06	20.95
Yield/100 Dfls	91.06	47.51	18.67

Heterosis in double crosses: The primary objective of rearing double hybrids is to get the desired quantitative and qualitative traits into one combination (Datta and Basavaraja, 1998). It is well known that survival and fecundity are affected greatly with increase in quantitative traits beyond threshold level. Although survival could be maintained in single hybrids, less number of eggs laid by inbred pure mother moths' handicaps them. Unless mother moth is a hybrid, the fecundity cannot be increased (Yokoyama, 1979). The increase in egg number is possible only with the foundation crosses, which are the parents of double hybrids. In addition, with clear advantage like easy rearing, superior to parental breeds in growth, vigour and other economic characters besides better in yield than single hybrids (Nirmal Kumar *et al.*, 1998), the double hybrids could be commercially exploited. Mukherjee (1998) stated that in general the heterotic manifestation is higher in case of single crosses than in the three-way and double crosses for all the characters except larval weight where higher level of heterosis was found associated. Yokoyama (1997) reported that the double crosses invariably manifest greater heterosis for fecundity. Nirmal Kumar *et al.* (1997) reported heterosis over mid-parent and better parent in double hybrids for pupation rate, cocoon weight, shell weight, filament length and raw silk % over foundation crosses with higher values in cocoon weight (Table 9.5).

Table 9.5: Heterosis of different characters in double crosses (Mean of three double crosses) (Source: Nirmal Kumar *et al.*, 1997)

Characters	*Heterosis %*	
	Mid parent	*Better parent*
Pupation rate	7.50	4.33
Cocoon weight	12.04	11.68
Shell ratio	2.56	0.90
Filament length	10.71	5.94
Raw silk	7.17	5.64

Improved silkworm strains which yield longer filament length tend to lay fewer eggs (Ohi *et al.*, 1970). On the other hand, in double cross hybrids, the eggs yield/female moth is 30% more than in single cross hybrids (Yokoyama, 1973). Hence, the usage of double cross hybrids was to an extent more than 40% in Japan, while such a use is yet to gain initiative in India. A model proposed by Minagawa and Ohtsuka (1975) can predict the performance of three-way and double cross hybrids from the performance of single cross hybrids of the constituent lines. Ghosh *et al.* (1996) reported heterosis in fecundity in double hybrids over foundation crosses (Table 9.6).

Table 9.6: Heterosis in fecundity over foundation crosses

Type of crosses	*Favourable*	*Unfavourable*	*Average*
Foundation crosses	479	399	439
Double crosses	509 (6.26%)	522 (30.82%)	516 (17.53%)

They stated that if foundation crosses were used at P1 level, it would eventually increase the commercial seed production. This approach may be adopted to bridge the gap of commercial seed production and quality. Also the benefit by the use of double hybrids is:

- Increased crop reliability if foundation crosses are raised and reared at P1 level especially in unfavourable seed crop season.

- Increase in number of eggs up to an extent of 20% promoting an enhanced production.
- Seed crop rearers will not hesitate to accept the foundation crosses because of crop assurance.

Mukharjee (1998) reported that in general heterotic manifestation is higher in case of single crosses than the three-way and double crosses (Table 9.7) and concluded that results are in conformity with Minagawa and Ohtsuka (1975). Moreover, his results have not confirmed the findings of Yokoyama (1957) who had reported that double crosses manifest greater heterosis for fecundity. Sengupta *et al.* (1974), Narasimhanna (1976) and Mukharjee (1997) reported lower degree of heterosis in multivoltine crosses. It is evident that the genetic background of Indian polyvoltine breeds is more or less similar in view of long inbreeding history. In the multi × Bi crosses, the cocoon characters have invariably failed to exceed the better parents. The negative heterosis might be due to the superiority of bivoltine strains. Udupa and Gowda (1988) and Gowda *et al.* (1993) also reported instances of negative heterosis in cocoon characters when multivoltine female parents crossed with bivoltine male parents. Mukharjee (1998) reported that performance of heterosis on individual cross basis in different crossing systems had good number

Table 9.7: Heterosis % in different crossing systems (Source: Mukherjee, 1998)

Characters	*Single crosses*	*Three-way crosses*	*Double crosses*
Fecundity	14.13	2.03	9.62
Larval duration	0.33	–4.22	–4.26
Larval weight	5.85	25.00	31.82
Yield / 10000 larvae	5.40	17.82	23.05
Single cocoon weight	18.63	26.98	25.99
Single shell weight	66.67	39.18	35.88
Shell ratio	52.98	21.62	19.48
Filament length	10.04	31.26	38.43
Denier	16.90	17.50	15.63

of crosses, which failed to exhibit heterosis, and thereby showed negative heterosis. Kantartankul *et al.* (1987), Sengupta *et al.* (1974) and Narasimhanna (1976) have also reported negative heterosis in silkworm. Egg productivity is positively correlated with number of eggs laid and number of effective moths capable of laying reasonable number of eggs but this character is negatively correlated with cocoon shell and raw silk percentage. Therefore, selection of inbred lines for high egg productivity without reducing the cocoon-shell per cent is a difficult task. Hence, breeders are hybridizing two or more inbred lines to get the desired result. Nirmal Kumar *et al.* (1998) observed no differences for shell ratio and neatness between pure breeds, foundation crosses (F1) and double crosses. However, major differences noticed by them were with respect to pupation rate, cocoon weight, filament length and raw silk recovery. The selection of suitable parents for foundation crosses is very important. If the foundation crosses with high degree of heterosis are used for double hybrid preparation, the hybrid vigour may decline. Therefore, the foundation cross which show low heterosis should be utilized to have more hybrid vigour in double hybrids. Relatively recently, Central Silk Board, Government of India, has authorized single, three-way and double cross hybrids for commercial exploitation in different regions and seasons of the country and besides India, there is also great demand for supply of these hybrids from other countries also.

Exploitation of heterosis: The phenomenon of heterosis or hybrid vigour has been fully exploited in both animals as well as in plant production. The classical example of the application of this phenomenon is corn in agriculture and silkworm in sericulture. Systemic and planned hybridization together with improved farming and rearing practices has helped a great deal to increase the productivity of corn and silk by many folds. In fact Japanese silkworm and American maize are two big stars of hybrid utilization. The exploitation of hybrid vigour in silkworm came to being slightly earlier than in the American maize.

Crossing of inbred lines has made a major contribution of today's high productive silkworm races; ever since the phenomenon of hybrid vigour was discovered and adopted for cocoon production. In this case the purpose of crossing is to produce a heterotic effect rather than to provide genetic variation for selection. Another purpose of crossing inbred line is to produce superior crossbreed or F1 hybrid. Therefore, heterosis depends on selection as well as on inbreeding and crossing. Since the introduction of heterosis, progress in silkworm breeding has depended on success or failure in identifying better combiners for a cross or a hybrid. One of the most important research activities for development of better hybrid varieties is the identification of inbred lines for specific cross combinations. Good combiners are distinguished by means of the combining ability test/line × tester analysis or D^2 analysis.

Heterosis and environment: Environmental factors known to influence growth and development play very important role in the expression of heterosis. For example, the level of heterosis expressed in a cross-bred population is determined by interaction between the genotypes environmental factors prevailing at that time. Lerner (1954) proposed the concept of genetic homeostasis in which heterozygous populations are expected to be less influenced by environmental factors in comparison to homozygous populations. Sang (1956), Gritting and Zsiros (1971), Knight (1951) and Orozco (1976) reported that the heterozygous populations are found to possess the required genetic architecture to withstand the adverse environmental factors better than the homozygote. Harada (1961) observed high degree of heterosis for various quantitative traits during spring compared to autumn season and stated that the difference in the expression of heterosis was due to the influence of environmental factors. The degree of heterosis over mid-parental value will mostly be less under favourable environmental conditions. For instance, when one of the parents involved is an exotic high yielding strain in MV × BV hybrids, the heterosis over the exotic parent will be negative when the exotic parent and hybrids are raised under similar favourable conditions. On the other hand, when both parental strains and hybrids are raised in unfavourable environmental conditions, performance of hybrids will be much superior to both the parental strains. Under such conditions the heterosis will be higher over both mid-parental and better parental values.

Silkworm breeding and heterosis: Hybridization followed by appropriate selection bringing together the economic characters of choice from defined sources and to synthesize genotypes of desirable constitution and expression is the main aim of breeding. By utilizing the known and established breeding material, the objective of synthesizing new breeds can easily be realized by the application of appropriate selection pressure for desirable combinations of genes. The reciprocal crossing of two breeds which are good in some characters and poor for some other characters to lead to the segregation of characters at indefinitely large number of loci in F2 generation (Lerner, 1954) enabling the breeder to select the desirable combination of characters and reject the individual with undesirable characters.

Evolution of improved races through inbreeding of hybrids is well-documented (Hirobe. 1968; Gamo, 1976; Yokoyama, 197). The distinct genotypic and phenotypic differences between the races utilized in the hybridization produce high degree of phenotypic variability enabling the breeder to step up selection for different characters in the polygenic system (Gamo and Ichiba, 1971 and Gamo, 1976) can be exploited by the application of systematic selection and bringing together some advantageous features of the parental races.

Exploitation of heterosis has played a vital role in increasing the silk production to a great extent. Continuous efforts are still being made to understand the mechanisms contributing to heterosis and to develop new hybrid combination for effective exploitation of heterosis and to increase productivity.

CORRELATION AND HERITABILITY

Correlation and heritability studies of quantitative traits are a prerequisite of judicious selection for genetic improvement of complex characters. The success of selection is governed by the degree to which the desired trait is transmitted to the next generation. Nature of correlation is to be given due consideration at appropriate developmental stage for pursuing selection in desired direction while improving or evolving high productive breeds or hybrids of the silkworm.

Characters showing high heritability and high genetic advance respond better to simple phenotypic selection while those having low heritability and low genetic advance may respond better to mass selection. Characters showing high heritability and low genetic advance may yield good response to hybridization and recurrent selection. An attempt has been made to emphasize the magnitude of correlation and heritability in selection strategies for the improvement of quantitative traits in desired direction in the silkworm.

The knowledge of interrelationship between quantitative characters of economic importance determining silk productivity is of paramount importance to the breeders, cocoon and egg producers, reelers, weavers, twisters and buyers. While egg producers favour strong potential genotypes producing more number of eggs, cocoon growers are interested in the genotype having high cocoon yield and healthy larvae. The filature industry favours high reelability, high percentage of raw silk and superior quality of cocoons and weaving industry requires neatness, denier, high tenacity and elongation.

For these, we cannot wait for favours from nature, but we must rest them from her and it is possible only through man's intervention to force any form of individual to change more quickly and in the direction desirable to them. Various methods are advocated for improving the quantitative characters in desired direction, which includes breeding (cross breeding, in-breeding), selection, mutation etc. However, whatever system is followed, genetic improvement of quantitative character is not possible without judicious selection. Considering the importance of selection, Wright (1921) pointed out that 'Selection is the measure of permanently changing the relative proportions of various genes present in the original stock.'

Estimation of correlation and heritability in the genetic studies of quantitative characters is of special significance for selection, as its magnitude indicates the accuracy with which a genotype can be recognized by its phenotypic expression. It also helps in deciding upon suitable selection criteria for the genetic improvement of complex characters. Thus, the knowledge of correlation and heritability of basic economic quantitative parameter is a prerequisite of selection while creating, evaluating, improving or evolving high productive breeds, hybrids or strains of silkworm.

Selection

There are two principal methods of selection:

I. Pedigree selection

Pedigree selection is useful only when adequate information is available about the genotype. Essentially, pedigree selection is only an extension of performance testing since each individual's performance is tested and performance records are used to evaluate the related genotypes.

II. Mass selection

(i) Tandem method of selection (Directional selection)

In this method, the selection is directed towards improvement of only one desired trait and is continued till the goal set for this character is achieved. Thereafter, selection is made for another trait till the goal set for that trait is also achieved. Thus, in such cases the traits are selected one after the other. This is highly inefficient method of selection, as unless the traits are genetically related, whatever achievement is made in the first trait in the first period is lost when attention is diverted to another trait. The rate of net improvement therefore becomes very small or sometimes negligible.

(ii) Independent culling method

In this method of selection, few parameters are considered it a time. For each parameter, minimum standard is set. The genotype must meet the minimum standard set for each of the trait; otherwise, it is to be rejected from the breeding population. If any genotype is exceptionally good in one parameter, but is bad in another parameter, it is being totally rejected. The effectiveness of this method, therefore, depends on the standard chosen for each of the traits. If very high standards are fixed, the number of genotypes selected to become the parents will be very few, resulting in gradual extinction of the genotypes. On the other hand, if very low standard is set, the selection of genotype based on merit will become difficult, as most of the genotypes fulfill the set standard. Besides, fixing an arbitrary standard for each trait, it is also necessary to determine as to how many traits are to be considered at a time. This is because selection for several traits at a time reduces the selection intensity of the trait. Therefore, selection for unimportant traits should be avoided as it reduces progress in important traits. Emphasis should be given on one or two traits, which are economically more important and have the capacity to respond.

(iii) Selection index (Simultaneous selection)

The most effective method of selection is by selection index. A selection index is used when the breeder simultaneously selects many desirable economic traits to improve it in a desired direction. The theory and practice of developing an index is what Kempthrone (1977) likes to call 'Applied Quantitative Genetics'. Procedure for calculation of selection index varies from breeder to breeder. Restricted selection index (Tallis, 1962), modified base index (Baker, 1986), weight-free index for ranking genotypes (Elston, 1963) are some of the methods in practice.

Various authors under different sets of restrictions have done theoretical comparisons among these types of selection. Finney (1962) suggested generalized formula for comparing the methods. According to him, expected change in genotypic worth in response to selection for a single trait is proportional to the ratio of co-variance. If any of these ratios is far larger than any other, tandem selection for that trait or independent culling with high selection intensity for that trait, should give response to overall genotypic value, which are close to that expected from index selection. Index selection is found to be better than tandem selection for improving genotypic value for negatively correlated characters but selection quite often does not follow the regular pattern predicted by 'Quantitative Genetics Theory'. One of the most striking manifestations of the irregularities is the 'Reversed Response' when selecting individuals for the increased value character results in a decreased value among their offspring and vice-versa. A reversed response in selection experiments is rarely being given serious consideration and its significance is usually dismissed with one of the two explanations—a sudden change in environmental conditions or random drift. Caution is needed, however, before either of the two explanations is accepted in a particular case because either of the explanations under the laboratory experiments is highly improbable where conditions are kept under control by the experimenter.

Therefore, in order to obtain desirable results, it is of paramount importance to find out the type of correlations existing between quantitative parameters and their heritability before initiating any form of selection.

Correlation

The degree of association or relationship between two variables is measured by correlation coefficient (r). The correlation coefficient may be positive or negative. Positive correlation indicates that the two variables are varying in the same direction. In other words, if one variable increases, the other variable also increases. In negative correlation, the two variables vary in opposite direction, i.e. if one variable increases the other decreases. There is very intimate correlation between some of the characters and an excellent character may bring down the merit of another character, if not given due consideration at the appropriate developmental stage. Correlation between different pairs of quantitative characters studied (Table 9.8) revealed high significant (P<0,01) positive values between cocoon weight and pupal weight (r = + 0.994), cocoon weight and shell weight (r = + 0.614), pupal weight and shell weight (r = + 0.527), while significant (P<0.01) negative values between pupal weight and cocoon shell -ratio (r =-0.827). This indicates that selection by cocoon weight would lead to increase of pupal weight and shell weight but selection by pupal weight would lead to decrease of cocoon shell ratio.

Table 9.8: Correlation co-efficient between some pairs of economic characters in *Bombyx mori* (after Singh *et al.*, 1994)

Correlation between	*Pupal weight*	*Shell weight*	*Cocoon-shell ratio*
Cocoon weight	+0.994**	+0.614**	–0.764**
Pupal weight		+0.527**	–0.827**
Shell weight			+ 0.035

** Significant at 1 % level of significance

Correlation studies performed to establish the relationship between female pupal weight and fecundity (Table 9.9) indicated highly significant (P< 0.01) positive correlation between the two, irrespective of their weight. Fecundity has been found increasing from lower pupal weight to higher pupal weight. Hence, selection by female pupal weight will automatically lead to increased fecundity. Positive values of correlation coefficient in the regression analysis also clearly indicated that selection of individuals for higher fecundity depends on its pupal weight but extreme pupal weight should be avoided as it may sometimes lead to bottleneck phenomenon. Therefore, selection of moderate pupal weight should only be encouraged for egg production, as it also determines increased larval weight, survival rate, filament length etc in the successive generations.

Table 9.9: Correlation and regression between female pupal weight and fecundity in the silkworm *Bombyx mori* (c.f., Singh, 1994)

Female pupal weight	*Average Pupal weight (X)*	*Average fecundity*	*Correlation coefficient (r)*	*Regressionof facundity on pupal weight (Y)*
1.000-1.20	1.12308	443.600	+ 0.8720**	Y=-38.7688 + 429.5053 X
1.201- 1.30	1.24280	468.040	+ 0.9209**	Y = 1873.5294 + 1884.1080 X
1.301-1.50	1.41356	487.880	+ 0.8646**	Y = 510.7906 + 706.4933 X
1.501-1.70	1.54728	535.360	+ 0.8456**	Y = 398.0606 + 603.2656 X
1.701-1.80	1.7440	559.280	+ 0.8366**	Y = 1794.1461 + 1349.1322 X
Pooled data 1.000-1.80	1.41422	498.831	+0.7820**	Y = 187.6987 + 220.0028 x

** Significant at 1 % level of significance

Fecundity, which has been found showing positive correlation with female pupal weight, has also shown highly significant (P< 0.01) positive correlation with cocoon weight and cocoon shell weight (Table 9.10). Hence, selection for higher cocoon weight, pupal weight and shell weight together would yield higher fecundity. Correlated quantitative traits of economic importance in the silkworm *Bombyx mori* is summarized in Table 9.11. As fecundity is positively correlated with pupal weight but negatively with productivity, cocoon-shell ratio and robustness every effort should be made for the improvement of negatively correlated characters without reducing the fecundity.

Table 9.10: Correlation between fecundity, cocoon weight and shell weight in *Bombyx mori* (c.f. Singh *et al.*, 1994)

Cocoon weight (gm)	*Shell weight (cg)*	*Fecundity (No.)*	*Correlation between fecundity and*	
			Cocoon weight	*Shell weight*
1.38 ± 0.162	24.1 ± 5.38	437 ± 143	+ 0.765**	+ 0.643**
1.52 ± 0.246	27.9 ± 5.15	453 ± 124	+ 0.867**	+ 0.769**
1.58 ± 0.149	28.9 ± 3.22	558 ± 66	+ 0.785**	+ 0.695**
1.76 ± 0.193	36.0 ± 4.64	566 ± 72	+ 0.866**	+ 0.715**
1.83 ± 0.197	35.0 ± 4.00	622 ± 64	+ 0.759**	+ 0.633**
1.88 ± 0.157	39.5 ± 4.84	632 ± 83	+ 0.584**	+ 0.625**

** Significant at 1% level of significance

Cocoon yield, a very important character linked directly with the earning of sericulturists is positively correlated with survival rate. Cocoon weight, which is being given always much emphasis in selection strategies, has shown positive correlation with shell weight, filament length and pupal weight. A high positive correlation is also established between shell weight and filament length/silkiness. Filament length has also been found positively correlated with shell ratio and neatness. Positive correlation is also being reported between lousiness and ratio of degumming loss. Therefore, when selection is enforced in the directions of high lousiness, the ratio of degumming loss increases. Generally, lousiness is more in Japanese strains and less in Chinese strains. It is more in cocoons with high shell weight. As degumming trait is closely correlated with cocoon shell weight, it is not quite easy to have a genotype showing low value for degumming trait without reducing the cocoon shell weight.

Reelability of cocoons is one of the most important parameters which needs attention in the improvement programme, but it is very complicated character to be improved upon, because it is negatively correlated with filament length and positively with neatness and the expression of which differs with environmental conditions viz., temperature, humidity, light and air current during spinning period.

The qualities of cocoons and fixation of price are usually assessed based on cocoon and shell weights but shell ratio is a better parameter for assessing the cocoon quality for reeling because higher shell percentage leads higher raw silk yield due to their positive correlation. A positive correlation is being established between shell ratio and cocoon quality, whereas cocoon weight and shell weight does not necessarily show positive correlation with reeling performance (Table 9.11).

It has been reported that there is a significant positive correlation between larval weight and cocoon weight, and larval weight and pupal weight. Therefore, selection should be done for robust larvae (disease-free) with higher larval weight. Usually, high productive worms show less viability, which is evident from the fact that poor productivity and higher resistance for diseases are associated together in indigenous genotypes, while high productivity and poor resistance for diseases in bivoltine races. Thus, the adoptive fitness, low silk content and polyvoltinism appear to be positively correlated in silkworms.

Genetic analysis of different quantitative traits indicated incomplete dominance for growth rate, raw silk percentage, filament length, filament size and reelability percentage; over dominance for pupation rate and cocoon weight and epistatic effect for pupation rate, cocoon weight,

Table 9.11: Significantly correlated characters in the silkworm *Bombyx mori*

Correlation between	*Correlation*	*References*
1	**2**	**3**
Fecundity and productivity	Negative	Kashiviswanathan, 1976
Fecundity and robustness	Negative	Gowda *et al.*, 1988
Fecundity and female pupal weight	Positive	Jayaswal *et al.*, 1991
Fecundity and moth weight	Positive	Gupta *et al.*, 1991
Cocoon yield and cocoon weight	Positive	Kashiviswanathan, 1976
Cocoon yield and pupation rate	Positive	Kashiviswanathan, 1976
Cocoon yield, filament weight and pupation rate	Positive	Ohi *et al.*, 1970
Cocoon yield and survival rate	Positive	Kashiviswanathan, 1976
Cocoon weight and larval weight	Positive	Satenahalli *et al.*, 1990
Cocoon weight and egg weight	Positive	Shamachary *et al.*, 1980
Cocoon weight and shell weight	Positive	Petkov, 1981 a
Cocoon weight and filament length	Positive	Petkov, 1981 c
Cocoon weight and pupal weight	Positive	Rajanna and Reddy, 1990
Cocoon weight and denier	Positive	Satenahalli *et al.*, 1990
Female pupal weight and egg weight	Positive	Shamachary *et al.*, 1980
Female pupal wt. and larval weight	Positive	Gowda *et al.* 1989

(Table (contd...)

Table 9.11: (Contd...)

1	2	3
Cocoon weight and cocoon silkiness	Positive	Grekov and Petkov. 1990
Shell weight and cocoon weight	Positive	Ozdzensky and Kremky, 1987
Shell weight and pupal weight	Positive	Singh *et al.*, 1992 a
Shell weight and cocoon silkiness	Positive	Long and Petkov, 1987
Shell weight and filament length	Positive	Petkov, 1981 b
Length and weight of filament	Positive	Ohoi *et al.*, 1970
Larval duration, reelability and neatness	Negative	Ohoi *et al.*, 1970
Shell weight and egg weight	Positive	Shamachary *et al.*, 1980
Shell ratio and raw silk yield	Positive	Sonawalkar, 1982
Shell ratio and cocoon quality	Positive	Singh *et al*, 1992 b
Shell ratio and pupal weight	Negative	Singh *et al*, 1992 a
Shell ratio and filament length	Positive	Petkov, 1981 b
Filament length and neatness	Positive	Kashiviswanathan, 1976
Filament length and reelability	Negative	Jayaswal *et al.*, 1990
Yield of cocoons of parent and their hybrids	Positive	Jonka, 1986
Reelability and tenacity	Positive	Liu and He, 1991
Length and size of filament	Positive	Miyahara, 1978

filament size and reelability percentage. Further, cytoplasmic effects were also observed in pupation rate and size of cocoon filament. As a result cocoon weight, pupation rate and cocoon yieldingness could be considered to improve by heterosis in F1 hybrids, while other characters are improved by selection. Especially, reelability of cocoons is expected to improve by the accumulation of dominant genes under the control of environmental conditions.

Heritability

Every character of an organism is both hereditary and environmental as it is manifested because of long chain interactions of genes either with each other or with the environment. In fact, characters cannot be developed until and unless the genes governing them have proper environment. Heritability of quantitative traits plays very vital role in the selection strategies. One of the most important functions of the heritability in genetic studies of metric character is its predictive role, expressing the reliability of the phenotypic value as a guide to the breeding value. With the genetic or environmental variations, the heritability estimates also change. The heritability of characters cannot be estimated from one population or one set of environmental conditions to another.

Determination of heritability: Heritability is determined in two ways:

A: **Broad sense heritability:** In broad sense, heritability is the ratio of the total genotypic variance to that of total phenotypic variance. It is useful in predicting the outcome of artificial selection among clones, inbred lines, varieties etc.

B: **Narrow sense heritability:** In narrow sense, heritability is the ratio of additive genetic variance (V A) to the total phenotypic variance (V P)'.

$$h^2 = \frac{V\,A}{V\,P}$$

(h^2 stands for heritability itself and not for its square).

It is used when artificial selection is practised in a randomly mating population. In narrow sense, generally, heritability of a character is smaller than the broad sense heritability. Heritability is expressed either 0-100 or 0 -1. Heritability estimates of different characters can be determined by the following three factors -

- Correlation regression analysis of close relatives (for example parent-offspring, full-sibs, half-sibs etc.).
- Correlation response in which both desired and undesired characters are selected.
- Analysis of variance components.

It is important to realize that the heritability is a property not only for a character but also of the population and of the environmental circumstances to which the individuals are subjected. Heritability studies (Table 9.12) conducted for some important quantitative traits reveals higher values for shell weight (80.20%), growth rate (79.30%), raw silk percentage (79.00%), pupal weight (78.50%), cocoon-shell ratio (72.40%) and cocoon weight (73.60%), while extremely low for reelability (28.00%) and pupation rate (19.00%).

Table 9.12: Heritability of some economic traits in Bombyx *mori* (Modified after Singh *et al.,* 1994)

Characters	*Heritability*
Cocoon weight	73.60
Pupal weight	78.50
Cocoon-shell ratio	72.40
Pupation rate	19.00
Shell weight	80.20
Growth rate	79.30
Raw silk %	79.00
Reelability	28.00

Heritability estimates (Table 9.13) for various quantitative traits in *Bombyx mori* reveal higher values for fecundity and filament length, cocoon weight and pupal

Table 9.13: Heritability of some economic characters in *Bombyx mori*

Economic traits	*Heritability*	*References*
Fecundity	High	Chatterjee *et al.*, 1990
Larval weight	High	Satenahalli *et al.*,1990
Larval duration	High	Kasivishwanathan, 1976
Growth rate	High	Rajanna and Reddy, 1990 b
Cocoon weight	High	Yan, 1983
Pupal weight	High	Yan, 1983
Shell weight	High	Tsuchiya and Kurashima, 1956
Shell ratio	High	Singh and Singh, 1993
Pupation rate	Low	Gamo and Hirabayashi, 1983
Pupal duration	Medium	Ashoka and Govindan, 1990
Filament weight	High	Ohi *et al.*, 1970
Filament length	High	Chatterjee et *al.*, 1990
Filament size	High	Singh and Saratchandra, 1994
Reelability (%)	Low	Gamo and Hirabayashi, 1983
Raw silk (%)	High	Gamo and Hirabayashi, 1983
Denier	High	Narasimharaju *et al.*, 1990
Neatness	High	Kasivishwanathan, 1976
E.R.R. %	High	Narasimharaju *et al.*, 1990
Cocoon yield by no. & wt.	High	Ashoka and Govindan, 1 990

weight, cocoon-shell weight, growth rate, raw silk percentage and cocoon-shell ratio, while low or extremely low for pupation rate and reelability percentage. These characters with low values of heritability are of little importance in selection strategies because here most variations are non-transmissible. Characters with high heritability as well as high genetic advance indicating possible operation of additive gene action and hence respond better to simple phenotypic selection than those having low heritability and low genetic advance. Therefore, individual selection for those having high heritability and high genetic advance has to be resorted to for obtaining results in desirable direction.

On the contrary, moth emergence, effective rate of rearing, larval and pupal duration show moderate to high heritability. But low genetic advance reveals operation of predominant non-additive gene action and hence respond better to hybridization and recurrent selection. Mostly, selection does not act on a single character but act on whole set of characters and when phenotypic correlation exists among characters, selection on a character may result in selection differentials on correlated characters. Since expression of economic characters depends upon a number of related attributes, genetic progress will be accelerated only if selection is performed simultaneously on more than one attribute, contributing to the theme. Seasons also have some influence on heritability of various characters. The traits like silk filament, size of the filament, silk content and cocoon-shell ratio has high heritability in favourable seasons compared to unfavorable ones. Thus, heritability is an important tool in predicting the magnitude and speed of population improvement. With the help of heritability estimates, a breeder can know how much more closely related organisms with similar genotypes resemble each other than less closely related organisms. It is also useful in predicting the outcome of artificial selection among the clones, inbred lines, and varieties besides production of superior genotypes.

Therefore, relations between different pairs of characters and the degree of its manifestation should be taken into consideration while performing selection keeping in view the magnitude of the objectives.

Selection order

Selection should not be conducted for all the traits at a time. The orders of selection for different economic traits during different generations are depicted in Table 9.14. In the early generation, selection should be enforced for neatness, reelability, wrinkle of cocoons, muscardine resistance etc. while during middle generation uniformity of cocoons, cocoon weight, shell weight, cocoon-shell ratio, cocoon color, raw silk per cent age etc. should be taken into consideration. Most of the reeling parameters should be considered in the later generations.

Table 9.14: Order of selection of important characters in the silkworm, *Bombyx mori*

Order	*Character*	*Generation*
1	Neatness	F1-F3
2	Reelability	F1-F4
3	Wrinkle	F2-F5
4	Double layered cocoon	F1-F5
5	Muscardine resistance	F2-F5
6	Diffusion of newborn	F2-F6
7	Hatchability	F4-F8
8	Uniformity of cocoon	F1-F8
9	Thin-waist cocoon	F4-F8
10	Thin end cocoon	F4-F8
11	Single cocoon weight	F2-F8
12	Raw silk percentage	F3-F8
13	Cocoon colour	F2-F9
14	Cocoon shell percentage	F2-F9
15	Cocoon shell weight	F3-F9
16	Filament length	F2-F15
17	Filament size	F2-F15
18	Size deviation	F2-F15
19	Double cocoon	F2-F15
20	Lousiness	F2-F15
21	Larval body size	F2-F15
22	Larval duration	F2-F15
23	Cocoon shell degumming loss	F2-F15
24	Tenacity and elongation	Unknown
25	Dyeing	Unknown

Selection strategies

The following are suggested for obtaining better results through selection in desirable direction:

- Elimination of weakened cocoons. Cocoons should be pressed from the two vertical ends and if they are pressed should be rejected.

- Elimination of double-layered cocoons. Double-layered cocoons should invariably be eliminated, as the second layer of such cocoons cannot be reeled properly. However, the shell weight of such cocoons is approximately 20% more, but is of no use because of problem during reeling.
- Urinated, stained, dead, melted, oversized, under-sized, Uzi infested and flossy cocoons should be eliminated.
- Cocoon shape is broadly classified into three types viz., spindle (one end pointed while the other blunt), oval (Chinese type) and peanut (Japanese type). Generally, the vertical ends are weak in Chinese type. Therefore, compact cocoons with elongated waist and having round vertical ends (more or less Japanese type) should invariably be selected.
- There is direct correlation between the grains and compactness of shell layers. Coarse grain leads to loose shell layers, whereas fine grain to compactness of shell layers. Therefore, cocoons with uniform, medium-sized and distinct grains should only be selected.
- Reeling result is very important for selection. Batches of the same genotype having better neatness should only be selected for further multiplication.
- Cocoons must be assessed individually for metric traits viz., cocoon weight, shell weight, pupal weight and cocoon shell ratio,
- Cocoons with higher shell weight and shell ratio should be selected as they have generally better robustness. Cocoon scoring above average for weight falling on the periphery of the average should only be selected. Extreme higher cocoon weight should be avoided as ultimately they have lower shell ratio and more than that lower robustness and leads to bottleneck phenomenon.

- Selection should be done not only at the cocoon stage but also at the egg stage, incubation stage and moth stage. The objectives of selection at different stages are different. At the egg stage, purpose is to have stability of voltinism, high fecundity, uniformity of hatching and more number of viable eggs; at the larval stage, objective relates to vitality, larval duration, uniformity in moulting, evenness of body colour and markings and at the cocoon stage, they are related to determination of mortality, vitality of pupae, occurrence of premature emergence, cocoon shape and colours, cocoon shell wrinkles, cocoon weight and shell weight, cocoon shell ratio, reelability, neatness, filament size and length, degumming loss and reelable filament length etc. At the moth stage, main objective of selections is health and uniform emergence.
- Handling of worms with bare hands should be avoided as far as possible because it is established that it reduces the effective rate of rearing 2-3%.
- In breeding lines at least, 60 cocoons (35 female and 25 male) should be selected for further multiplication, which may be able to produce at least 20 Dfls for further selection.
- It is not advisable to carry forward all the batches brushed. If any batch is found not yielding desirable result, forthwith be rejected.
- Quicker decision is very important for the evolution and utilization of genotypes. General pattern of selection in this case should be F1 to F4 mass rearing, F5 to F9 single line rearing and then onwards maintenance.
- Any individual cannot be judged only on the basis of its phenotypic expression for its variability in future generations, as it can store small or large potentialities to change by balancing the beneficial (+) and non-beneficial (-) genes. Therefore,

selection in the early generation when high degree of heterosis persists should be avoided because it is very difficult to judge the true value of observed characters at this stage. If it is done, it may be possible to select the genotypes, which have no survival value and as such may not prove ultimately useful.

- Brushing of stabilized genotypes for maintenance should be conducted in the 'composite form' (prepared from collection of known number of eggs from at least 50 individual laying).
- Low intensity of selection should be performed in stabilized genotypes and genetic markers, whereas high intensity for lines which are under purification or evolution.
- Selected genotypes for further utilization should be tested for genetic divergence before preparation of hybrids. Genetically diverse parent should be crossed for obtaining desirable results.
- Multilocational trial should invariably be conducted before releasing selected hybrid genotypes for the purpose of commercial exploitation.

10

SILKWORM DISEASES AND PESTS

Mulberry silkworm is a domesticated variety of silkworm. It is susceptible to various diseases and attacked by pests and parasites. The diseases of silkworms together cause considerable damage to the silk industry. It has been proven that one silkworm disease 'pebrine' can destroy entire industry of a country. This threat imposed by silkworm diseases necessitates extreme care in handling of the silkworms. It is very well established that there is no practical way available for curing infected larvae. Therefore, precaution, identification and strong disinfections are the only methods available for preventing diseases.

In general, outbreak of diseases during silkworm rearing and continuous crop failure have been usual phenomena associated with tropical sericulture. The threat of diseases is related to the factors like poor quality of mulberry leaf, unfavourable weather conditions, lack of independent rearing houses for effective disinfections, poor hygiene and above all faulty rearing practices. Although several years of research in the field has highlighted certain preventive measures for the major silkworm diseases, the occurrence is on a very high scale in India causing a considerable loss of cocoon crop every year.

Classification of silkworm diseases: Silkworm diseases are broadly classified into two broad categories viz., infectious and non-infectious diseases.

A. **Infectious Diseases:** Infectious diseases are those caused by bacteria, virus, fungi, protozoa and similar microorganism, which enter and harm the body of the silkworm. The diseases can be transmitted from infected larvae to healthy larvae.

(a) **Bacterial Diseases:** Bacterial septicaemia, Bacterial toxicosis and Bacterial diseases of digestive tract.

(b) **Fungal diseases:** White Muscardine, Green Muscardine, Black Muscardine, Brown Muscardine and Aspergillosis.

(c) **Viral Diseases:** Nuclear polyhedrosis, Cytoplasmic polyhedrosis, Infectious flacherie and Densonucleosis.

(d) **Protozoan Disease:** Pebrine.

B. **Non-Infectious Diseases:** Non-infectious diseases are those which are caused by arthropods, agricultural chemicals and mechanical injuries and that cannot be transmitted from infected larvae to healthy larvae.

(a) **Arthropod diseases:** *Acarid* infestation

(b) **Strings:** *Euprgctis similes. Setora postornata*

(c) **Poisoning:** Agricultural chemicals, Exhaust fumes, Coal gas etc.

(d) **Physiological ailments**

Major diseases of silkworm prevailing in India and other countries are presented in Table 10.1 and discussed separately in this chapter.

BACTERIAL DISEASES

Bacterial diseases affecting silkworms are collectively known as 'Flacharie' or 'Kalashira'. Its occurrence is associated with environmental factors like temperature and relative humidity and unevenness in these factors creates physiological and metabolic abnormalities in silkworm larvae. The incidence of flacharie is high during hot and humid seasons. However, the massive outbreak of this disease is not common but depending upon the poor disinfections, accumulation of contaminated mulberry leaves, improper handling and unsafe use of bacterial

Table 10.1: Status of diseases of mulberry silkworm in India and other countries

S.N.	Disease	Pathogen	Prevalence in		Season
			India	*Other countries*	
1	**Protozoan**				
	Pebrine	*Nosema bombycis*	Prevalent	Prevalent	Al seasons
		Nosema sp M -1 1	Prevalent	Prevalent	
		Nosema sp. M -1 4	Not Rep.	Prevalent	
		Vairomorpha sp, M-12	Prevalent	Prevalent	
		Pleistophora sp. M-24	Not Rep.	Prevalent	
		Pleistophora sp. M-25	Not Rep.	Prevalent	
		Pleistophora sp. M-27	Not Rep.	Prevalent	
		Thelohania sp. M-32	Not Rep.	Prevalent	
		Leptomonas sp.	Not Rep.	Prevalent	
2	**Viral**				
	Nuclear polyhedrosis	BmNPV	Prevalent	Precvalent	Summer & rainy season
	Cytoplasmic Ployhedrosis	BmCPV	Rep. but not confirmed		
	Infectious flacherie	BmIFV	Prevalent	Prevalent	
	Denso-nucleosis	BmDNV1	Prevalent	Prevalent	
		BmDNV2	Not Rep.	Not Rep.	
		BmDNV3	Not Rep.	Not Rep.	

(Table (contd...)

Table 10.1: (Contd...)

S.N.	Disease	Pathogen	Prevalence in		Season
			India	Other countries	
3	**Bacterial**				
	Bacterial diseases of digestive tract	*Streptococcus sp.* *Pseudomonas sp*	Prevalent	Prevalent	Summer & rainy season
	Bacterial septicaemia	*Bacillus sp.* *Serratia marcescens*	Prevalent	Prevalent	
	Bacterial toxicosis	*Bacillus thuringiensis*	Prevalent	Prevalent	
4	**Fungal**				
	White muscardine	*Beauveria bassina*	Prevalent	Prevalent	Winter Season
	Green muscardine	*Nomuraea rileyi*	Prevalent	Prevalent	
	Yellow muscardine	*Paecilomyces farinous*	Not Rep.	Prevalent	
	Red muscardine	*Sporosporelle uvella*	Not Rep.	Prevalent	
	Orange muscardine	*Sterigtnatocystis japonica*	Not Rep.	Prevalent	
	Aspergillosis	*Aspergillus flavus*	Not Rep.	Prevalent	
		Aspergillus oryzae	Prevalent	Prevalent	

pesticides, sometimes causes large-scale loss in crops. Other attributed causes are high temperature, high humidity, bad ventilation, bad quality leaves (dirty leaf, coarse leaf, leaf not suited to the age and stage of the larvae, wet and fermented leaf etc.), overfeeding, decreased alkalinity.

Infection takes place due to some disturbances in the metabolic activity of the caterpillar. When the alkalinity of the gut is reduced, the bacteria, which are normally present on the mulberry leaves, find a medium in which they multiply rapidly. Matsura, renowned scientist, reported that worms fed on leaves containing little chlorophyll also suffer from flacharie. Improper feeding also renders silkworms susceptible to the diseases. Infected worms become soft, skin elasticity is lost and vomit yellowish fluid. Initially larvae become yellowish in colour, then turn brown and finally become dark black after death. That is why the disease is also known as Kalashira. Due to bacterial purification, internal organs of diseased larvae become liquidified ailing all sorts of dysenteries. In general vomiting, diarrhoea, thickening of peritrophic membrane, brown/yellowish colour of gut contents, discolouration of body and purification accompanied by blackening of body is the symptoms of larvae suffering from flacharie.

Flacharie disease of silkworms is caused not by any special bacterium but by sets of bacteria, which occur on mulberry leaves. The important ones are *Streptococcus pastorlanus, Streptococcus bombycis, Bacillus megatehum, Bacillus sotto, Bacillus A, Bacillus coli, Bacillus mycoides, Micrococcus A etc.* Bacterial diseases of silkworms are divided into three major types:

A. Bacterial septicemia

B. Bacterial diseases of digestive tract,

C. Bacterial toxicosis

A. Bacterial septicemia: Bacteria reside and multiply enormously in haemolymph of larvae, pupae and moths. Septicemia during larval stages leads to larval mortality, whereas infection during pupal stage leads to a large number of melted cocoons, thus affecting egg production on the one hand and making it unsuitable for reeling on the other.

Causal agents: Septicemia is caused by multiplication of large number of bacteria in haemolymph. The principal pathogenic bacteria are large and small Bacilli, Streptococci, and Staphylococci etc. Septicemia is of two types:

(i) **Black thorax septicemia:** It is caused by 'Bacillus' species belonging to the family Bacillaceae of the order Eubacteriales. These are gram positive, spore-forming rod shaped bodies occurring either singly or in chains. Septicemia spreads very quickly. It takes just 10 hrs to kill the larvae at 28°C. At higher temperature and under epidemic conditions, the infected larvae will die within 5-6 hrs. The size of Bacillus is 1-1.5 microns, spores sub-terminal and flagella peritrichate.

(ii) **Red septicemia:** The disease is also known as 'Court' in Europe and 'Rangi' in India. It is minor bacterial disease. Serratia marcescens occurred singly or in small chains causes it. They are gram negative and non-sporulating. The genus *Serratia* usually produces a characteristic red or pink pigment, although sometimes white or rose strain also occurs. They are 0.6-1.0 × 0.5 microns in size and look like small rods, flagella peritrichate with rose red colonies.

Differences between black and red septicemia: In black septicemia blackening starts from thorax and extends to the dorsal vessel till the whole body darkens and rots. In red septicemia the whole body softens taking a slightly reddish tinge. The disease is identified by the crimson red colour of the affected silkworm larvae and pupae at the time of death or after death.

Symptoms: Silkworms affected with septicemia disease have the following characteristics:

Sluggish movement, decreased appetite, straightened body, swollen thorax, shrinkage of abdominal segments, vomiting and soft or bead-like excreta, loss of clasping power of legs, soft and discoloured body, body wall ruptures easily emitting foul smelling fluid. In general, the fore intestine may be swollen and the posterior part shrunken in dead larvae.

Pathogenesis: The bacteria exist mainly in the natural environment, in the soil and adhering to the dust particles, on mulberry leaves, in the rearing rooms and appliances. Warm and humid environment (high temperature and humidity) is most favourable for the propagation of these bacteria. These diseases occur mostly at the later part of the larval life.

Prevention: High temperature and high humidity conditions are most favourable for the propagation of the bacteria responsible for the disease. Therefore, this disease occurs in the seasons having high temperature and humidity. Irrespective of the health of the larvae, the disease is transmitted mainly through injury or wound and multiplies in haemolymph disrupting the normal physiological functions causing septicemia. The disease can be controlled by taking the following steps:

- Maintenance of hygienic conditions.
- Avoid injury of larvae.
- Avoid overcrowding of larvae.
- Avoid accumulation of faeces in rearing beds.
- Affected silkworm larvae should be isolated from the healthy ones as soon as possible.
- Destroy the affected worms by burning or burying deep in soil.
- Disinfections of rearing rooms, appliances etc should be done with 2% formalin without fail at the end of each rearing.

B. **Bacterial diseases of digestive tract:** The disease is also known as 'Transparent Head Disease'. Various theories have been advocated as the cause of this disease. These are—the bacterial theory, the non-bacterial theory and the intermediate theory. The intermediate theory has been widely accepted. Multiplication of bacteria in digestive tract leads to the swelling and transparency of head. The bacteria associated with the progress of disease are gram-positive *Streptococcus* sp. belonging to the family Streptocceae. Under poor nourishment and adverse environmental and rearing conditions, the physiological metabolic activity of the digestive tract is disturbed which is responsible for the disease. There is no doubt that poor quality of mulberry leaves provided to the larvae particularly during the chawki rearing is one of the major reasons for the outbreak of the disease during the final stage of fifth instars larvae. For example, if weather remains cloudy or rainy for a long time or temperature is much higher than the desired level or if just before brushing unhealthy conditions prevail, the quality of mulberry leaves deteriorates fast and if these leaves are supplied to the silkworms during 1st to 3rd instars the larvae become victim of the disease during fifth instars.

Symptoms: Symptoms are not always uniform. It varies according to the time and occurrence, kind of bacteria multiplying in digestive system, the race of silkworm, environmental conditions and quality of leaf. In general, the symptoms are poor appetite, sluggish movement, transparent head, stunted body size and retarded body growth. The diseased worms often hide under the mulberry leaves. In case of late stage attack, worms remain in the spinning tray for a long period without spinning cocoon till they die. In majority of cases, the body becomes black but sometimes it turns red due to presence of *Bacillus prodigiosus* or green because of presence of *Bacillus pyocyaneus*. Mixed propagation of bacteria may result sometimes some other colour also. This disease occurs mostly in young silkworms and just after moulting

Prevention

- Feed nutritious and suitable foliage according to the age and stage of the larvae to raise healthy and stable silkworm crops. Leaves grown under shade, lack of fertilizers, muddy, dusty and withered leaves and leaves poor in food value should be avoided for feeding.
- Maintain hygienic conditions.
- Diseased larvae should be removed from the rearing bed.
- Maintain optimum temperature and humidity.
- Addition of chloramphenicol to the diet has been observed to bring considerable improvement.
- Incubation and hatching should be performed at proper temperature, photoperiod and humidity. Silkworm becomes weak if incubated at higher temperature or greater dryness.
- Cold storage of freshly hatched larvae should be avoided as far as possible.
- Selection of suitable race, resistance to adverse conditions is also very much essential for successful cocoon crop.
- Silkworm should be handled carefully during moulting phase and it should be ensured that they do not starve for a long time particularly if the temperature is high.

C. **Bacterial toxicosis:** Bacterial toxicosis is also known as 'Soto' disease and is caused when silkworms encountered toxin-producing bacilli. The disease is particularly caused by *Bacillus thuringiensis sotto*) belonging to the family Bacillaceae of the order Eubacteriales. It produces toxin substance and hence the disease is known as toxicosis. The infection is usually per-oral but can also take place through wounds or injury. After entering into the silkworm body, the toxin crystals are dissolved in alkaline digestive fluid and absorbed through the gastric wall. It affects the nervous system leading to paralysis. The pathogens not only multiply in the body of silkworm but also in the pupae.

In Bt strain 7 different toxins have been reported -

(i) Phosphalipase (BT- exotoxin)

(ii) Thermostable exotoxin (BT B-exotoxin)

(iii) Enzyme-may not be toxin (BT Y-exotoxin)

(iv) Protein parasporal crystal (BT- endotoxin)

(v) Labile toxin

(vi) Water soluble toxin isolated from commercial formulate

(vii) A mouse factor exotoxin

Acute bacterial toxicosis: The symptoms are lack of appetite, sluggishness, lack of skin tension followed by shrinkage of body, diarrhoea, constipation, loss of clasping power of legs, lifting of head, paralysis followed by death. The death may occur within 10 minutes to a few hours. The body of insect becomes black shortly after death. The time from initial infection to death is shorter when temperature and humidity are higher. The corpse becomes dark brown and the inner organs of body are liquidified. If the skin bursts, a black foul smelling liquid oozes out.

Chronic bacterial toxicosis: It is caused by ingestion of small quantity of BT crystal toxin. Mulberry leaf intake is reduced, faeces become irregular shaped and occasional vomiting occurs. Thorax and abdominal tips become transparent and muscles develop paralysis. The other symptoms of infected larvae are loss of clasping power of the legs, softness of skin, retarded growth and light brown colouration.

Prevention

- Diseased larvae must be removed from the healthy ones and be destroyed.

- As usual, rearing house and equipments must be thoroughly disinfected.
- Larvae should be prevented for swelling of toxic substances.
- In order to destroy and eliminate the disease by disinfections, it has been found that the conidia of *B. thuringiensis* are killed within 10 minutes of treatment with 1% corrosive sublimate or within 3 hrs of treatment with 2% formaldehyde.
- Treatment with 0.05 and 1% Sodium hypochlorite for 1-30 minutes reduced both the viability and infectivity.
- Streptomycin sulphate, Gentacixcin, Cloxocillin and Kanamycin at 0.05 and 1% concentration supplemented through mulberry leaf as feed to silkworm leads to lowering the occurrence of the disease.

Gattine: The disease is caused by the combination of a non-inclusion type virus and a bacterium *Streptococcus bombycis*. It is popularly known as Sapla (Bengal) and Hasirumoto (Karnataka) disease. *Streptococcus bombycis* plays a significant role in the development of gattine, although it is not the principal cause. Gattine virus affects the cylindrical epithelial cells of the mid-gut causing nuclear lesions followed by the bacterial infection. The virus excreted along with faeces causes contamination during rearing.

A submicroscopic virus causes the gattine but it alone does not significantly alter the pH of the intestinal contents of the diseased larvae from that of healthy silkworm. Due to invasion of *Streptococci* the intestinal contents characteristically become more alkaline. The symptoms of gattine manifested, only when the combination of *Streptococcus* and virus occurs in the susceptible silkworm.

Symptoms: The anterior or cephalic end of the insect becomes swollen and almost transparent. In addition to this, the other symptoms of gattine are lack of appetite, ejection of a clear ropy liquid from the mouth, which is slightly alkaline than the normal secretion. Further, the digestive tract in the thorax and fore part of the abdomen does not contain any mulberry leaf but only gastric juice. Therefore, these areas become transparent.

Techniques for bacterial staining: Crystal-violet saffranin method:

- Make a bacterial smear on a slide and heat it by passing the slide on the flame.
- Immerse the slide in ammonium oxalate crystal violet stain for one minute.
- Rinse the slide in running tap water for 5 seconds.
- Rinse quickly with 'Gram iodine' solution and immerse in it for one minute.
- Dip the slide in 'n-propyl alcohol' for one minute and give three changes separately for one minute in each.
- Counter stain in saffranin for one minute.
- Mount in DPX and observe under oil immersion.
- Gram-positive bacteria take blue stain and gram-negative red stain.

Preparation of solution

(a) Ammonium oxalate crystal violet solution

Solution A: Dissolve 2 gm of crystal violet in 40 ml of 95% ethyl alcohol.

Solution B: Dissolve 1.6 gm of ammonium oxalate in 160 ml of distilled water. Mix solutions A and B.

(b) Grams' iodine solution

First dissolve 2 gm of potassium iodide in 5 ml of distilled water; add 1 gm of iodine and dissolve. To this solution add 295 ml of distilled water.

Immune responses to bacterial infection

Immunity is a type of resistance to disease in which an organism is resisting a pathogen and thus resisting the development of the disease. Immunity is an added ability acquired naturally and or artificially. Immunity can be divided into two categories:

(a) Naturally acquired (Active and passive)

(b) Artificially acquired (Active and passive)

Immunity is the result of the role played by numerous factors largely mechanical and physiological in nature. An immunity that has been gained by an organism during its lifetime is known as acquired immunity. Naturally an infectious agent acquires acquired immunity as a result of an attack and artificially acquired immunity is due to infectious agents or vaccines inoculated into the insect. All of these in turn may be active or passive.

Active immunity is one in which the host has a direct or active participation. Along with the production of antibodies by the host itself, there is usually an accompanying increased cellular reactivity and a general increase in resistance to the microorganism concerned. Passive immunity occurs to a host that is the recipient of antibodies formed in the body of animal of the same or different species. It involves no active generation of protective substances by the immunized insect.

FUNGAL DISEASES

Fungal diseases (mycosis) in silkworm are caused by parasitic fungi. Two major kinds of such diseases are Muscardine and Aspergillosis. There are more than 10 types of fungi, which cause Muscardine, and signs of the disease vary with the type of infecting fungus. Depending on the colour of the spores of fungus which covers the body of the silkworm giving characteristic colour have been named as white muscardine, green muscardine, yellow muscardine, black muscardine, red muscardine etc. The different types of muscardine and their causal organism is presented below:

White muscardine: The white muscardine disease is known by different names viz., sunnakaddi, sunnakattu, chitti and chenakatu. This disease occurs mainly during

Different kinds of muscardines infecting silkworm

Muscardine type	*Causal organism*
White muscardine	*Beauveria bassiana*
Green muscardine	*Spicaria prasina*
Yellow muscardine	*Paecilomyces farinosus*
Black muscardine	*Beauveria brongniartti* *Metarrhizium anisopliae*
Red muscardine	*Sporosporella uvella*
Yellow red muscardine	*Paecilomyces fumosorosea*
Purplish-red muscardine	*Spicaria rubida*
Orange muscardine	*Sterigmatocystis japonica*
Aspergillosis/Brown muscardine	*Aspergillus flavus*
	Aspergillus tamari
Pencillosis	*Penicillum citrinum* *P. granulatum*

rainy and winter seasons under moderate to low temperature and high humidity conditions. The disease is mostly caused by fungus *Beauveria bassiana* belonging to the family Moniliaceae, order Moniliales of the class Fungi Imperfecti. The developmental cycle of *Beaueria bassiana* consists of three stages—conidium, vegetative mycelium and aerial mycelium. At the initial stage, it is very difficult to differentiate the infected larvae from the healthy ones. However, as the disease progresses, the larvae gradually loss appetite and become inactive, skin elasticity is lost, larvae stops movement and finally die. Before death symptoms of diarrhoea and vomiting appear. Initially the body of dead larva is elastic but gradually it hardens due to low water content in the body. Now mycelia start growing from the spiracles and inter-segmental membranes covering the body except head. When the entire body becomes covered with white powdery material becomes the source of further contamination. As the infected silkworms are covered with white powdery material, the disease is called white muscardine. Larvae unlike other diseases do not rot or decay but remain hard as the fungus secretes double oxalate-crystal of ammonium and magnesium. During moth stage, the body is hardened and the wings fall off easily.

The spores of white muscardine penetrate through an open wound on the skin of silkworm larvae and germinate under optimal thermal conditions. However, the temperature and humidity both promotes germination of spores but role of humidity is the uppermost. Under optimum conditions, germination of spores takes 6-8 hrs. The spores of *Beaueria bassiana* can survive in the natural environment for a few months to a year. The time duration between infection and death is generally 2-3 days for the 1st and 2nd instar larvae, 3-4 days for 3rd instar, 4-5 days for 4th instar and 5-6 days for final instar depending on the temperature, humidity and health of larvae.

Source of infection: *Beaueria bassiana* is a facultative parasite having a variety of source of infection and chief being the exuviae and faeces of the diseased silkworms. The spores of *Beaueria bassiana* are light and fine and hence can be blown by the wind to silkworm rearing units and their surroundings making them the site of infection.

Mode of infection: The primary mode is contact followed by wound infection. No infection occurs by ingestion.

Predisposing factor: Susceptibility varies according to the different stages of the silkworm. The young stages are more susceptible than the later stages and within the same instars freshly moulted larvae are more susceptible than those entering into the moult. The infection rate decreases with the advancement in the development but the ripe larvae and pupa again show increased susceptibility. A relative humidity of 90-100% is more favourable for the germination of conidia, which does not occur below a relative humidity of 70%. Disease tends to occur when the ceiling of the rearing room is low, ventilation poor or when the rearing house is located near the water source.

Prevention and control

- Rearing rooms, rearing surroundings, rearing equipments etc. should be thoroughly disinfected with 2% formalin or 5% bleaching powder solution.

- Avoid low temperature and high humidity during rearing.
- Rearing bed should be kept thin and dry to avoid germination of spores.
- Bed refuse and diseased larvae should be disposed of properly.
- Anti-Muscardine powder can fruitfully check the spread of disease, which included application of formalin chaff and Dithane M-45.

Formalin chaff application: For preparation of formalin chaff paddy husk is charred or burnt either by roasting or burning without making ash. Depending on the stage of larvae, the required strength of formalin (I and II instars-0.4%, III instars-0.5%, IV instars-0.6% and V instars-0.8%) is mixed with the burnt paddy husk in the ratio of 1:10 by volume and mixed thoroughly. The mixture is sprinkled evenly on the larvae, which are then covered with paraffin paper. After half an hour, the paraffin paper is removed and feeding is given. Application can be done after each moult but half an hour before the resumption of the feed.

Dithane M- 45 or Captan application: Dithane M-45 and Captan are the two commonly available fungicides used for the control of Muscardine in combination with levigated china clay at the concentration of 1% during I, II and III instars and 2% during IV and V instars. The mixture is dusted on newly born larvae and also after each moult half an hour before the resumption of feed. The quantity required is 2-3 gm per 100 sq.cm. area during I, II and III instars and 4-5 gm during IV and V instars. It should not be dusted when the larvae are either in mould or in feeding stage.

(ii) **Green Muscardine:** This disease is caused by the infection of *Spicaria prasina* and *Nomuraea rileyi* belonging to family Moniliaceae of the class Fungi Imperfecti. The cause of its infection is more or less same as in the case of white Muscardine. At serious infection stage larvae vomits fluid, shows symptoms of diarrhoea and finally dies. Initially

the dead bodies are soft but gradually harden. In two or three days, mycelia emerge from inter-segmental membranes and spiracles. Subsequently the body becomes covered with mycelia and conidiospores. A few days later green conidiophores cover the entire body. Generally, 4-5 days after infection, the larva loses appetite, turns yellowish in colour and appears sick. On progress of the disease large moist blackish spots appear all over the body. The dead body of the larva appears white in colour initially, which turns green at a later stage. The appearance of the green colour of the dead body is due to the formation of conidia, which are also green in colour. Optimum temperature for germination of conidia is 22-24°C. Temperature above 25°C is not favourable for germination. Treatment with bleaching powder containing 0.2% active chlorine for 5 minutes can inactivate germination. The course of the disease is longer than that of white muscardine and death takes place 7-10 days after infection. Prevention and control are same as in the case of white Muscardine.

(iii) **Yellow Muscardine:** This disease is caused by the infection of yellow Muscardine fungus *Isaria farinosus* or *Paecilomyces farinosus*. It affects both young and late stage larvae. Their death rate is very high particularly during 5th instars and mounting or during cocooning. The symptoms of this disease are more or less same as of white Muscardine except the formation of large number of yellow conidiophores. The spores are oval or spherical in shape. The incidence of disease is greater during autumn.

(iv) **Black Muscardine:** The disease is caused by the infection of *Oospora destructor* or *Beauveria brongniartti* or *Metarrhizium anisopliae*. Its incidence compared to other Muscardine disease is much lower. This disease occurs mainly during

hot summer and autumn silkworm rearing. Symptoms are same as in white Muscardine except formation of large number of black conidiophores leading to black appearance of the diseased larvae.

Aspergillosis: *Aspergillus* species causing aspergillosis of silkworm have been extensively studied, as they are also capable of infecting plants, animals, leather materials, storage grains, animal feeds and dairy products in addition to being pathogenic to a variety of insects. The disease is prevalent in young instar larvae during high humidity conditions. The fungi responsible for the disease are included in Aspergillus and Sterigmatocystis group belonging to the family Moniliaceae of class Fungi Imperfecti. *Aspergillus flavus, A. sojae, A. parasiticus, A. fiavipes, A. nidulans, A. melleus, A. fumigates, A. etegans, A. niger, A. oryzae* and *A. ochraceus* are pathogenic to silkworm.

Classification: Anamorphic stage classification (Domsch *et al.*, 1980)

Kingdom	: Fungi
Division:	: Eumycota
Sub-division:	: Deuteromycotina
Class	: Hyphomycetes
Order	: Moniliales
Family	: Moniliaceae
Genus	: *Aspergillus*

Though Aspergilli are saprophytic, they are reported to be pathogenic to several insects in addition to *B. mori* (Table 75). Patil (1989) reported *A. flavus* on *B. mori* from India. Freshly hatched larvae are the most susceptible to these fungi. With the larval development, the resistance of the larvae gradually decreases and the resistance is maximum during the peak growth period of 5th instars. Thereafter, it once decreases again soon after pupation. Silkworms are very susceptible to these fungal infections. Usually the susceptibility increases with the increase in humidity. When the humidity is 70%, the disease is rare but as the humidity increases, the incidence of disease also increases. The favourable temperature for germination of conidia is 30-35°C. Infected larvae stops eating of mulberry leaf, becomes lethargic, show body tension, lustrousness and then die. Of all the fungi that cause diseases in the silkworm, the conidia of *A. flavus* are the most resistant to environmental factors, being able to survive up to one year or more.

Table 10.2: Lepidopteron host range of *Aspergillus* sp. pathogenic to silkworm and reported from India

Name of insect	*Pest on*	*References*
A. *Aspergillus flavus*		
Nephantis serinopa	Coconut palm	Oblisami *et al.* (1969)
Azogophieps scalaris	Sesbania	Oblisami *et al.* (1969)
Amsacta albistriga	Groundnut	Oblisami *et al.* (1969)
Utethesia pulchella	Sun hemp	Oblisami *et al.* (1969)
Achoea janata	Castor	Oblisami *et al.* (1969)
Euproctis fraternal	Plum	Batra & Sinha (1971)
Parasa lepida	Coconut	Pillai & Ayyar (1969)
Spilosoma oblique	Agricultural crops	Battu *et al.* (1971)
Spodoptera litura	Agricultural crops	Battu *et al.* (1971)
Pelopidas mathias	Rice	Veluswamy *et al.* (1973)
Chilo parteilus	Maize & Sorghum	Atwal *et al.* (1973)
Lymantria obfuscata	Cacao	Nair & Premkumar (1974)
B. *A. parasiticus*		
Drosicha magniferae	Citrus & Mango	Saxena & Rawatt (1968)
C. *A. candidus*		
Indarbela sp.	Guava & Plum	Singh & Singh (1984)
Utethesia pulchella	Crotalaria	Mathur *et al.* (1970)
D. *Aspergillus tamarii*		
Azygophleps scalaris	Sesbania	Sithanantham (1970)
Dasychria menctosa	Mulberry	Chinnaswamy *et al.* (1986)
E. *Aspergillus nidulans*		
Samia cynthia ricini	Eri	Devaiah *et al.* (1982-83)

(v) **Brown muscardine:** This is known to be caused by more than 10 species of the genus *Aspergillus*. Most of these fungi are distributed in the environment. They are saprophytic and become pathogenic only when conditions are favourable. Aspergillosis caused by fungus *Aspergllius* is called brown muscardine. Young larvae are very much susceptible to this and die within 2-3 days of infection. Conidiospore are greenish-yellow mixed with brown. It is capable of growing and producing spores even on rearing equipments, walls and floors of rearing rooms besides moist chopping board. All these materials should be disinfected thoroughly to check the occurrence of this disease.

***Aspergillus oryzae* disease:** This type of aspergillosis is caused by *A. oryzae.* Symptoms of the disease resembles to those of brown muscardine except the formation of spores on the surface, which show light yellow colour mixed with dirty brown.

***Aspergillus coracles* disease:** The disease is very rare compared to other muscardine diseases. The infection level is also very mild. The spores produced are usually orange yellow in colour.

Red muscardine disease: This type of aspergillosis is caused by *Isaria fumosorosea.* This fungus has very weak pathogenecity to silkworm. The bodies of the infected worms occasionally show red coloured patches a few hours before death. When insect is cut opened, a black red powdery mass of spores is seen. The spore germinates upon exposure to moisture. The parasite destroys the functional organs completely. The 'Kojic acid' has been reported to be produced by *Aspergillus oryzae, A. flavus,* A. *candidus, A. fumigatus, A. giganteus. A. niger.* There is close relationship among Kojic acid production, resistance to formalin and virulence to the silkworm larvae. The isolate with a high productivity of kojic acid showed a high resistance to formalin and severe virulence to silkworm larvae.

Dilthiocarbamate fungicides were found to be effective for bed disinfections. Also disinfections by organosulfurous fungicides such as 2% Maneb, 2% Zineb and 2% Mancozeb resulted in above 90% survival of silkworm larvae. Bavistin, Bayleton, Vitavax, Dithane M-45, Daconil and formalin were found controlling the aspergillosis of silkworm. Though more than ten Aspergillus sp. is known to infect silkworm *Bombyx mori,* fungi belonging to *A. flavus* group mostly cause the disease in Japan. Whereas in India, natural infection of silkworm with only *A. tamarii* is considered to be prevalent though infection with *A. flavus* and *A. niger* also occurs. So far many silkworm breed have been screened for their susceptibility to *A. flavus* and *A. tamarii.* It is a boon to tropics that multivoltine genotypes are less susceptible to *Aspergillus* compared to bivoltine as the former are usually used as maternal parents in hybrid egg production.

VIRAL DISEASES

A virus is a biological entity, which lacks metabolism but undergoes multiplication at the expense of host cells. Disease caused by virus poses a great problem to sericulture industry. Insect viral diseases are of two types:

A. **Inclusion type:** It includes Nuclear polyhedrosis and Cytoplasmic polyhedrosis.

B. **Non-inclusion type:** It includes infectious flacherie and gattine.

Inclusion type (nuclear and cytoplasmic polyhedrosis} can easily be identified through ordinary microscope while the non-inclusion type can be detected only through electron/fluorescent microscope and serological tests.

A. Inclusion type

(i) **Nuclear polyhedrosis:** It is one of the serious diseases in tropical countries and occurs throughout the year. The disease is also known by various names viz., grasserie/jaundice/milky disease/fatty degeneration disease/hanging disease. The silkworms, which mostly fail to spin cocoons, are found to suffer from this disease. The disease prevails throughout the year but is intensive during summer and rainy seasons.

Causes of the disease: *Borrelina bombycis* virus belonging to the family Baculoviridae, which is a parasite principally on the nuclei of certain cells (trachea/epithelial cells, adipose tissue cells, dermal cells and blood cells), causes the disease. Occasionally, the nucleus of middle and posterior portion of silk gland cells are also affected. It initiates the morbid process and ends in the elaboration of polyhedral bodies. The virus is rod shaped. The polyhedra are usually octadecahedral or hexahedral but rarely tetragonal or trigonal. Infection mostly takes place through feeding to polyhedra contaminated mulberry leaf but sometimes also through wounds. Factors influencing the outbreak of disease are high temperature and high humidity, their sudden fluctuations, bad ventilation, ineffective disinfections, feeding of tender leaves during late stages, use of surface contaminated laying, inadequate larval spacing, larval starvation, excessive moisture in rearing bed etc.

Infection: Disease begins with the digestion of infectious material. It has been assumed that alkaline reaction of the silkworm gut as well as certain enzymes present there dissolve the polyhedra resulting in the release of virus, which then passes through intestinal wall into the body cavity of the insect and invades the cells of susceptible tissues. It has been shown that grasserie virus reproduces very actively when the silkworm is weak.

Symptoms: No external symptoms are noticed during early part of the disease except slightly sluggishness of the larvae. As the disease advances, appetite decreases and skin loses its tension. Initially, skin shows oily shining appearance, then it becomes thin and fragile and body becomes milky white with inter-segmental swellings. The diseased larvae in the final stage of attack shows pronounced swellings at the inter-segments resulting in bamboo cane-like appearance of the larvae with distinct nodes. The fragile skin is prone to rupture easily, liberating liquefied body contents containing innumerable number of polyhedra, which becomes the source of secondary contamination. If the disease occurs just before moulting, larvae do not enter into moult and infact many victims do not moult at all. Another characteristic symptom of the disease is that the infected larvae becomes restless and crawl aimlessly along the ridges or rims of rearing trays and subsequently fall off from the rearing tray on the ground, where they usually crawl in a circle and die. Death takes place after 4-5 days of infection in earlier stages and often 5-7 days in the later or grown-up stages. Diseased larvae also lose clasping power of the pseudo and true legs except the caudal legs by which it hang with the head downward. Hence, the disease is also known as hanging disease. No external change is observed in pupae at the initial stages. However, towards the end skin is easily ruptured on handling as the poorly, infected worms fail to spin cocoons and die, whereas, if the infection is late, infected larvae are able to spin cocoons but die inside producing melted cocoons.

Prevention

- Silkworm rearing rooms, mulberry storage rooms, mounting rooms, equipments and rearing premises should be thoroughly disinfected besides surface disinfection of laying before brushing as precautionary measure.
- Larvae should be reared under strict hygienic conditions.
- Temperature and humidity should be maintained according to age and stage of silkworm. In other words, low or high temperature and humidity must be avoided during rearing period.
- Nutritious quality leaves should only be fed to the silkworms.
- Proper spacing and required quantity of leaves should be provided.
- Proper bed drying is necessary before each feed.
- Great care should be taken in removing the dead and sick caterpillars. They should be removed avoiding breaking of skin and must be disposed

suitably either by burning or by burying. The litter pit should be away from the rearing house.

- Ensure proper ventilation.
- Pupal body is almost homogenized and sometimes black markings are observed on the body at the time of death, if the infection is heavy.

In addition to the above preventive measures, use of certain bed disinfectants are also being reported to prevent secondary contamination and spread of disease viz., Resham Keet Oushad (RKO), Vijetha, Labex, Resham Jyothi etc.

(ii) **Cytoplasmic polyhedrosis:** It is one of the major diseases, which occurs mainly during summer season.

Causes of the disease: *Smithies* virus belonging to the family Reoviridae causes the disease. It infects and forms polyhedra mainly in the cell cytoplasm of the mid-gut cylindrical cells. The infection in the midget starts from the posterior portion and slowly proceeds towards the anterior portion. The polyhedra varies greatly in size from 1-10μ. The shape is usually tetragonal or hexagonal but rarely trigon.

However, the infection takes place through the feeding of contaminated mulberry leaf but the major factor influencing the outbreak of the disease is the inferior quality of mulberry leaf, high temperature and fluctuations in temperature and humidity. The major source of contamination and spread is the rearing bed itself as the virus with the polyhedra excreted along with the faecal matter.

Symptoms: Affected larvae show symptoms of slow growth, stunted body, reduced mulberry leaf consumption and dull white colour. Individual sizes vary greatly and larvae show delayed moulting. The infected larvae excreta appears soft whitish containing numerous polyhedra. Occasionally the larval anal region is soiled with rectal protrusion. On dissection of infected larvae, mid gut is seen as whitish and opaque compared to the greenish and transparent mid gut of the healthy larvae.

Prevention and control: The cytoplasmic polyhedral virus, occluded in the polyhedra can persist for more than one year inside the rearing room, appliances and surroundings and hence thorough disinfection is very much essential. The infected larvae, faecal matter and bed refuse should be destroyed either by burning or by decomposition in a manure pit. Care should be taken to rear silkworms under proper temperature, humidity and hygienic conditions. On appearance of disease trays, seat papers, nets and foam pads should be replaced. Silkworms should be fed with good quality of mulberry leaf procured from plants grown under optimal conditions of sunlight and manure. Ensure proper disinfection of egg surface. Evolution of highly resistance breed will play an important role in minimizing the incidence of this disease. Chemicals like 1% calcium hydroxide can be sprayed on mulberry leaf and fed to larvae to reduce the occurrence of cytoplasmic polyhedrosis.

B. Non-inclusion type (Flacherie): Flacherie is a 'sub-chronic' disease resulting primarily due to physiological disorders and secondarily by the infection of bacterium. The term flacherie is a general one used to include dysentery conditions due to microbial and amicrobial factors in silkworm. Flacherie may be due to virus, bacteria and physiological disorders.

(i) **Infectious flacherie:** It is highly contagious and disastrous disease found in the entire silkworm rearing areas.

Causes of disease: Non-occluded Morator virus belonging to the family Picornaviridae causes the disease. The virus is globular and measures 24-28nm. Infection usually takes place per-orally. As infection advances, the virus is dispersed in the lumen of the digestive tract and excreted with the faeces. Similar to cytoplasmic polyhedrosis the infection starts from the anterior region of the mid gut and progresses towards the posterior region but never exhibits the chalky white appearance.

Symptoms: Symptoms include loss of appetite, transparent cephalothorax, shrinkage of the body, retarded growth and empty foregut followed by vomiting of gastric juice and diarrhoea. The infected worms are sluggish and sticky with head and thorax upheld motionless. Infected larvae evacuate excreta in chain or string or irregular shaped or sometimes exhibit diarrhoea. They omit fluid often. The skin characteristically becomes pale with very light reddish tinge. Shrinkage of the body is also a characteristic symptom of the disease. Some individuals do exhibit rectal protrusion. However, the diagnosis of this disease is neither possible through external appearance nor through ordinary microscope but can be detected by fluorescent antibody technique or by staining the infected cells with pyronine methyl green. Latex agglutination and other serological tests are also being used for the detection of this disease.

Prevention and control: As the virus exhibits high virulence and may retain its pathogenicity in the body of dead larvae for 2-3 years, the rearing rooms, appliances and surroundings must be thoroughly disinfected by using 2% formalin and 0.5% calcium hydroxide or bleaching powder containing 1% active chlorine in it. Silkworm rearing under optimum climatic and hygienic conditions and better-feed arrangement helps in the reduction of the incidence of the disease. The diseased larvae with bed refuse should be burnt or put in manure pit for thorough decomposing. Leaves used for feeding should be good. Nutritionally too mature leaves at early instars and tender leaves at the later instars should be avoided. Soiled and diseased leaves moist with raindrops should also be avoided for feeding. Yamatari (1977) reported that 5% of infected larvae in a batch in early instars could lead to complete failure of crops. Thus, it is advisable to destroy such batches.

(ii) **Densonucleosis:** The disease is caused by a non-occluded virus belonging to the genus *Densovirus*

of the family Parvoviridae. Infection usually takes place orally. The major source of cross contamination is the virus excreted along with the faeces by the silkworm. The *Bombyx mori* DNVs are categorized into three groups' viz., BmDNVI, BmDNV2 and BmDNV3. The size of BmDNVI, BmDNV2 and BmDNV3 is approximately 22 ± 0.5 nm, 21-23 nm and 23-24 nm respectively.

Symptoms: Retardation of growth and shrinkage of body takes place in the infected larvae. Lack of flaccidity of flacherie-infected worms is the other major symptom of the disease.

Prevention and control: The larvae have been found to be highly thermo labile and when the larvae reared at 25-28°C were transferred to a temperature of 37°C the multiplication of virus in the body of the larvae is greatly reduced. Susceptibility of DNV was also found to be genetically controlled with some varieties and crosses made were found non-susceptible to the disease.

Staining procedure for Polyhedra of NPV and CPV: For identification of polyhedra of NPV and CPV following procedure is adopted -

- Make a smear of polyhedra on a slide and air dry.
- Fix in methyl alcohol for 5 sec and air dry.
- Stain in Giemsa for 45-60 minutes (1 or 2 drops of stock giemsa stain to 1 ml of distilled water).
- Wash in distilled water.
- Air dry or blot dry and mount in DPX.
- Examine under high power of microscope.
- Polyhedra stained in violet blue.

PROTOZOAN DISEASE

Pebrine disease of silkworm is one of the most serious maladies, which determines success, or failure of sericulture industry in any country. This is evidenced by the historical fact that the rise and fall of the pebrine disease corresponds with ups and downs of the sericulture industry in silk producing countries of the world. At one time or the other, it has severely damaged sericulture in all the silk producing countries of the world. The evidence showed that the pebrine outbreak started in France during 1845. France total production, which had reached 26,000,000 kg in 1853, fell to only 4,000,000 kg in 1865. During this time the disease was so rampant that sericulture in France was on the verge of collapse (Tatsuke, 1971). The history of research on pebrine disease progressed with the advancement of microbiology in 19th century. The name 'pebrine' was coined by De Quadrefages (1860) because of the appearance of pepper-like spots in the diseased larvae. The disease-causing microorganism was first observed in haemolymph of silkworms and was given the name 'Hematozoid' (Guerin-Menaville, 1849). Later Nageli of Germany stated that the disease is caused by a protozoan parasite and named this pathogen *Nosema bombycis*. Louis Pasteur called the disease as 'Corpuscles disease', made a detailed study on its growth and transmission, discovered that disease is contracted through transovam transmission within the body of mother moth, and suggested the method of preventing the disease. Balblain made it known that the pathogen of pebrine disease belongs to Protozoa. Later on in 1909, Stempell published the detailed of his study on the life history of the pathogen of pebrine disease. Based on the microsporidians unusual cytological and molecular characteristics such as primitive type of nuclear division, devoid of mitochondria, prokaryotic sized ribosome's and ribosomal RNAs, they have been phylogenetically considered as one of the earliest known eukaryotes (Vossbrinck *et al.*, 1987).

Classification

Phylum	: Protozoa
Sub-phylum	: Cnidospora
Class	: Sporozoa
Sub-class	: Neosporidia

Order	: Microsporidia
Sub-order	: Monocnidina
Family	: Nosematidae
Genus	: *Nosema*
Species	: *bombycis*

Causative agent

A microsporidian *Nosema bombycis* and strains of *Nosema* sp., NIK-2r, NIK-3h and NIK-4m.

Life cycle

- The life cycle of *Nosema bombycis* Nageli includes three stages namely, spore, planont and meront. Mature spore is oval or ovocylindrical and measures 3-4 microns by 1.5-2 microns with three-layered membrane, the inner, middle and outer. They can be observed at 600 magnifications under a microscope. The spores consists of:

  - Spore membrane, which encloses the sporoplasm.
  - Sporoplasm in the form of a girdle across the width of the spore.
  - Anterior and posterior vacuoles.
  - Two nuclei in the sporoplasm.
  - Posterior capsule.

The spores are highly refractive, appearing light green under the microscope. The outline is smooth and the spores are heavier than the water. The spore belongs to the dormant stage of pathogen and possesses great resistance. For example, they can remain infective after three years in the dried body of the female moth and remain active after being submerged in water for five months. The spore germinates in digestive juice of silkworm larva and produces a long polar filament having a length of more than 30 times that of the lengthwise dimension of the spore, on the end of which grows a sporoplasm (germs). The sporoplasm is having two nuclei and other cell organs and possesses the limiting membrane. The sporoplasm multiplies through fission, comes out of the haemolymph through intracellular spaces spreading to every part of the body, and lives in various systems particularly in the fat body and muscular tissue, becomes a nucleus and form spore after multiplication through fission. Spore formation is apansporoblastic, disporous and dimorphic. One type of sporoblast of the long polar tube type turns into single spore and many coil of polar tube. The other type is the sporoblast of the short polar tube, which turns into single spore with few coils of polar tube. Spores of short polar tube hatches directly in the host cell. The mature spore is unicellular endomembranous differentiation of its sporoblast. The pathogen of pebrine disease is capable to complete its life cycle within 4 days.

The pathogen parasitizes the ovary first and when 4th or 5th instar larvae after pupation and emergence becomes moth they move into egg and after deposition of eggs undergo multiplication and develops into a disease in the embryo or in the body of silkworm in next generation. After the deposition of eggs the pathogen grows and multiplies within the egg. The spores of different microsporidia infecting silkworms differ in their morphological characters, some are larger than mature spore, some are long, thin, and pear shaped with different size, shape and luster. Growth and multiplication of pathogen are influenced by the growth of its host. When egg enters into diapause, the growth and multiplication of pathogen stops simultaneously and when egg starts growing the pathogen also starts growing and multiplying.

When the degree of infection of the disease in egg is relatively high, the egg often becomes sterile or dead, but when the contamination is of low degree, the egg hatches and disease develops at larval stage causing the death of larvae at later stage of development. Most of the larvae infected through trans-ovum transmission show irregular moulting and growth before they reach to 2nd or 3rd instar and become tiny or undergrown larvae and die after discharging spores. If these larvae infected through trans-ovum transmission are reared together with healthy larvae, the spore discharged by infected larva : provide the source of contamination and digestion of spores by healthy silkworm results in spread of the disease. This process takes place in and around the 1st-2nd instars and contamination at these instars is called first stage of contamination.

The silkworms in the first stage of contamination show comparatively normal growth until the third instar but show symptoms from the later half of the 4th instar to the first half of the 5th instar and die by the time of mounting. Contamination rate differs from season to season. It is usually more in summer and autumn season than in spring season. The minimum amount of spores required for contamination through per oral infection varies with each instar. The silkworm infected at 2nd instars usually dies at the 5th instar, but infection at 3rd instar results death in cocooning frame or inside the cocoon and most of the larvae infected at 4th-5th instar undergo normal emergence, deposit eggs and transmit the disease to the next generation.

Physiological stability: Generally, large number of factors viz., temperature, humidity and abiotic components of the substrate influence the survival of microsporidians (Kramer, 1976). The spores belong to the dormant stage of pathogen and possess great resistance, can remain infective after 3 years in the dried body of the female moth and remain active after being submerged in water for 5 months (Lee, 1995). When kept in dark, the spores are reported to remain viable for as long as seven years, but when spores are directly exposed to sunlight, they remain viable for 6-7 hrs and when treated with hot water remain viable for just 5 minutes. Studies conducted on the viability of pebrine spores in soil and compost under tropical conditions showed survival of spores for a maximum period of 225 days in wet soil and a minimum of 135 in wet compost (Patil, 1993). Srikanta (1986) found that spores remained infective even after 150 days of refrigeration and after 90 days in moist soil and faeces and viability is lost in 60 days in dry soil and in 5 days when stored at room temperature. Resistance of spores to different disinfectants indicates that it can remain viable for 10-30 minutes in a solution of corrosive sublimate, for about 5 hrs in formalin and for about 10 hrs in chlorinated lime solution (diluted 10,000 times). Bleaching powder containing 1% and 3% active chlorine can render spore inactive in 30 minutes and 10 minutes respectively.

The growth and multiplication of pathogen in the eggs are influenced by the growth of the host. When the egg diapauses, the growth and multiplication of the pathogen stops simultaneously and when the eggs start growing by incubation, the pathogen also starts growing and multiplying. When the degree of infection is relatively high, the egg often becomes sterile or dead, but when the contamination is of low degree, the egg hatches and the disease develops at larval stage and cause death of larvae at later stages of development.

Alternate host

Most microsporidians prefer to have alternate hosts because of many advantages for them viz., dispersal, transmission and survival. The perpetual incidence of microsporidian infection in silkworms may be due to various sources of secondary contaminations including alternate hosts in and around mulberry garden. In addition to *N. bombycis,* seven other microsporidians belonging to the genera *Nosema, Pleistophora, Thelohania, Vairimphora* and *Leptomonas* sp. have been isolated from the silk moth (Govindan *et al.*, 1998). They differ in their spore morphology, target tissue and virulence and have been designated as M11, M12 and M14 *(Nosema* sp.), M24, M25, M27 *(Pleistophora* sp.) and M32 *(Thelohania* sp.) (Fujiwara, 1985) as indicated below:

Nosema bombycis is reported to infect *Samia cynthia ricini* and Indian tropical tasar, muga and Chinese tasar silkworms (Talukdar, 1980). *N. bombycis* is also found to infect a number of other insect species like *Telchinia violae, Pieris rapae, Brachyhinus lingustici, Choristoneura fumiferana, Bombyx mandarina, Glyphodes phyloalis, Chilo suppressalis, Arctia caja, Chilo simplex, Pieris rapae,*

Table 10.3: Different types of *Nosema* spores

Microsporidian	*Spore size (μm)*	*Site of infection*	*Virulence*
Nosema bombycis	3.8 × 2.2	Systemic	High
Nosema sp. (M11)	3.9 × 1.9	Various tissues	Low
Nosema sp. (M12)	4.2 × 2.7	Various tissues	Low
Nosema sp. (M14)	5.1 × 2.0	Various tissues	High
Pleistophora sp. (M24)	2.7 × 1.6	Mid gut	Low
Pleistophora sp. (M25)	3.2 × 1.8	Mid gut	Low
Pleistophora sp. (M27)	5.4 × 3.0	Various tissues	Low
Thelohania sp. (M32)	3.4 × 1.7	Muscle	Low

P. brassicae etc. (Samson *et al., 1999b)*. The lawn grass cut worm, *Spodoptera depravata* serves as a natural reservoir for the pathogen (Ishihara and Iwano, 1991), which shares the surface specific antigens with *N. bombycis* from *B. mori*. Its infection is systemic and results in transovarial transmission but is less virulent.

Epidemiology

Source of infection: The sources of pebrine infection are many including diseased larvae and wild insects affected by the diseases, excreta and faeces, urine of the ripe larvae and moths, discarded egg shells, pupal skin and scales, epicuticle and cocoon shell.

Routes of infection: These are mainly oral and transovarian transmission. Orally eating mulberry leaves contaminated by pathogen,infects silkworm. Trans-ovarian transmission occurs when the pebrine pathogen infects the 4th and 5th instar larvae, then invades the epithelial cells of the ovaries, from where the parasites are transferred to the oogonia, oocytes and nutritive cells. Parasitism of the oocytes results in the death of the eggs. The result of the embryonic infection, however, differs according to the stage when invasion of the embryos occurs. If infection takes place during the formation of embryos, then no embryonic development takes place and the eggs die.

Transmission within the rearing tray is caused by sick silkworms in which large quantities of pebrine spores formed are excreted with the faeces or attaches to epicuticles, thus contaminating the rearing tray and transmitting the disease to the healthy worms. Infection inside the rearing tray may be divided into two categories i.e. primary and secondary contamination. Primary contamination refers to that occurring in the 1st and 2nd instar and the excretion of spores taking place in the 3rd or 4th instars. Ingestion of these spores by other healthy larvae constitutes secondary contamination. Secondary contaminated silkworms are able to feed normally and become adult moths but they lay infected eggs. Young silkworms infected in the 1st or 2nd instars usually die in the 3rd instars but rarely in 4th instars. If infection occurs in 4th instars, development may proceed to the adult stage with laying of eggs but the eggs laid will be infected with pebrine. Young silkworms freshly moulted and starving larvae are more susceptible to the disease and show high mortality.

Symptoms

Symptoms of disease can be observed in developmental stages of silkworm viz., egg, larva, pupa and adult. In the egg stage poor egg number, piling of eggs one over the other, lack of gluey substance responsible for adherence of eggs to the substratum, lack of egg uniformity, more unfertilized and dead eggs, poor and irregular hatching are some of the symptoms of the disease. Poor appetite, retarded growth and development, unequal larvae, irregular moulting, sluggishness, wrinkled skin and rusty brown colour besides sometimes black pepper like spots on larval skin are the symptoms of the disease at larval stage. Pupae are flabby and swollen with lusterless and softened abdomen. Highly infected pupae fail to metamorphose into adult. Irregular moth emergence, clubbed wings, distorted antennae, improper mating, eggs with less gluey substance resulting in their detachment from the egg sheets, easily coming off of scales from wings and abdominal area are some of the symptoms of the disease at moth stage. Severely diseased eggs cannot hatch or if they do hatch, the larvae soon die. Slightly infected eggs do not show any special symptoms.

Examination of infection: Following procedures of examination is to be adopted for the identification of spores in order to monitor it:

- Take 20 larvae/pupae or moth in a cup of mixer.
- Add 80 ml of 0.6% potassium carbonate solution.
- Homogenize the larvae/pupae or moth by using mixer for 1-2 minutes at medium speed.
- After homogenizing, the contents are transferred into a glass beaker and are allowed to settle for 2-5 minutes.
- Filter the homogenate by using cotton or muslin cloth. Volume of filtrate recovered will be around 70 ml.
- Transfer the filtrate into 100 ml capacity of centrifuge tube. All the centrifuge tubes should be evenly balanced, capped and loaded into the centrifuge machine.
- Centrifugate at 3000 rpm for 5 minutes.
- Remove the centrifuge tube from the centrifuge machine.
- Discard slowly the supernatant.
- Suspend the sediment by shaking with a few drops of K_2CO_3 or by using a cyclomixer or with a glass rod, which facilitates uniform dissolving.
- Take smear from the centrifuge tube on the micro-slide, put the cover slip and examine under 600 magnification of microscope.
- Minimum 5 microscopic fields should be examined per smear.
- Two moth testers to ensure the detection of pebrine spores may perform examination.

Disposal of refuse

Refuse derived from the processes of examination should be dumped into a pit after disinfection with 5% bleaching powder solution or dumped and disinfected.

Depending on the intensity of spores, the infection is graded and recorded as:

Number of spores/field	*Grade*
1 - 3	±
4 - 10	1 +
11 - 30	2 +
31 - 100	3 +
101 - 300	4 +
301 - above	8

Prevention and control

- Produce healthy eggs to avoid embryonic infection. This can be achieved through scientific processing and inspection method of mother moth examination in silkworm egg production center.
- Dead eggs, dead larvae, dead pupae in the cocoon, dead moths, excrement of larvae from infected trays, exuviae of infected larvae and other possible sources of infection such as contaminated litter should be removed and destroyed.
- Conduct effective disinfections of rearing rooms, equipments, seed production units and surroundings.
- Maintain hygienic conditions during rearing and seed production.
- Laying should be surface sterilized with 2% formalin for 10 minutes before incubations in the rearing house.
- Inspection of eggshells and sample larvae by standard procedure during each instar for possible presence of pebrine.
- Immediate destruction of infected crops, if noticed pebrine.
- Synchronization of rearing to facilitate effective monitoring.
- Monitoring and examination of unequal larvae in the rearing.

- Seed legislation in the true sense needs to be implemented.
- Rearing and grainage operations in same place should be discouraged at all costs.
- Practice of hiring rearing appliances should be discouraged.
- Integrated approach is the need of the day for proper disease management in sericulture.
- Destruction of disease causing microsporidians at various levels is the general method of preventing and controlling disease.

Preparation of permanent slide of pebrine spores

- Make a thin smear on a glass slide and air dry.
- Fix in methyl alcohol for 2-3 minutes.
- Air-dry or blots dry the smear.
- Dilute giemsa stock solution (1 drop giemsa + 1 ml of distilled water) and stain the smear for 45-60 minutes.
- Wash in distilled water.
- Air dry or blot dry.
- Mount in DPX and examine under 600 magnification of microscope.
- In giemsa stain, pebrine spore appears as pinkish violet or bluish oval body.

Detection of pebrine spores in soil/dust

- Collect dust from the rearing house/egg production centers and equipments.
- Take 5 gm of the soil sample in a beaker and add 20 ml (1:4) of 0.6% potassium carbonate solution. Stir it thoroughly for 2 minutes. Allow the suspension to settle for 15-20 minutes.
- Centrifuge the supernatant for 5 minutes at 10,000 r.p.m.
- Collect the sediment.

- Take a drop of distilled water on a glass slide and a small quantity of sediment with a glass rod or brush.
- Add a tiny drop of Indian ink, mount and examine.

Detection of pebrine spores on mulberry leaves

- Wash 10-15 mulberry leaves in 100 ml of water.
- Centrifuge the wash for 8-10 minutes at 10,000 r.p.m.
- Discard the supernatant.
- Take a drop of distilled water on a glass slide and small quantity of the sediment with a glass rod or brush.
- Add a tiny drop of Indian ink, mount and examine.

Detection of pebrine spores in egg-shell/eggs/unhatched eggs

- Collect head/body pigmented stage eggs/hatched eggshells/unhatched eggs into a porcelain/glass mortar and add 0.6% Potassium carbonate solution and grind thoroughly.
- After settling, filtering and centrifuging, examine the sediments after dissolving the same.

Detection of pebrine spores in litter

- Collect 5 gm of litter in a mortar and add 40 ml 0.6% potassium carbonate solution (8 times the weight of litter) and homogenize by grinding. If the resultant homogenate turns out to be viscous, add a few drops of HCl to reduce viscosity.
- After settling, filtering and centrifuging dissolve the sediment and observe under microscope.

Adoption of this method in stock race rearing, seed areas and also at commercial silkworm rearing to detect spores will help to take up early remedial measures to contain the spread of the disease. The advantages are:

- Total elimination of wasteful sacrifice of larvae/ pupae.
- Repeated faecal pellet examination may be conducted to ensure detection of infection in the silkworm population without additional cost.
- Random sampling method for faecal pellet collection instar-wise (Table 10.4) and centrifugation of homogenate sample enables accurate detection of spores to minimize the incidence of trans-ovarian transmission.

Table 10.4: Faecal pellet sample size for 100 Dfls

Age Instar		*No. of trays per*	*Sample size*	
Instar	*Day*	*Instar (4.5' dia)*	*No.of samples of 10gm each*	*Total weight of faecal matter (gm)*
I	2	2	1	10
II	2	2	1	10
III	2	4	2	20
IV	2	8	2	20
IV	4	10	3	30
V	2	18	4	40
V	4	25	6	60
V	6	30	8	80

Source: Patil *et al.* (2001)

Forced eclosion test

Sample cocoons from a lot are selected randomly and kept at constant temperature of 33°C to facilitate 1 or 2 days early emergence. The emerged moths are examined and if the lot is noticed infected, are rejected immediately.

Delayed mother moth test

After oviposition, the mother moths are collected in groups in perforated cardboard boxes/cover. Alternatively, they can be left on dummy sheets in the oviposition trays itself. The boxes/oviposition trays are properly numbered as per egg sheets and preserved in well-ventilated room at

Table 10.5: Probability of detection of pebrine in 20% sampling method (Index)

No. of egg cards	Population	Pebrine	Samples	Probability Non Detectable	Probability Detectable
20	400	2	80	0.6400	0.3600
30	600	3	120	0.5120	0.4880
40	800	4	160	0.4096	0.5904
50	1000	5	200	0.3277	0.6723
60	1200	6	240	0.2621	0.7379
80	1600	8	320	0.1678	0.8322
100	2000	10	400	0.1074	0.8926
150	3000	15	600	0.0352	0.9648
200	4000	20	800	0.9885	0.9885
250	5000	25	1000	0.9620	0.9620
300	6000	30	1200	0.9988	0.9988
500	10000	50	2000	1.0000	1 .0000

Rate of pebrine infection = 0.5% in female moths. (Refer Dr. T. Fuziwara, 1992).

25 ± 1°C for a period of 3-4 days. After stipulated period, moth testing is done as per procedure described.

NON-INFECTIOUS DISEASES

Common arthropod diseases of silkworm include *Exorista myiasis, Acarid* infestation, *Sturmia myiasis* and wasp parasitism. The non-parasitic conditions include injury by poisonous hairs of larvae of *Euproctis* similes and *Setora postornata.* Poisoning is another type of non-infectious disease induced by toxic substances that cats on the body of the silkworm and disrupts normal physiology and metabolism. Most common toxic substances are agricultural chemicals and factory exhaust. The common agricultural chemicals causing considerable damage include rganophosphorous (dipterex, DDVP, parathion), organochlorine (benzene hexachloride, chlordane, heptachlor), organo-nitrogen and pesticides (DDT, BHC etc.).

The symptoms of poisoning by agricultural chemicals are erratic movement, enlargement of thoracic region, lifting of head, vomiting, shortened body and tremor. The best method of prevention of poisoning by agricultural chemicals is in cutting off their application. Residual toxicity and shelf life should be ascertained. Mulberry leaves should not be fed to the silkworms after spraying of chemicals. However, if it rains following the spray, the toxicity usually disappears in about two weeks. To avoid contamination from the factory exhaust (smoke), effort should be taken not to plant mulberry around these factories. Because of smoke, mulberry leaves become dark brown or black and distorted in shape and in real sense not suitable for feeding. However, the severity of poisoning effect is influenced by the nature of the poisonous substances present in the smoke.

UZIFLY PESTS

Major pests infecting mulberry silkworm in India and other countries are presented in Table 10.5. However, Uzi fly, the major pest causing considerable damage to the silkworm, is discussed hereunder.

Table 10.6: Status of pests of mulberry silkworm in India and other countries

Sl.No.	*Pests*	*Country*	*Incidence*
1	**Uzi fly**		
	Exorista bombycis, Exorista sorbilans, *Exorista myiasis*	Bangladesh, China, Japan, India, Korea, Thailand and Vietnam	Throughout the year
2	**Dermestid beetle**		
	Dermestis sp.	India and Japan	Throughout the year
3	**Silkworm Tachnid fly**		
	Crossocosmia zebina *Stumla sericariae*	Japan	Seasonal
4	**Himefly**		
	Dtenophorocera pavide	Japan	Seasonal
5	**Mite**		
	Pediculoides ventricosus	China, India and Japan	Seasonal
6	**Hair caterpillar**		
	Euproctis similes *Setora postomata*	China & Japan	Seasonal

Among the insect pests of mulberry silkworm, the Uzi fly, *Exorista bombycis* (Louis) a primary larval endo-parasitoid of silkworm *Bombyx mori* is a member of a tribe Exoristini under the sub-family Goniinae belonging to the family Tachinidae of the order Diptera. It is distributed in silk producing countries viz., China, India, Japan, Korea, Thailand, Srilanka, Burma and Bangladesh, Vietnam etc. The other three commercially reared silkworms namely tasar, muga and eri are also reported to be parasitized by this fly. There are more than 55-recorded alternate hosts of this fly in nature but mulberry silkworm *Bombyx mori* is most preferred host. The extent of damage ranges from 10-20 per cent.

Life cycle: The fly is considerably larger than a housefly and is blackish gray in colour with four prominent longitudinal lines on the thoracic region and broad bands on the abdomen. The abdomen is conical. Male fly is generally larger than female with a body length of about 12 mm in male and 10 mm in female. Life span of adult fly varies with *sex* and season. Males survive for about 10-18 days while female lives for 20-25 days. Moreover, survival is least during summer seasons. The differences between male and female flies are:

- Longitudinal lines on the thorax of male are more prominent than in female.
- Pulvilli of male are larger than female.
- Width of frons of male is narrower than that of female.
- Lateral regions of the abdomen are covered with bristles, which are denser in male than in female.
- Males have external genetalia covered with brownish orange hairs on the abdominal top.

In nature, these flies copulate in air, live on nectar of flowers, and honeydew excreted from aphids and scale insects. The adults are polygamous. They mate 1-2 times within 24 hrs of adult emergence. They can mate 3-7 times during the adult life. Minimum 1 hr mating is essential for better fecundity and hatchability. In nature, mating duration ranges from half an hour to two and half hours. Oviposition starts approximately 2 days after emergence. A single mated female fly can lay about 300-1000 eggs in its life span. Usually 2-3 eggs are laid on per silkworm larvae and the oviposition continues until death. The fly prefers later stages of silkworm for egg laying. Though it can lay eggs anywhere on the body surface of larvae but the incidence on the ventral side and inter segmental joints are noticed very less. There are four distinct stages in the life cycle of the fly viz., egg, maggot, pupa and adult. Eggs are oval, macro type, creamy white in colour, which measures about 0.45-0.56 mm in length and 0.25-0.30 mm in width. The shape of eggs is oblong which depending on the season hatches out within 2-5 days after oviposition and tiny maggots enter the body of silkworm larvae by making a perforation on the integument leaving its shell outside. At the point of penetration the parasitized silkworm larvae shows a characteristic black scar. The marking alone is sufficient for the diagnostic purpose of Uzi fly infestation.

Maggot has a pair of pharyngeal hooks at the anterior end and passes through three instars within the body of the host. The first two instars are yellowish white in colour while third instars maggots are creamy white. Maggots have 11 body segments. It feeds on fat bodies leaving silk glands and lives for 4-6 days inside the body of silkworms. Full-grown maggots' cuts the integument of host with pharyngeal hooks leading the death of the host. After coming out from the body of the host, maggots crawl in search of cracks and crevices, soil or darker regions where it forms puparium. Maggot just before pupation becomes motionless and body shrinks. The pupal period is 10-12 days. Pupae are oblong in shape, light reddish brown to dark reddish brown in colour. Male adult emerges out earlier than the female. The fly completes 10-14 generations in a year in tropical regions. In temperate regions it complete 6-7 generations while in arctic regions hardly these complete 4-5 generations.

Period of occurrence

The pest occurs throughout the year. However, its incidence is maximum from August-September.

Symptoms and nature of damage

Infestation of this fly in 3rd, 4th and early 5th instar results in death of larvae before they reach to spinning stage. If parasitization occurs after middle of 5th instar, the mature maggot comes out by piercing the cocoons and thereby rendering the cocoons unsuitable for seed production or even reeling. Bivoltine cocoon shells are compact and stiff, therefore, if its larvae are parasitized in late 5th instar, maggots fail to come out and hence pupate inside the cocoon and flies dies there itself.

Management of Uzi fly

Since Uzi fly has many alternate hosts in nature, it cannot be eradicated instead it can only be managed. For management beside its prevention and control following points should be taken into consideration:

(i) Exclusion method

- Use Uzi fly-proof wiremesh or nylon nets on doors, windows and ventilators, which should be kept closed.
- Antechamber must be attached to each rearing house for preventing entry of Uzi fly in the rearing apartment.
- Use nylon net on the individual rearing trays for preventing the fly from getting access to the silkworm for oviposition.
- Transportation of only healthy cocoons in new seed areas to prevent Uzi fly entry into these areas.
- Covering of individual rearing stands with fly proof wire mesh.

(ii) Cultural/mechanical method

- Pick Uzi-infested silkworm larvae and emerging maggots in rearing trays and kill them.

- Make floor of rearing houses free from cracks and crevices to avoid pupation of maggots at unnoticed places.
- Uzi-infested larvae spin cocoons a day or two earlier than other silkworms. Such cocoons should be harvested separately and stifled.
- Simultaneous skipping of silkworm rearing by all the farmers in a locality helps in non-availability of silkworms for continuous multiplication.
- Maggots falling from mountages should be collected and destroyed.
- Sorting out of Uzi-pierced cocoons before transportation to cocoon markets helps in preventing further spreading of Uzi maggots besides fetching higher price for the good cocoon, which is free from Uzi infestation.

(iii) Physical method

- Use light-cum-sticky trap to attract adult flies and get caught on the sticky board.
- Use of kerosene water trap near doors and windows to attract and kill ovipositing adults.
- Use of fishmeal trap outside the rearing room to trap adult flies.
- Use of food bait trap and propoxur bail trap

(iv) Chemical method

- Use Uzi trap, uzicide or Uzi-powder in the rearing house.
- Diflubenzuron in low concentration (100 ppm) has been reported to have ovicidal activity and is used to kill the eggs of Uzi fly.

Uzi trap: Uzi trap is a mixture of indigenous chemical, does not contain any insecticide and is available in the form of tablet. It is a chemo trap used for attracting and killing the adults. Dissolve one tablet of Uzi trap in one liter of water. The solution prepared should be put in light coloured flat trays and placed near the windows both inside and outside at the height of the base of the window. The solution should be used from 3rd instars onwards till spinning. One packet of Uzi trap containing 12 tablets is sufficient for use in rearing of 100 Dfls. When solution becomes dirty due to accumulation of dust, dead insects, silkworm litter etc., it should be discarded and fresh solution should be prepared for further use. Uzi trap solution is safe to silkworms, pets and to human beings. It is very simple to adopt besides highly cost-effective. It can be used along with other control strategies of Uzi fly in IPM.

Uzicide: It is a liquid ovicidal formulation sprayed on the body of the silkworm in each instars from 3rd stage onward on alternate days except the period of moulting. It is sprayed on the 2nd and 4th day of IV instar and 2nd, 4th and 6th days of V instars. Silkworm should be given feeding half an hour after spraying. Four to five liters of uzicide is required for rearing of 100 Dfls larvae. Uzicide kills the eggs when it is sprayed on the uzi-infested silkworms, resulting in non-emergence of Uzi maggots from the eggs. Spraying of uzicide can be performed with any ordinary hand sprayer.

Uzi powder: It is an ovicidal dust formulation, which kills the Uzi eggs when dusted on the silkworms. It is dusted on the body of the silkworm from 3rd instars onwards. Uzi powder should be taken in a muslin cloth and dusted uniformly after bed cleaning. Silkworm should be fed half an hour after dusting. Four to five kilogram of uzi powder is required for rearing of 100 Dfls larvae. Uzi powder should be kept out of the reach of the children. Bed disinfectant should not be applied when uzi powder is dusted. Uzi powder contaminated silkworm litter should not be fed to the cattle and facemask should be used while dusting the uzi powder.

(v) Biological method

Biological control of the pests is the most safe and eco-friendly approach in pest management. In biological control, natural enemies of the pest concern that have high searching ability, synchronomous with host life, host specificity, and adaptations to field conditions, easy rearing and multiplication methods are preferred.

Natural parasitoids viz., *Nesolynx thymus, N. dipterae, Trichopria, Exoristobia phillipinensis, Dirhinus anthracia* etc have been identified and used to control uzi fly. So far, 20 larval/pupal parasitoids are known (Table 10.7). Among these *N. thymus* is one of the most popular biological control agents of uzi fly today, because of its high reproductive rate and higher female ratio. One lakh adult females should be released in three doses corresponding to IV and V instars and within one or two days after cocoon harvest at 8000, 16,000 and 76,000 adults respectively. Parasitoids should be released immediately after sunset in the rearing houses, places of mountage storage, near mountages with spinning larvae and also near the manure

Table 10.7. Natural parasitoids of uzi fly

Sl. No.	*Parasitoids*	*Family**	*Nature of parasitoid***
1	*Brachymeria intermedia*	Chalcididae	Solitary pupal
2	*Brachymeria lugubris*	Chalcididae	Solitary pupal
3	*Dirhinus anthracia*	Chalcididae	Solitary pupal
4	*Dirhinus himalayanus*	Chalcididae	Solitary pupal
5	*Exoristobia philippinensis*	Encyrtidae	Gregarious pupal
6	*Marmoniella vitripennis*	Chalcididae	Solitary pupal
7	*Nesolynx dipterae*	Eulophidae	Gregarious pupal
8	*Nesolynx thymus*	Eulophidae	Gregarious pupal
9	*Pachycrepoideus veeranai*	Pteromalidae	Solitary pupal
10	*Pachycrepoideus vindimmae*	Pteromalidae	Solitary pupal•
11	*Pleurotropis* sp.	Pteromalidae	Solitary pupal
12	*Spalangia cameroni*	Eulophidae	Solitary pupal
13	*Spalangia endues*	Diapriidae	Gregarious larval
14	*Tetrasticus howardii*	Eulophidae	Gregarious larval
16	*Trichopriya khandalus*	Diapriidae	Gregarious larval
17	*Trichospilus diaptraeae*	Chalcididae	Gregarious larval
18	*Brachymeria* sp	Chalcididae	Solitary pupal
19	*Dirhinus* sp.	Chalcididae	Solitary pupal
20	*Trichopriya* sp.	Diapriidae	Gregarious pupal

*Order – Hymenoptera ** Endoparasitoid

pits. *N. thymus* has been the choice of exploitation in the control of uzi fly due to various reasons. However, its host searching ability and parasitization potential has kept it on the top of the other parasitoids (Table 10.8).

Table 10.8: Searching ability and parasitization potential of parasitoids of Uzi fly

Sl. No.	*Parasitoids*	*Searching ability (distance in feet)*	*Parasitization range*
1.	*Nesolynx thymus*	200	33-94
2.	*Exoristobia phillippinensis*	90	0 – 9
3.	*Trichopriya* sp.	90	0 – 3
4.	*Dirhinus* sp.	200	0 – 66

An IPM package comprising an ovicide (uzicide) against eggs, augmentation release of indigenous gregarious *(N. thymus)* and solitary *(Dirhinus* sp.) parasitoids against pupae and dusting of dimilin on maggots/puparia to suppress the reproductive efficiency of adults has been developed and recommended.

Between IPM, biological control is most successful than any other methods. Biological control where biological agents are used to control pests, begin as an environmentally safe alternative to the chemical means of control. It is very effective method of control offering a long-term protection and is environment-friendly, therefore, highly suitable for sericulture in India.

Economics: Economics of use of chemical and biological methods separately and in combination is presented below:

Expenditure

Item	*Quantity*	*Unit rate*	*Amount*
Uzi trap	1 packet	10.00	10.00
Uzicide	4.5 liters	15.00	67.50
Uzi powder	4.5 kg.	20.00	90.00
N. thymus 1 lakh adults		20.00	20.00
Total expenditure (without uzi powder)			97.50
Total expenditure (without uzicide)			120.00

B. Receipts

(a)	Average recovery of cocoons/100 Dfls	: 5.1 Kg.
(b)	Value of cocoons @ Rs. 130/= per Kg.	: Rs. 663.00
(c)	Net gain (without Uzi powder)	: Rs. 565.50
(d)	Net gain (without Uzicide)	: Rs. 543.00
(e)	Cost benefit ratio (without Uzi powder)	: 1: 6.80
(f)	Cost benefit ratio (without Uzicide)	: 1: 5.52

Genetic control: Genetic control is by sterilization of male and female through exposing the maggots and puparia to gamma rays or treatment of maggots, pupae and adult with chemosterilents to affect their reproductive potential have also been reported. Apholate, Tepa, Thiotepa, Penfluron and Diflubenzuron chemosterilent is known to bring sterility in Uzi fly besides affecting eclosion, longevity, mating, competitiveness and fecundity.

Semiochemicals (pheromones and allelochemicals), essential oils (lemon, lime and orange), aqueous extracts of plant products (Eucalyptus oil) and quarantine measures are also useful to control Uzi fly.

BIBLIOGRAPHY

Akai, H. (1958) Observations of the micropylar region of the chorion in the silkworm, *Bombyx mori* L. *Acta Sericol.*, 2:619-21.

Akutsu, S. and Yoshitake, N. (1977) Electron microscopic observation on the vitelline membrane formation in the silkworm, *Bombyx mori* L. *J. Seric. Sci. Japan*, 46:509-514.

Alenkseenork, A. (1986) Nosematol for control of nosematosis of bees and pebrine of silkworm. *Veterinariya*, USSR, 10:45-47.

Ando, Y. (1974) Egg diapause and ambient oxygen tension in the false melon beetle, *Atrachya menethesi* (Coleoptera: Chrysomelidae). *Appl. Ent. Zool.*, 9:261-270.

Anitha, T.; Shirimani, P.; Meena and Nithe Rani, R. (1994) Isolation and characterization of pathogenic bacterial species in the silkworm, *Bombyx mori* L. *Sericologia*, 34:97-102.

Anonymous (1995) Authorization of silkworm hybrids. *Indian Silk*, 34:26

Arakawa, A. (1988) Western-blothing method for the detection of nuclear polyhedrosis virus of the silkworm, *Bombyx mori*. *J. Seric. Sci. Japan*, 57:475-499.

Arakawa, A. (1991) Quantitative assay of cytoplasmic polyhedrosis virus in the faeces of the silkworm, *Bombyx mori* using enzyme linked immunosorbent assay (ELISA). *J. Seric. Sci. Japan*, 60:105-111.

Arataka, Y. (1973) Strain differences of silkworm, *Bombyx mori* L. in the resistance to a Nuclear Polyhedrosis Virus. *J. Seric. Sci. Japan*, 42:230-238.

Arnold, S. J. and Wade, M. J. (1984) On the measurement of natural and sexual selection: Theory. *Evolution*, 38:709-719.

Ashoka, J. and Govindan, R. (1990) Genetic estimates for quantitative traits in bivoltine silkworm, *Bombyx mori* L. *Mysore J. Agric.Sci.*, 24:371-374.

Askari, S. and Sharan, R. K. (1984) Studies on different copulating duration on pre-oviposition, fecundity and fertility of mulberry silkworm, *Bombyx mori* L. (Bombycidae: Lepidoptera). *J. Adv. Zool.*, 5:114-119.

Attathom, T. and Sinchaisri, N. (1987) Nuclear Polyhedrosis Virus isolated from *Bombyx mori* in Thailand. *Sericologia*, 27: 287-295.

Atwal, A. S.; Singh, B. and Battu, G. S. (1973) *Chilopartellus* (Swinhoe) a new host of *Aspergillus flavus* Link and *Fusarium* sp, *Curr. Sci.*, 42:585.

Austrurov, B. L; Baburashvli, E. L; Bedniakova, T. A.; Vereiskaia, V. N.; Labzhanidze, V. I. and Ovanesyan, T. T. (1969) Thermal intravital disinfections of eggs with simultaneous of the embryonic diapause as a new method of control of silkworm pebrine disease. *Zvakad. Nauk., SSSR,. Ser. Bio.*, 6:811-818.

Azuma, M and O. Yamashita (1985) Immunohistochemical and biochemical localization of trehalase in the developing ovaries of the silkworm, *Bombyx mori. Insect Biochem.*, 15:589-596.

Babu, G. K. S.; Subramanya, G. and Magadum, S. B. (1991) Effect of preservation conditions of pupae on moth emergence and fecundity in *Bombyx mori. Current Research* (University of Agricultural Sciences, Bangalore), India, 20:37-39.

Baig, M.; Datta, R. K.; Nataraju, B.; Samson, M. V. and Sivaprasad, V. (1992a) Protein-A linked Latex Antisera test for the detection of *Nosema bombycis* Nagali spores. *J. Invertebr. Pathol.*, 60: 310-313.

Baig, M.; Gupta, S. K.; Nataraju, B.; Mohd Sha, M. M.; Sivaprasad, V.; Datta, R. K.; Gupta, R. and Samson, M. V. (1992b) Latex agglutination test for the detection of pebrine in the silkworm, *Bombyx mori* L. *Indian J. Seric.*, 31:141-145.

Baig, M.; Nataraju, B. and Samson, M. V. (1990) Studies on the spread of diseases in the rearing of silkworm, *Bombyx mori* L. through different sources of contamination. *Indian J. Seric.*, 29:145-146.

Baig, M.; Samson, M. V.; Sharma, S. D.; Balavenkatasubbaiah, M.; Sasidharan, T. O. and Jolly, M. S. (1993) Efficacy of certain bed disinfectants in certain combinations against the nuclear polyhedrosis and white muscardine in the silkworm, *Bombyx mori* L. *Sericologia*, 33:53-60.

Baig, M.; Sharma, S.D.; Balavenkatasubbaiah, M.; Samson, M.V.; Sasidharan, T.O. and Noamani, R. (1991) Relative susceptibility of different races of silkworm, *Bombyx mori* L. to Nuclear Polyhedrosis under natural and induced conditions. *Sericologia*, 31:417-420.

Baig, M.; Samson, M. V.; Sasidharan, T. O.; Sharma, S. D.; Balavenkatasubbaiah, M. and Jolly, M. S. (1988a) Study on the spread of pebrine after introduction of transovarially infected worms in a colony of silkworm, *Bombyx mori* L. *Sericologia* 28:75-80.

Baig, M.; Samson, M. V.; Sharma, S. D.; Balvenkatasubbiah, M.; Sasidharan, T. O. and M. S. Jolly (1988b) Effect of certain disinfectants as surface sterilants against pebrine in surface contaminated layings. *Sericologia* 28:81-87.

Balinsky, B. I. (1981) An Introduction to Embryology-Saunders College, Philadelphia.

Balvenkatsubbaiah, M.; Datta, R. K.; Baig, M.; Nataraju, B. and Iyengar, M. N. S. (1994) Efficacy of bleaching powder as a disinfectant against the pathogens of silkworm, *Bombyx mori* L. *Indian J. Seric.*, 33:23-26.

Barker, R. J. (1986) Selection indices in plant breeding. CRC Press, Inc. New York.

Basavaraja, H. K.; Suresh Kumar, N.; Mal Reddy, N. and Datta, R. K. (1998) New approaches to bivoltine silkworm breeding; in *Silkworm Breeding*. G. Sreerama Reddy (ed.), pp.131-139, Oxford and IBH Publishing Co. Pvt. Ltd., New Delhi.

Basu, R.; Roychoudhury, N.; Shamsuddin, M.; Sen, S .K. and Senguta, K. (1992) Effect of larval feeding and subsequent starvation on development and cocoon characters in *Bombyx mori*. L. *Environment & Ecology*, 10:937-941.

Batra, R. C. and Sinha, M .K. (1971) A fungal parasite of Plum hairy caterpillar, *Euproctis fraternal* Moore (Lepidoptera: Lymantriidae). *Labdev. J. Sci. Tech.*, 9-B:228-229.

Battu, G. S.; Bindra, O. S. and Rangarajan, M. (1971) Investigations on microbial infections of insect pests in Punjab. *Indian J. Entomol.*, 33:317-325.

Bedniakova, T. A. and Vereiskaia, V. N. (1958) The disinfection action of high temperature on eggs on mulberry silkworm (B. mori L) infected with Pebrine (*N. bombycis*) at different stages of the diapausal cycle of development (in Russian). *Doklady Akad. Nauk, USSR, Biol. Sci. Sect.*, 122:760-763.

Benchamin, K. V. (1992) Chawki silkworm rearing—an evaluation. *Indian Silk*, 31:18-20.

Benchamin, K. V.; Holkar, P. S. and Rao, V. (1990) Studies on the separation of fertile and unfertile eggs in silkworm. *Indian J. Eco.*, 17:79-80.

Benchamin, K. V.; Krishna Reddy, R. and Naseema Begum, A. (1989) On the grading and pricing of seed cocoons in silkworm, *Bombyx mori* L. *Indian J. Seric.*, 28:168-177.

Benchamin, K. V. and Krishnaswami, S. (1981) Studies on the egg production efficiency in silkworm, *Bombyx mori* L. II. Egg production efficiency in hybrid parents and its effective application. *Proc. Seric. Symp. Sem.*, 7-14.

Benchamin, K. V. and Magdum, S. B. (1990) Sex separation of silkworm pupa on the basis of weight differences. *J. Rec. Adv. Appl. Sci.*, **5**:11-15.

Benchamin, K. V.; Magdum, S. B. and Shivashankar, N. (1990) Mating capacity of male moths of pure breeds and hybrids in silkworm, *Bombyx mori* L. *Indian J. Seric.*, 29:182-187.

Bhargava, S. K.; Venugopal, A.; Choudhury, C. C. and Ahsan, M. M. (1995) Productivity in bivoltine breeds. *Indian Text. J.*, 105:112-114.

Bhattacharya, J.; Krishnan, N.; Chandra, A. K.; Prakash, O. and Sengupta, K. (1993) Use of slide agglutination test for the detection of nuclear polyhedrosis virus of silkworm, *Bombyx mori* L. *Current Science*, 65:638-639.

Biram Saheb, N. M.; Gaur, J. P.; Samson, M. V. and Rajanna, K. L. (1998) Behaviour of male moths in *Bombyx mori* L. *Indian Text. J.*, 108:46-49.

Biram Saheb, N. M.; Rajanna, K. L.; Jayaram Raju, P.; Samson, M. V. and Gaur, J. P. (1997) Silkworm seed production. *Indian Text. J.*, 107:40-45.

Biram Saheb, N. M.; Sengupta, K. and Vemananda Reddy, G. (1990) *A Treatise of the Acid Treatment of Silkworm Eggs*. CSR&TI, Mysore, India.

Biram Saheb, N. M.; Vinod, K.; Negi, B. B. S.; Sengupta, K. and Noamani, M. K. R. (1991) Comparative study on age-specific responses of hot and cold hydrochlorization methods on the diapausing eggs of silkworm, *Bombyx mori* L. *Indian J. Seric.*, 30:151-153.

Biram Saheb, N. M.; Vinod, K.; Negi, B. B. S. and Samson, M. V. (1996) Acid treatment in relation to refrigeration of silkworm, *Bombyx mori* eggs. *Indian J. Seric.*, 35:77-79.

Bliss, C. I. (1927) The oviposition rate of the grape leafhoppers. *J. Agric. Res.*, 34:847-852.

Borovsky, D. and Van-Handel E. (1980) Synthesis of ovary specific proteins in mosquitoes. *Intl. J. Invertebr. Reprod.*, 2:153-164.

Boswell, R. E. and Mahowald, A. P. (1985) Cytoplasmic determinants in embryogenesis. in *Comprehensive Insect Physiology, Biochemistry and Pharmacology*, Kerkut, G. A. and Gilbert, L.I. (eds.), Vol. II., pp. 387-405, Pergamon Press, Oxford.

Bowman, J. C. (1958) Selection for heterosis. *Animal Breeding Abstracts*, 27:261-273.

Brady, U. E. (1983) Prostaglandin in insects. *Insect Biochem.*, 13:443-451.

Byrareddy, M. S.; Devaiah, M. C.; Narayanaswamy, T. K.; Govindan, R. and Shyamala, M. B. (1991) Comparative efficacy of some rearing tray disinfectants in prevention of silkworm white muscardine caused by *Beauveria bassina* (Bales). *Sericologia*, 31:533-535.

Chandra, A. K. and Sahakundu, A. K. (1993) The effect of drug on pebrine infection in *Bombyx mori* L. *Indian J. Seric.* 21 & 22:67-69.

Chandrasekharaiah (1994) Silkworm Breeding. In *Lectures on Sericulture.* Ed. Boraiah, G., pp.102-111.

Chatterjee, S. N.; Nagaraja, C. S. and Giridhar, K. (1990) An approach to silkworm breeding. *Workshop on Biometrical Genetics*-CSR&TI Mysore, 7-8, September, pp:11-16.

Chattopadhyay, S. (1995) Mating duration and production of viable eggs of mulberry silkworm (*Bombyx mori* L). *Environ. Ecol.*, 13:460-461.

Chattopadhyay, S.; Das, S. K.; Roy, G. C.; Sen, S. K. and Sinha, S. S. (1995) Heterosis analysis on silk productivity of three-way crosses in *Bombyx mori* L. *Sericologia*, 35:549-551.

Chaturvedi, M. L. and Upadhyay, V. B. (1990) Effect of cold storage on the hatchability of silkworm (*Bombyx mori*) eggs. *J. Adv.*

Chen, J.; Teng, J.; Hu, C. and Michael, M. (1989) Production of monoclonal antibodies to densovirus of silkworm (*Bombyx mori*) and their application in diagnosis. *Chinese J. Virol.* 5:77-81.

Chen, P. S. (1971) *Biochemical Aspects of Insect Development.* S.

Chen, Q.; Tao, T.; Li, S. and Sheng, J. (1994) Studies on the three-step refrigeration system of the hibernating silkworm eggs. *Bull. Seric. (China)*, 25:11-14.

Cheng, K. Y.; Han, K. S. and Min, B. Y. (1981) Genetic studies on silkworm characters by diallel cross. II. Analysis of heterosis and combining abilities. *Seric. J. Korea*, 22:1-7.

Cheng, L.J. and Hou, R. F. (1992) Factors enhancing *Bombyx mori* nuclear polyhedrosis virus infection in-vitro. *J. Appl. Ento.*, 113:103-106.

Chinaswamy, K. P. and Devaiah, M. C. (1986) Studies on the control of *Aspergillosis* of the silkworm, *Bombyx mori* L. *Indian J. Seric.*, 25:63-69.

Chinaswamy, K. P.; Gowda, B. L. V. and Devaiah, M. C. (1993) Silkworm seed cocoon crop management. *Indian Silk*, 32:40-43.

Chinaswamy, K. P.; Reddy, D. N. R.; Govindan, R. and Narayanaswamy, T. K. (1986) Pathogenecity of *Aspergillus tamarii* Kita to *Dasychira mendosa* Hubner (Lepidoptera: Lymantriidae), a pest of mulberry. *Entomon,* 11:67-68.

Chino, H. (1957 a) Carbohydrate metabolism in diapause eggs of the silkworm, *Bombyx mori.* I. Diapause and change of glycogen content. *Embryologia,* 3:295-316.

Chino, H. (1957 b) Conversion of glycogen to sorbitol and glycerol in the diapause eggs of the *Bombyx mori* silkworm. *Nature,* 180:606 -607.

Chino, H. (1958) Carbohydrate metabolism in diapause eggs of the silkworm, *Bombyx mori.* II. Conversion of glycogen into sorbitol and glycerol during diapause. *J. Insect Physiol.,* 2:1-12.

Chitra, C.; Karanth, N. G. K. and Vasantharajan, V. N. (1975) Diseases of the mulberry silkworm, *Bombyx mori* L. *J. Sci. Indust. Res.,* 34:386-401.

Choudhury, P. C.; Shukla, P.; Ghosh, A.; Mallikarjuna, B. and Senguta, K. (1991) Effect of spacing, crown height and method of pruning on mulberry leaf, quality and cocoon yield. *Indian J. Seric.,* 30:46-53.

Christiana, S. T. and Kamble, C. K. (1995) Loose egg preparation and adoption—an appraisal. *J. Seric.,* 32:40-45.

Coulon, M. (1988) Comparative changes of ecdysteroid content in *Bombyx mori* eggs in diapausing and non-diapausing development. *Comp. Biochem. Physiol.,* 89:503-509.

Dandin, S. B. (1997) Mulberry improvement programmes—An overview. *Indian Silk,* 36:5-9.

Dar, H. U. and Singh, T. P. (1991) Influence of population density of silkworm, *Bombyx mori* (L) on some economic traits. Entomon, 16:269-273.

Das, K. K.; Sahu, P. K. and Das, N. K. (1999) Adoption of recommended package of practices in sericulture—myths and realities. *J. Interacademicia,* 2:297-304.

Das, S.; Saha, A. K. and Samsuddin, M. (1996) High temperature induced sterility in silkworms. *Indian Silk,* 35:26-28.

Das, S. K.; Ghosh, B.; Pattanaik, S.; Das, N. K.; Singh, T.; Sen, S. K. and Rao, G. S. (1997) Hybrid vigour in three-way crosses of mulberry silkworm, *Bombyx mori* L. *Indian J. Genet.,* 57: 447-453.

Das, S. K.; Patnaik, S.; Ghosh, B.; Singh, T.; Nair, B. P.; Sen, S. K. and Subba Rao, G. (1994) Heterosis analysis in some three way crosses of *Bombyx mori* (L). *Sericologia,* 34:51-61.

Das, S. K. and Sengupta, K. (1991) Proper incubation of eggs ensures proper hatching and successful cocoon crop. *Indian Silk*, 29: 28-29.

Datta, R. K. (1984) Improvement of silkworm races (*Bombyx mori* L.) *Sericologia*, 24:393-415.

Datta, R. K. (1988) Embryological studies on non-diapause silkworm, *Bombyx mori* L. *Indian J. Seric.*, 27:1-6.

Datta, R. K. and Basavaraja, H. K. (1998) Silkworm breeding in Japan, China and India; in *Silkworm Breeding*. Sreerama Reddy, G. (ed.), pp.18-38, Oxford and IBH Publishing Co. Pvt. Ltd., New Delhi.

Datta, R. K.; Sengupta, K. and Biswas, S. N. (1972) Studies on the preservation of multivoltine silkworm eggs at low temperatures. *Indian J. Seric.*, 11:20-27.

Davey, K. G. (1985) The male reproductive tract. In *Comprehensive Insect Physiology, Biochemistry and Pharmacology*, Kerkut, G. A. and Gilbert, L. I. (eds.), Pregamon Press, Oxford, Vol. I., pp. 15-36.

Devaiah, M. C. and Krishnaswami, S. (1975) Observations on the seasonal incidence of pebrine disease of the silkworm, *Bombyx mori* L. *Indian J. Seric.*, 14:27-30.

Devaiah, M. C.; Rajashekharagowda, R. and Chinnaswamy, K. P. (1983) A new fungal pathogen *Aspergillus nidulans* on the eri silkworm, *Samia cynthia ricini* (Lepidoptera: Saturniidae). *Indian J. Seric.*, 21 & 22:71-72.

East, E. M. and Hayes, H. K. (1912) Heterozygosis in evolution and plant breeding. USDA. Bur. Plant Ind. Bull., 243:1-58, in *The relationship of heterosis and genetic divergence in maize*. Moll., R. H., Lonnguist, J. H., Fortune, V. J. and Johnson, P. (1965), *Genetics*, 52:139-144.

Elston, R. C. (1963) A weight-free index for the purpose of ranking or selection with respect to several traits at a time. *Biometrics*, 19:85.

Englemann, F. (1970) *The Physiology of Insect Reproduction.*

Enomoto, S.; Moriyama, H. and Iwanami, S. (1987) *Septicemia* occurrence in cocoons as related to silkworm rearing conditions. *J.A.R.Q.*, 21:117-121.

Falconer, D. S. (1981) *Introduction to Quantitative Genetics*, 2nd Edition, Longman Inc., New York, p. 340.

Finney, D. J. (1962) Genetics gains under three methods of selection. *Genet. Res.*, 3:417.

Fonseca, T. C.; Almeida, J. E. de. and Fonseca, A. S. (1990) Effect of mulberry selection on silkworm feeding. *Sericologia*, 30: 460-477.

Fu, W. and He, M. (1993) Relationship between the maturity of mother moths and amount of laid eggs. *Bull. Seric.* (China), 24:29-30.

Fugo, H. and Arisawa, N. (1992) Oviposition behavior of the moths, which mated with males, sterilized by high temperature in the silkworm, *Bombyx mori. J. Seric. Sci. Japan*, 61:110-115.

Fujieda, T. (1986) Effect of reduced feeding and premature mounting in the 5th instars on the emergence and diapause in the silkworm, *Bombyx mori* L. *Gunma J. Agric. Res. Series (B), Seric.* (Japan), 3:43-48.

Fujimoto, N. (1951) Laying of eggs on the inclined plane in the silkworm moth. *J. Seric. Sci. Japan*, 20: 258.

Fujiwara, T. (1979) Infectivity and pathogenecity of *Nosema bombycis* to larvae of the silkworm. *J. Seric. Sci. Japan*, 48:376-380.

Fujiwara, T. (1980) Three Microsporidians (*Nosema* spp.) from silkworm *Bombyx mori. J.Seric. Sci. Japan*, 49:229-236.

Fujiwara, T. (1984a) A Pleistophora – like microsporidian isolated from the silkworm, *Bombyx mori. J. Seric. Sci. Japan*, 53: 398-402.

Fujiwara, T. (1984b) Thelohania sp. (Microsporidia – Thelohanidae) isolated from the silkworm, *Bombyx mori. J. Seric. Sci. Japan*, 53:459-460.

Fujwara, T. and Kagawa T. (1984) Control of Nosema bombycis parasitizing silkworm eggs by treatment with hydrochloric acid on exposure to various temperatures. *J. Seric. Sci. Japan.* 53:394-397.

Fukuda, S. and Tekeuchi, S. (1967) Diapause-factor producing cells in the suboesophageal ganglion of the silkworm, *Bombyx mori* L. *Proc. Jap. Acad.*, 43:51-56.

Furasawa, T. and Shikata, M. (1982) Temperature dependent changes of polyols and glycogen content in the eggs of silkworm, *Bombyx mori. J. Seric. Sci. Japan*, 51:77-83.

Furasawa, T.; Shimizu, K. and Yano, T. (1987) Polyol accumulation in non-diapause eggs of the silkworm, *Bombyx mori. J. Seric. Sci. Japan*, 56:150-156.

Furasawa, T.; Yaginuma, T. and Yamashita, O (1992) Temperature-induced metabolic shifts in diapause and non-diapause eggs of the silkworm, *Bombyx mori. Zoo/. Jb. Physiol.*, 96:169-178.

Furasawa, T. and Yang, Won-jin (1987) Fluctuations of free sugars with embryonic developments of non-diapause eggs of the silkworm, *Bombyx mori. J. Seric. Sci. Japan*, 56:143-149.

Furuta, Y. (1983) Multiplication of the infectious flacherie virus and the densonucleosis virus in cultured silkworm embryos. *J. Seric. Sci. Japan*, 52:245-246.

Gamo, T. (1976) On the concept and trends in silkworm breeding. *Farming Japan*, 10:11-12.

Gamo, T. and Hirabayashi, T. (1983) Genetic analysis of growth rate, pupation rate and some quantitative characters by diallel cross in the silkworm, *Bombyx mori. Jap. J. Breed.*, 33:178-190.

Gamo, T. and Ichiba, S. (1971) Selection experiment on fibroin hydrolyzing ratio in silkworm cocoons, its effects on the environmental characters. *Jap. J. Breed.*, 21:87-92.

Gangwar, S. K.; Somasundaram, P. and Thangavelu, K. (1993) Feeding behavior of silkworm, *Bombyx mori* L. *J. Adv. Zool.*, 14:115-118.

Geetha Bai, M.; Patil, C. S. and Kasturi Bai, A. R. (1985) A new method for easy detection of pebrine spores. *Sericologia*, 25: 297-300.

Ghosh, B.; Rao, P. R. T.; Sengupta, A. K.; Sen, S. K. and Saratchandra, B. (1996) Utilization of hybrid vigor—An approach. *Indian Silk*, 34:9-12.

Ghosh, C. C. (1949) *Silk production and weaving in India.* Govt. Printing Press, Calcutta.

Giebultowicz, J. M.; Raina, R. A. and Uebel, E. G. (1990) Mated-like behavior in senescent virgin females of Gypsy moth, *Lymantria. J. Insect Physiol.*, 36:495-498.

Gimelfarb, A. (1986) Multiplicative genotype-environmental interaction as a cause of reversed response to directional selection. *Genetics*,

Goldsmith M. R.; Paule M.; Weare B. and Clermont-Rattner, E. (1978) Development of the chorion in *Bombyx mori. J. Cell Biol.*, 79:32.

Govindan, R.; Narayanaswamy, T. K. and Devaiah, M. C. (1998) *Principles of Silkworm Pathology.* Seri Scientific Publishers, Bangalore, India, pp.420.

Govindan, R.; Narayanaswamy, T. K. and Ashoka, J. (1990) Influence of pupal weight in multivoltine silkworm, *Bombyx mori* (L) on some metric parameters. *Mysore J. Agric. Sci.*, 24:499-502.

Govindan, R.; Veeresh, G. K.; Shyamala, M. B.; Devaiah, M. C.; Narayanaswamy, T. K. and Sasthry, M. N. (1990) Effect of simultaneous infection of silkworm, *Bombyx mori* L. with

Kenchu virus and *Straphytococcus aureus* Rosenbach. *Indian J. Seric.*, 29:273-278.

Gowda, B. L. V.; Narayanaswamy, T. K. and Munirajappa, R. (1989) Impact of pupal weight on growth and development of the following generation in the silkworm Indian race NB7 (*Bombyx mori*). *Sericologia*, 29:481-489.

Gowda, B. L. V.; Sannaveerappanayar, V. T. and Shivayogeshwar, B. (1989) Fecundity and hatchability in mulberry silkworm, *Bombyx mori* (L) as influenced by pupal weight. *Intl. Cong. Trop. Seric. Prac.* Bangalore, Feb. 18-23, Part VI:21-24.

Gowda, P. and Jolly, M. S. (1987) Acid treatment of silkworm eggs made easy. *Indian Silk*, 26:33-36.

Gowda, R. R.; Gopalan, M.; Jayaraj, S. and Natarajan, N. (1993) Heterosis in selected single cross hybrids of silkworm, *Bombyx mori* L. *J. Seric.*, 1:50-55.

Grekov, D. (1989) Selection-genetic evaluation of some white cocoon races of the silkworm (*Bombyx mori*). I. Variability and correlations of quantitative traits. *Zhivotnov's Nauki*, 26:70-73.

Grekov, D and Petkov, N. (1990) Correlation between some traits and possibilities for prognostication heterosis of F1 crosses on hybridization of *Bombyx mori* L. *Zhivotnov's Nauki*, 27:80-85.

Griffing, B. and Ziros, E. (1971) Heterosis associated with genotype environment interactions. *Genetics*, 68:443-455.

Grobov, O. F. and Rodionova, Z. E. (1985) Identification of spores of Nosema bombycis from silkworm. *Veterinarira*, Moscow, USSR, 12:70-71.

Guerine-Meneville (1849) cit. in Pebrine disease of silkworm, a technical report, Tatsuke, K. (ed) (1971), Overseas Technical Co-operation Agency, Tokyo, Japan.

Guo, X. J.; Qiwan, Y. J. and Hu, X. F. (1985a) The diagnosis of the densonucleosis disease of the silkworm (*Bombyx mori*) in the early stage of infection by immuno-peroxidase histochemical method. *Scientia Agricultura Sinica*, 8:82-85.

Guo, X. J.; Qiwan, Y. J.; Hu, X. F. and Wang, H. L. (1985 b) Studies on the infection site of the densonucleosis virus in the diseased silkworm (*Bombyx mori* L.) in China. *Canye Kexue*, 11:93-98.

Gupta, V. K.; Chatterjee, K. K. and Sinha, A. K. (1992) Floating behavior of silkworm eggs. *Indian Silk*, 30:24-26.

Gupta, V. K.; Kharoo, V. K. and Sahani, N. K. (1990) Effect of different laying sheets on number of eggs laid by silkworm (*Bombyx mori*). *Bioved*, 1:79-80.

Gupta, B. K.; Sinha, A. K. and Das, B. C. (1991) Studies on egg yielding capacity of different races of silkworm (*Bombyx mori* L). *Giobios*, 18:173-176.

Han, M. S. and Watanabe, H. (1987) Immunoperoxidase-staining method for discrimination of microsporidian spores in the pebrine infection of silkworm mother moths. *J. Seric. Sci. Japan*, 56:431-435.

Han, M. S. and Watanabe, H. (1988) Transovarian transmission of two microsporidia in the silkworm, *Bombyx mori* and disease occurrence in the progeny population. *J. Invertebr. Pathol.* 51: 41-45.

Han, M. S.; Nguyen, M. T. and Lim, J. S. (1997) Establishment of simplistic moth inspection system to prevent *Nosema bombycis* infection of the silkworm, *Bombyx mori. Korean J. Seric. Sci.*, 36:69-75.

Harada, C. (1961) On the heterosis of quantitative characters in silkworm. *Bull. Seric. Expt. Stn.*, 17:50-52.

Harvey, W.R. (1962) Metabolic aspects of insect diapause. *Ann. Rev. Ent.* 7:57-80.

Hartwig, A. and Mieczkowski, K. (1990) Diseases of silkworm – pebrine (*Nosema bombycis*) mycotic diseases. *Med. Weter* 46:21-23.

Hasegawa, K. (1957) The diapause hormone of the silkworm, *Bombyx mori. Nature*, 179:1300-1301.

Hashimoto, Y.; Watanabe, A. and Kawase, S. (1984) Preliminary studies of terminal structures of infectious flacherie virus RNA. *Microbiologica*, 7:91-96.

Hashimoto, Y.; Watanabe, A. and Kawase, S. (1986). Evidence for the presence of a genome-linked protein in infectious flacherie virus. *Arch. Virol.*, 90:301-312.

Haundov, Z.I. (1968) Effect of light factors on the oviposition and quality of silkworm eggs of *Bombyx mori. Dokl. Acad. Nauk. Azerb.* SSR, 24:70-75.

Hayasaka, S. and Ayuzawa, C. (1987) Diagnosis of microsporidians, *Nosema bombycis* and closely related species by antibody-sensitized latex. *J. Seric. Sci. Japan*, 56:169-170.

Hayman, B. L. and Mather, K. (1955) The description of genetic interactions in continuous variations. *Biometrics*, 11:69-82.

Hinton H. E. (1969) Respiratory system of insect eggshells. *Annu. Rev. Ent*, 14:343-368.

Hinton, H. E. (1981) *Biology of Insect Eggs*. Vol. I, Pergamon Press, Oxford, pp.413.

Hirobe, T. (1968) Evolution of differentiation and breeding of the silkworm—the Silk Road, past and present. *Genetics in Asian countries. XII Intl. Cong. Genet*, pp. 25-36.

Hirobe, T. (1985) On the recent advancement of silkworm breeding in Japan. A Report, pp. 150.

Hitoshi, I. and Ishihara, R. (1981) Inhibitory effect of several chemicals against the hatch of *Nosema bombycis* spores. *J. Seric. Sci. Japan*, 50:276-281.

Huang, G. R. (1983) Influence of relative humidity and air currents in the mounting room on the cocoon quality of *Bombyx mori* in China. *Canye Kexue*, 9:90-92.

Hurkadli, H. K. and Manjula, A. (1991) Artificial of bivoltine silkworm eggs, *Bombyx mori* at different hours of oviposition for tropical conditions. (Lepidoptera: Bombycidae). *Sericologia*, 31:345-347.

Hurkadli, H. K. and Manjula, A. (1992) Safe period of acid treatment for bivoltine silkworm (*Bombyx mori* L) hybrid eggs at different hours of oviposition for varying temperatures. *Indian J. Seric.*, 31:97-100.

Indrasith, L. S.; Sasaki, T. and Yamashita, O. (1988 a) A unique protease responsible for selective degradation of yolk protein in *Bombyx mori*-Purification, characterization and cleavage profiles. *J. Biol. Chem.*, 263:1045-1051.

Indrasith, L. S.; Izuhara, M.; Kobayashi, M. and Yamashita, O. (1988 b) In-vitro translation of the protease catalising *Bombyx mori* egg specific protein and identification of peptide with biological activity. *Arch. Biochem. Biophy*, 267:328:333.

Irie, K. and Yamashita, O. (1980) Changes in vitellin and other yolk proteins during embryonic development in the silkworm, *Bombyx mori*. *J. Insect Physiol.*, 26:811-817.

Ishihara, R. and Iwano, H. (1991) The lawn grass cutworm, *Spodoptera depravata* (Butter) as a natural reservoir of *Nosema bombycis* Nageli. *J. Seric. Sci. Japan*, 60:236-337.

Iwano, H. and Ishihara, R. (1981) Inhibitions effect of several chemicals against hatching of *Nosema bombycis* spores. *J. Seric. Sci. Japan*, 50:276-281.

Jadav, L. D. and Gajare, B. P. (1978) Studies on the effect of mating durations on the viability of silkworm (*Bombyx mori* L.) eggs. *Indian J. Seric.*, 17:28-32.

Jayaswal, K. P.; Singh, T. and Das, B. D. (1991) Sex association and orientation pattern of pupae in double cocoons of *Bombyx mori*. *Indian J. Seric.*, 30:145-147.

Jayaswal, K. P.; Singh, T. and Sen, S. K. (1990) Correlation between some economic parameters and their application in silkworm breeding. *Indian Silk*, 29:25-27.

Jayaswal, K. P.; Singh, T. and Subba Rao, G (1991) Effect of female pupal weight on fecundity of mulberry silkworm *Bombyx mori*. *Indian J. Seric.*, 30:141-143.

Jolly, M. S. (1986) *Pebrine and its Control*. CSB publication, Bangalore, India.

Jolly, M. S., Subba Rao, S. and Krishnaswamy, S. (1964) Studies on the mating capacity of male of mulberry silkworm and the possibility of utilizing polygamy in sericulture. *Indian J. Seric.*, 1:25-32.

Jolly, M. S., Subba Rao, S. and Krishnaswamy, S. (1964) Effect of plane of inclination on egg laying by *Bombyx mori* L. *Indian J. Expt. Biol.*, 2:165-166.

Jonaka, N. (1986) Some parameters of basic quantitative breeding characters in silkworm, *Bombyx mori*. II. Correlations between the basic breeding characters. *Genet. Sel.*, 19:144-150.

Joshi, K. C. (1984) A new record of natural enemies of tent caterpillar, *Malacosoma indica* Wlk. *Science & Culture*, 47:356.

Jura, C. (1972) Development of apterygote insects. In *Developmental Systems-Insects*, Counce, S. J. and Waddington, C. H. (eds.), Vol.1., PP 49-94, Academic Press, London.

Kagawa, T. (1980) The efficacy of formalin as disinfectant of *Nosema bombycis* spores. *J. Seric. Sci. Japan*, 49:218-222.

Kageyama, T. (1976) Pathways of carbohydrate metabolism in the eggs of the silkworm, *Bombyx mori*. *Insect Biochem.*, 6:507-511.

Kai, H. and Haga, Y. (1978) Further studies on 'esterase A' in *Bombyx mori* eggs in relation to diapause development. *J. Seric. Sci. Japan*, 47:125-133.

Kai, H and Hasegawa, K. (1973) An esterase in relation to yolk cell lysis at diapause termination in the silkworm, *Bombyx mori*. *J. Insect Physiol.*, 19:799-810.

Kai, H.; Kawai, T. and Kawai, Y. (1987) A time interval activation of 'esterase A' by cold relation to the termination of embryonic diapause in the silkworm, *Bombyx mori*. *Insect Biochem.*, 17: 367-372.

Kai, H and Nishi, K. (1976) Diapause development in *Bombyx mori* eggs in relation to 'esterase A' activity. *J. Insect Physiol.*, 22:1315-1320.

Kamble, C. K.; Acharya, P. K. and Singh, G. B. (1995) Maintenance and management of basic seed farms (P3 and P2). *J. Seric.*, 3:59-66.

Kanada T.; Matsumura H. and Ohtsuki Y. (1974) Surface structure of silkworm (*Bombyx mori*) egg. I. Fine structure of micropylar apparatus. *J. Seric. Sci. Japan*, 43:379-383.

Kang, P. O.; Ryu, K. S.; Hong, K. W. and Sohn, B. H. (1993) Studies on occasional artificial hatching of hibernated eggs, *Bombyx mori* L. (I). The early hatching of post-hibernation of hibernated eggs, PDA. *J. Agric. Sci.* (Korea), 35:725-729.

Kantaratanakul, S.; Tharvornanukkulkit, C.; Wongthong, S.; Chareonying, S.; Campiranon, A. and Saksoong, P. (1987) Diallel cross with polyvoltine strains of Thai silkworm (*Bombyx mori* L.). *Sericologia*, 27:279-286.

Kasiviswanathan, K. (1976) Sericulture industry in Japan. VI. Silkworm Breeding & Genetics. *Indian Silk*, 14:13-21.

Kasturibai, A. R.; Mahadevappa, D.; Nirmala, M. R., and Jyothi, H. K. (1986) Control of uzifly by semiochemicals. *Curr. Sci*, 55:1038.-1040

Kataoka, H.; Yuhara, Y.; Tanaka, S. and Sawai, M. (1973) The sex separation at pupal stage of silkworm by means of an electric capacity measurement. *J. Seric. Sci. Japan*, 42:454-462.

Kawaguchi, E. (1926) Polyspermy in *Bombyx mori* L. *Sangyo Simpo.*, 34:38-41.

Kawamura, N. (1978) The early embryonic mitosis in normal and cooled eggs of the silkworm, *Bombyx mori*. *J. Morphol.*, 158: 57-72.

Kawarabata, T. and Ishihara, R. (1984) Infection and development of *Nosema bombycis* in cell lines of *Antheraea eucalypti*. *J. Invertebr. Pathol.* 44:52-62.

Kawarabata, T. and Hayasaka, S. (1987) An enzyme-linked immunosorbent assay to detect alkali-soluble spore surface antigens of strains of *Nosema bombycis* (Microspora: Nosematidae). *J. Invetebr. Pathol.* 50:118-123.

Kim, S. E.; Lee, S. M. and Seong, S. I. (1992) Long-term preservation of *Bombyx mori* stocks by frozen gonad storage. *Korean J. Seric. Sci.*, 34:1-7.

Kim S. E.; Shikata M. and Akai H. (1981) Eggshell lipids in relation to water evaporation and diapause in the silkworm, *Bombyx mori*. *J. Sericult. Sci. Japan.*, 50:94-100.

Kitazawa T.; Kanada T. and Takami T. (1963) Changes in the mitotic activity in the silkworm eggs in relation to diapause. *Bull. Sericult. Exp. Stn.* 18:283-295.

Kitazawa, T.; Kiguchi, K.; Sugiyama, H. and Ohtsuki, Y. (1989) Selection of egg sensitivity to the hydrochloric acid treatment and its effect to diapause in the silkworm, *Bombyx mori*. *J. Sericult. Sci. Japan.*, 58:511-516.

Knight, R. (1951) A multiple regression analysis of hybrid vigor in single crosses of *Docyylis glomerata* L. *Theor. Appl. Genet.*, 41:306-311.

Knight, R. (1973) The relation between hybrid vigour and genotype and environment interaction. *Theor. Appl. Genet.*, 43:311-318.

Kobayashi, M. and Chaeychomsri, S. (1993) Thermal inhibition of viral diseases in the silkworm, *Bombyx mori* L. *Indian J. Seric.*, 32:1-7.

Koga N. and Osanai M. (1967) Der Gehalt and Tryptophane. Kynurenin, 3-Hydroxy-kynurenin and ommochromen ber den uberwinternden Eiern des Seidenspmners *Bombyx mori*. *Hoppe-Seyler's Z. Physiol. Chem.*, 348:979-982.

Kotoku, K. (1993) On the mounting for saving labour by the improved rotary cocooning frame in the silkworm, *Bombyx mori. Res. Rep. Ehimeken, Seric. Expt. Stn.*, 14:34-38.

Krishna Prasad, N. K.; Dilipkumar; Sannappa, B. and Rukmananda, A. (2000) Impact of seed cocoon transportation on grainage performance of *Bombyx mori* L. *Proc. Natl. Semi. Trop. Seric.*, Vol. II, pp. 54-60.

Krishnaswamy, S. (1986) *Appropriate Rearing Technology.* Published by CSB, India

Krishnaswamy, S. (1987) A new concept of a three-way cross in place of conventional Mysore × Bivoltine hybrids. *Indian Silk*, 27:21-26.

Krishnaswamy, S.; Jolly M. S. and Subba Rao, S. (1964) Diallel analysis of quantitative characters in multivoltine races of silkworm. *Indian J. Genetics*, 24B:213-222.

Krishnaswamy, S.; Narasimhanna, M. N.; Suryanarayan, S. R. and Kumararaj, S. (1973) *Sericulture Manual-2. Silkworm Rearing*, FAO, Agricultural Services Bulletin, 15/3, Rome, Italy.

Kubota, I.; Isobe, M.; Imai, K.; Goto, T.; Yamashita, O and Hasegawa, K. (1979) Characterization of the silkworm diapause hormone-B. *Agric. Biol. Chem.*, 43:1075-1078.

Kumar, P.; Jolly, M. S. and Sharma, S. D. (1987) Uzicide-a new product of universal applicability to contain uzifly. *Indian Silk*, 25:13-15.

Kumar, P.; Prasad, K. S.; Kishore, R.; Manjunath, D. and Datta, R. K. (1993) Efficacy of introduced indigenous parasitoid against uzifly, *Exorista sorbillans. Proc. Natl. Semi. Uzifly and its control.* KSSRDI, Bangalore, page 127-133.

Kumar, P.; Sathya Prasad, K.; Kishor, R.; Katiya, R. L.; Ahsan, M. M. and Datta, R. K. (1996) IPM approach to optimize silkworm cocoon production. *Global Silk Scenario*-2001; 351-258.

Kumar, V. and Benchamin, K. V. (1989) Evaluation of mulberry leaf quality under two systems of pruning for silkworm rearing. *Nutri. Eco. Insect & Environment*, 65-66.

Kumar, V.; Mathur, V. B.; Rajan, R. K. and Datta, R. K. (1993) Transportation boxes for silkworm eggs. *Indian Silk*, 32:30-31.

Kumaresan, P.; Vijaya Prakash, N. B. and Rajan, R. K. (1999) An economic evaluation of different methods of silkworm rearing. *Productivity*, 40:139-141.

Kunkel J. G. and Nordin J. H. (1985) Yolk Proteins. In *Comprehensive Insect Physiology, Biochemistry and Pharmacology*, Kerkut, G. A. and Gilbert, L. I. (eds.), Vol. I., pp. 83 -111, Pergamon Press, Oxford.

Kurata S.; Koga K. and Sakaguchi B. (1979) RNA content and RNA synthesis in diapause and non-diapause eggs of *Bombyx mori. Insect Biochem*, 9:107-110.

Kurata S.; Yaginuma T.; Kobayashi Y.; Koga K. and Sakaguchi B. (1980) DNA content and cell number during the embryogenesis of *Bombyx mori. J. Sericult. Sci, Japan*, 49:107-110.

Kurisu, K. (1986) Simplified calculation of the operating characteristics in the pebrine inspection of the grouping mother method. *J. Seric. Sci. Japan*, 55:351-352.

Kurisu, K.; Nakasone, S.; Dohi, M. and M. Hamazaki (1985) Studies on the pebrine inspection of the mother moth in the silkworm, *Bombyx mori* for commercial eggs. III. Practical application of sampling inspection table. *Bull. Fac. Text. Sci., Kyoto Univ.* 11: 19-30.

Kuroida, K. and Nihei, K. (1979) Studies on the cold storage of silkworm eggs treated with hydrochloric acid after chilling. *J. Seric. Sci. Japan*, 48:401-403.

Lande, R and Arnold, S. J. (1983) The measurement of selection on correlated characters. *Genet. Sel.*, 20:58-62.

Lee, H. N.; Lee, K. Y.; Kim, T. J.; Sin, S. B.; Cho, J. S. and Kwon, S. I. (1992) Insecticidal characterization of thirteen *Bacillus thuringiensis* strains from soil. *Korean J. Microbiol.*, 30:438-443.

Legay, J. M. (1989) Contribution to the typological analysis of the laying behaviour in *Bombyx mori* L. *Sericologia*, 29:163-166.

Lerner, I.M. (1958) *The Genetic basis of Selection.* John Wiley & Sons, Inc. New York.

Li, D. (1985) Studies on the serological diagnosis of the pebrine of silkworm, *Bombyx mori*, by slide agglutination test. *Sci. Seric.* 11:99 -102.

Linzen, B. (1974) The tryptophane-ommochrome pathway in insects. *Adv. Insect Physiol.*, 10:117-246.

Liu, S.X. (1984) A summary of the techniques for the control of *Nosema bombycis* in *Bombyx mori* with instant acid treatment at high temperature. *Guangdong Agric. Sci.*, 3:20-21.

Liu, S. X.; Zhu, D. Z.; Zheng. W. Y.; Huo. Y. C.; Wu, Y. N. and Liang J. Y. (1991). A summary of the techniques for the control of *Nosema bombycis* Negeli in *Bombyx mori* with instant acid treatment at high temperature. *Guangdong Agric. Sci.*, 3:20-21 (Chinese).

Liu, S. X. and Xhong, W. B. (1989) The research channels in the prevention and control of silkworm diseases. *Sericologia*, 29: 287-295.

Liu Q-X and He S-m (1991) Studies on the efficiency of selection for improving technological characters of cocoon filament of *Bombyx mori* L. *Canye Kaxue*, 17:75-79.

Loasesthakul, W. and Kuribayashi, S. (1975) Sex separation of silkworm pupa by means of brine assortment. *Bull. Thai Seric. Res. & Training Center*, 6:81-83.

Long, N. V. and Petkov, N. (1987) Breeding-Genetic studies in some silkworm (*Bombyx mori*) breeds. I. Variability and correlations of quantitative characters. *Genet. Sel.*, 20:58-62.

Malone, L. A. and McIvor, C. A. (1995) DNA probes for the microsporidia, *Nosema bombycis* and *Nosema costelytrae*. *J. Invertebr. Pathol.* 65:269-273.

Manjula, A. (1993) Oviposition behaviour in silkworm moths under tropical conditions. *Indian Text. J.*, 103:102-104.

Manjula, A. and Hurkadli, H. K. (1986) Cold acid treatment of bivoltine silkworm eggs, *Bombyx mori* for tropical country. *Sericologia*, 26:26-29.

Manjula, A. and Hurkadli, H. K. (1993) Effect of cold storage of multivoltine and multi × bivoltine silkworm eggs, *Bombyx mori* L. (Lepidoptera: Bombycidae) at low temperature on hatching performance. *Sericologia*, 33:615-620.

Manjula, A. and Hurkadli, H. K. (1995) Chilling of silkworm eggs. *Indian Text. J.* 106:70-74.

Manjula, A. and Hurkadli, H. K. (1996) Studies on the hibernation schedule for bivoltine pure and hybrid silkworm eggs, *Bombyx mori* (Lepidoptera: Bombycidae) aestivated from twenty days under tropical conditions. *Sericologia* 36:665-675.

Manjulakumari, D. and Geethabali (1991) Ovipositional response of *Bombyx mori* (L) to different textures of the substratum. *Entomon*, 16:11-15.

Mano, Y. (1994) *Comprehensive report on silkworm breeding.* Central Silk Board, Bangalore, India, pp. 180.

Margaritis, L. H. (1985) Structure and physiology of eggshell. In *Comprehensive Insect Physiology, Biochemistry and Pharmacology,* Kerkut, G. A. and Gilbert, L. I. (eds.), Vol. I. pp.153-230, Pergamon Press, Oxford.

Martin, P. A. W. and Travers, R. S. (1989) Worldwide abundance and distribution of *Bacillus thuringiensis* isolates. *Appl. Environ. Microbiol.* 55:2437-2442.

Mathew, G. and Mohammed Ali, M. I. (1987) Microbial pathogen causing mortality in the carpenter worm, *Cossus cadambae* Moore (Lepidoptera: Cossidae), a pest of teak (*Tectona grandis*) in Kerala, (India). *J. Trop. Forestry,* 3:349-351.

Mathur, B. N.; Singh, V. and Sharma, S. K. (1970) Occurrence of parasitic *Aspergillus fumigatus* Free on *Utethesis pulchella* L. (Arctiidae: Lepidoptera) in Rajasthan. *Indian J. Ent,* 32:393-394.

Mathur, S. K.; Kumar, K.; Rao, G. S.; Singh, B. D. and Lall, S. B. (1992) Hot water treatment to break diapause in silkworm eggs. *Indian Text. J.,* 103:46-48.

Mathur, S. K.; Roy, A. K. and Mukherjee, P. K. (1988) Studies on the effect of number of eggs per laying on the development of silkworm race—Nistari, *Bombyx mori* L. (Lepidoptera: Bombycidae). *Indian J. Seric.,* 27:168-170.

Mathur, S. K.; Roy, A. K.; Sen, S. K. and Subba Rao, G. (1995) Fecundity and *Bombyx mori* L. - Light effects on silkworms. *Indian Text. J.,* 106:74-76.

Mathur S. K.and Singh T. (1990a) Abnormal eclosion in silkworm, *Bombyx mori. Indian Text. J.,* 100:150-151.

Mathur, S. K. and Singh, T. (1990b) The uzifly resistant breed of silkworm can be evolved. *Indian Silk,* 28:49-50.

Mathur, S. K. and Singh, T. (1991) Effect of multiple use of male moths. *Indian Text. J.,* 101:166-167.

Mathur, V. B.; Singh, G. P. and Kamble, C. K. (1995) Effect of photoperiod on the rearing and diapause in the silkworm, *Bombyx mori* L. *J. Seric.,* 3:46-49.

Matsumoto, T.; Yafeng-Zhu and Kazuhiko, K. (1985) Mixed infections with flacherie virus and bacteria in *Bombyx mori. J. Seric. Sci. Japan,* 54:453-456.

Matsuzaki, M. (1968) Electron microscopic studies on the chorion formation of the silkworm, *Bombyx mori. J. Seric. Sci. Japan.,* 37:483-490.

Mattews, R. E. F. (1982) Classification and nomenclature of viruses. *Intervirology,* 17:1-5.

Mazur, G. D.; Regier, J. C. and Kafatos, F. C. (1982) Order and defects in the silk moth chorion, a biological analogue of a cholesteric liquid crystal. In *Insect Ultrastructure*, King, R. C. and Akai, H. (eds.), Vol. I., pp. 150-185, Plenum Press, New York.

Mehrunnessa, J. and Barman, A. C. (1996) Simplified method of hot water treatment for breaking diapause of bivoltine silkworm eggs. *Bull. Seric. Res.*, 7:91-93.

Mill, P.J. (1985) Structure and physiology of respiratory system. In *Comprehensive Insect Physiology, Biochemistry and Pharmacology*, Kerkut, G. A. and Gilbert, L. I. (eds.), Vol. III., pp. 518-593, Pergamon Press, Oxford.

Minagawa, I. and Otsuka, Y. (1975) Relationships of actual performance of double cross hybrids and predicted value based on the mean value of the single crosses concerned in the silkworm, *Bombyx mori* L. *Japan. J. Breed.* 25:251-257.

Miya, K. (1978) Electron microscopic studies on the early embryonic development of the silkworm, *Bombyx mori*. I. Architecture of the newly laid eggs and the changes by sperm entry. *J. Fac. Agric. Iwate Univ. Japan*, 14:11-35.

Miya, K. (1984) Early embryogenesis of *Bombyx mori*. In *Insect Ultrastructure*, King, R.C. and Akai, H. (eds.), Vol. II., pp. 49-72, Plenum Press, New York.

Miya, K.; Kurihara M. and Tanimura I. (1972) Changes in the fine structure of the serosa cell and the yolk cell during diapause and post-diapause development in the silkworm, *Bombyx mori* L. *J. Fac. Agric. Iwate Univ. Japan*, 8:11- 87.

Miyahara, T. (1978) Selection of long filament length basic variety. I. Effect of selection in the later generations. *Acta Sericologia*, 106:73-78.

Mizuno, T. (1920) On the cold storage of silkworm eggs. *Sanshi Shikenjo Hokoku*, 4:205-262.

Mizuta, Y.; Honouse, T. and Wada, T. (1969) Relationship between weight of pupae and number of eggs by moth of silkworm, *Bombyx mori*. *Bull. Sericult. Expt. Stn.* 23:515-532.

Mladenov, G. (1990) Effect of heterosis on interlineal, intra-breed and inter-breed crosses of the silkworm (*Bombyx mori* L). *Zhivotnov'D Nauki*, 27:99-104.

Morohoshi, T. (1979) *Developmental Physiology of the Silkworm*. Gakkai Shupan Center, Tokyo.

Mummigatti, S. G. and Raghunathan, A. N. (1988) Production of *Bacillus thuringiensis* var. kursatakiby three methods and its relative toxicity to *Bombyx mori*. *J. Invertebr. Pathol.* 55:115-118.

Mukherjee, P. (1998) Hybrid vigour in different crossing system in silkworm, *Bombyx mori*; in *Silkworm Breeding*. Sreerama Reddy, G. (ed.), pp.197-208, Oxford and IBH Publishing Co. Pvt. Ltd., New Delhi.

Nagaraju, J. (1990) Studies on some genetic aspects of quantitative characters in tropical silkworm, *Bombyx mori*. Ph.D. Thesis, University of Mysore, India.

Nagaraju, J.; Raje Urs and Datta, R. K. (1996) Crossbreeding and heterosis in the silkworm, *Bombyx mori*. *Sericologia*, 36:1-20.

Nagatomo, T. (1953) On the significance of Im-type in the silkworm. *Japanese J. Breed.*, 13:60.

Nair, R. R. and Premkumar, T. (1974) *Aspergillus flavus* Link, a parasite on the leaf eating caterpillar, *Lymantria obfuscata* Wlk. *Current Science*, 45:563.

Nakada, T. (1932) The resistance of silkworm embryo to abnormal high temperature and dryness on the external morphology of the embryo. *Bull. Fukuoka Sweicult. Exp. Stn.* 1:1 -26.

Nakagaki, M.; Tsuda, H.; Kajiura, Z. and Takei, R. (1993) Localization of DNV infection in the mid gut of the silkworm, *Bombyx mori*. *J. Seric. Sci. Japan*, 62:405-411.

Nakasone, S. (1979) Changes in lipid components during the embryonic development of the silkworm, *Bombyx mori*. *J. Seric. Sci. Japan.*, 48:526-532.

Narasimhanna, M. N. (1976) *Contribution to the genetics of silkworm*. Ph.D. Thesis, University of Mysore, India.

Narasimhanna, M. N. (1988) *Manual on silkworm egg production*. Central Silk Board, Bangalore, India, pp. 169.

Narasimhanna, M. N., Chandrasekharaiah, Geetadevi, R. G. and Prabha, G. (1976) Ecogenetic attributes of the newly evolved bivoltine hybrid 'Nandi' in *Bombyx mori* L. *Proc. Dunn-Dobzan sky Symp. Genet*, 379-386.

Narayanaswamy, T. K.; Surendra, H. S. and Govindan, R. (2000) Relationship between weight components and egg parameters in silkworm, *Bombyx mori*. *Proc. Natl. Semi. Trop. Seric.*, Vol. II., pp. 79-81.

Nataraju, B., Baig, M., Balavenkatasubbaiah, M., Venkatareddy, S., Singh, B. D. and Noamani, M. K. R. (1993) Comparative toxicity and infectivity titer of *Bacillus thuringiensis* to silkworm, *Bombyx mori* L. *Indian J. Seric.*, 32:103-105.

Nataraju, B., Balavenkatasubbaiah, M., Baig, M., Singh, B. D. and Sengupta, K. (1991) A report on the distribution of *Bacillus thuringiensis* in Sericultural areas of Karnataka. *Indian J. Seric.*, 30:56-58.

Nataraju, B., Datta, R. K. Baig, M., Balavenkatasubbaiah, M.; Samson, M. V. and Sivaprasad, V. (1998). Studies on the prevalence of nuclear polyhedrosis in sericultural areas of Karnataka. *Indian J. Seric.*, 37:154-158.

Nirmal Kumar, S.; Ramesh Babu, M.; Basawaraja, H.K.; Mai Reddy, N. and Datta, R.K. (1998) Double hybrids for improvement of silk production in silkworm, *Bombyx mori* L. in *Silkworm Breeding*, Sreeram Reddy, G. (ed.), Oxford and IBM Publishing Co. Pvt. Ltd., New Delhi, pp. 209-217.

Obara, Y. (1979) *Bombyx mori* mating dance: An essential in locating the females. *Appl. Entomol. Zool.*, 14:130-132.

Oblisami, G.; Ramamoorthi, K. and Rangaswamy, G. (1969) Studies on the pathology of some crop pests of South India. *Mysore J. Agric. Sci.*, 3:86-98.

Ohio, H.; Miyahara, J and Yamashita, A. (1970) Analysis of practically important characteristics in the silkworm in early breeding generations of hybrids. Variations among strains, correlation between parents and offspring as well as relation between each character. *Tech. Bull. Sericult. Expt. Stn. Japan*, MAFF, 93:39-49.

Ohtsuki, Y. (1979) Silkworm Eggs-In '*A General Textbook of Sericulture*' edited Sericultural Society of Japan, pp. 156-173, Nihon Sanshi Shinbun-sha, Tokyo, Japan.

Ohtsuki, Y.; Kanada T. and Matsumura H. (1977) Surface structure of silkworm (*Bombyx mori*) eggs. II. Characteristics of different areas of egg surface. *J. Seric. Sci. Japan*, 46:45-50.

Ohtsuki, Y. and Murakami, A. (1968) Nuclear division in the early embryonic development of the silkworm, *Bombyx mori* L. *Zool. Mag.*, 77:383- 387.

Ohtsuki, Y.; Mori S.; Kanada T. and Kitazawa, T. (1976) Morphological observation on the embryonic moult in the silkworm, *Bombyx mori. J. Seric. Sci. Japan.*, 45:225-231.

Okada, M. (1970 a) Electron microscopic studies on diapause embryos of the silkworm, *Bombyx mori* L. *Sci. Rep. Tokyo Kvoiku Daigdku* Sect B, 14:95-111.

Okada, M. (1970 b) Changes in affinity of lysosomes to acridine organge during diapause and development of embryos of the silkworm, *Bombyx mori* L *Zool. Mag.*, 79:204-210.

Okada, M. (1971) Role of chorion as a barrier to oxygen in the diapause of the silkworm, *Bombyx mori* L. *Experientia*, 27:658-660.

Omura, S. (1939) Oviposition mechanism of the silkworm moths. I. Stimulation to elicit the oviposition. *J. Seric. Sci. Japan*, 10: 47-49.

Ono, T. (1980) Role of the scales as a releaser of the copulation attempt in the silkworm moth (*Bombyx mori*). *Kontyu*, 48: 540-544.

Orozoco, F. (1976) Heterosis and genotype environment interaction. Theoretical and experimental aspects. *Bull. Tech. Dept. de Genetique Anim. Nat. de la Recher. Agronom*, 24:43-52.

Ozdzenska, B. and Kremky, J. (1987) Estimation of heritability and genotypic, phenotypic and environmental correlations in outbred populations of mulberry silkworm, *Bombyx mori* L. *Sericologia*, 27:633-638.

Pallavi, S. N. and Kamble, C. K. (1997) Disinfections and hygiene in sericulture—A review. *Sericologia*, 37:401-415.

Patil, C. S. (1989) New record of fungal pathogen *Aspergillus flavus* Link. On mulberry silkworm, *Bombyx mori* L. from India. *Current Science*, 58:683.

Patil, C. S. (1993) Review on pebrine-a microsporidian disease in the silkworm, *Bombyx mori* L. *Sericologia*, 33:201-210.

Patil, C. S. and Geethabai, M. (1985) *Guidelines for identification of pebrine spores in grainages*, KSSRDI publication, Bangalore, India.

Patil, C. S. and Geethabai, M. (1989) Studies on the susceptibility of silkworm races to pebrine spores. *J. Appl. Entomol.* 108: 421-423.

Patil, C. S.; Jyothi, N. B. and Dass, C. M. S. (2001) Silkworm faecal pellets examination as diagnostic method for detecting pebrine. *Indian Silk*, 39:11-12.

Paul, D. C. and Kishor Kumar, C. M. (1995) Influence of male age on mating capacity, fecundity and fertility of mated female silk moth, *Bombyx mori* L. under high temperature and high humidity conditions. *Entomon*, 20:253-255.

Perk, K. E. (1973) The fine structure of the diapause regulator cell in the suboesophageal ganglion in the silkworm, *Bombyx mori*. *J. Insect Physiol.*, 19:293-302.

Perk K. E. and Yoshitake N. (1970a) A radio autographic study of diapause in the silkworm, *Bombyx mori*. *J. Insect Physiol.*, 16:1655-1663.

Perk, K. E. and Yoshitake N. (197 b) Function of the embryo and yolk cells in diapause of the silkworm eggs (*Bombyx mori*). *J. Insect Physiol.*, 16:2223-2239.

Peters, T. M. and Barbosa, P. (1977) Influence of population density on size, fecundity and developmental rate of insect in culture. *Rev. Entomol.*, 22:431-450.

Petkov, N. (1981a) The possibility of forecasting the effectiveness of selecting lines of the silkworm, *Bombyx mori* based on weight and silk content of cocoons. *Selskotopanska Nauka*, 19:92-96.

Petkov, N. (1981b) Variability and correlations between some characteristic features of silkworm (*Bombyx mori* L). *Zhivotnov'd Nauki*, 18:83-86.

Petkov, N. (1981c) Phenotypic correlations and regressions between some silkworm (*Bombyx mori*) breeding characters. *Genet. Sel.*, 14:386-390.

Petkov, N. and Mladenov, G. (1979) Studies on the multiple use of silk moth (*Bombyx mori*) male individuals in the production of pedigree and commercial silkworm seed. *Anim. Sci.*, 16:107-115.

Petkov, N.; Yolov, A.; Mladenov, G. and Nacheva, I. (1979) Influence of mating length of silk moths of some inbred silkworm (*Bombyx mori*) line on silkworm seed quality and quantity. *Anim. Sci.*, 16:116-122.

Pillai, K. S. and Ayyar, G. R. (1969) Biology of *Parasa lepida crom*, a pest of coconut in Kerala. *Agric. Res. J. Kerala*, 6:101-104.

Punitham, M. T.; Haniffa, M. A. and Arunachalam, S. (1987) Effect of mating duration on fecundity and fertility of eggs in *Bombyx mori* (Lepidoptera: Bombycidae). *Entomon*, 12:5-8.

Purohit, K. M. and Pavan Kumar, T. (1996) Influence of various agronomical practices in India on the leaf quality of mulberry. *Sericologia*, 36:27-39.

Quadrefague, A. De. (1860) cit. in Pebrine diseases of silkworms, a technical report, Tatsuke, K. (1971) Overseas Technical Co-operation Agency, Tokyo, Japan.

Rahman, S. M.; Raza, M. A. S.; Salem, M. A. and Bari, A. (1991) Effect of larval population density on the fecundity and hatchability of silkworm, *Bombyx mori* (L). *Bull. Seric. Res.*, 2:7-12.

Rahaman, S. M. and Ahmad, S. U. (1989) Artificial hatching of hibernated eggs of the silkworm, *Bombyx mori* L. by warm water treatment. *Bangladesh J. Zool.*, 17:117-122.

Rajanna, G. S. and Reddy, G. S. (1990) Studies on the variability and interrelationship between some quantitative characters in different breeds of silkworm, *Bombyx mori* L. *Sericologia*, 30: 67-74.

Raju, S.; Dharmapandit, S. K. and Datta, R. K. (1993) A simple technique of sex separation in mulberry silkworm. *Indian Silk*, 31:16-18.

Ram, K. and Singh, D. (1992) Role of mating disruption in the production of viable silkworm (*Bombyx mori*) eggs. *J. Entomol. Res.*, 16:206-210.

Randel, J. M. (1953) Heterosis. *American Naturalist*, 87:129-138.

Rao, G. S.; Das, S. K. and B. Ghosh (1989) Heterosis effect on some new silkworm hybrids evolved by three-way cross. *Pros. Cyto. Genet.*, 6:373-378.

Rao, P. R. M.; Singh, R.; Nagraja, C. S. and Vijayaraghavan, K. (1997) Studies on foundation hybrids in silkworm, *Bombyx mori* L. *Uttar Pradesh J. Zool.*, 17:75-81.

Rapusas, H. R. and Gabriel, B. P. (1976) Suitable temperature, humidity and larval density in the rearing of *Bombyx mori*. *Phillipp. Agric.*, 60:130-138.

Ravindra Singh, Chaturvedi, H. K. and Datta, R. K. (1994) Fecundity of mulberry silkworm, *Bombyx mori* L. in relation to female cocoon weight and repeated mating. *Indian J. Seric.*, 33:70-71.

Ravindra Singh, Nagaraju, J. and Vijayaraghavan, K. (1990) Effect of hot water on the prevention of diapause in the silkworm, *Bombyx mori*. *Sericologia* 30:443-447.

Reddy, G. S. and Raju, P. J. (1998) Exploitation of heterosis in silkworm, *Bombyx mori*; in *Silkworm Breeding*. Sreerama Reddy, G. (ed.), pp.186-196, Oxford and IBH Publishing Co. Pvt. Ltd., New Delhi.

Regier, J. C. and Kafatos, F. C. (1985) Molecular aspects of chorion formation. in *Comprehensive Insect Physiology Biochemistry and Pharmacology*, Kerkut, G. A. and Gilbert, L. I. (eds.), Vol. I., pp. 113- 151, Pergamon Press, Oxford.

Regier, J. C.; Mazur G. D. and Kafatos, F. C. (1980) The silk moth chorion: Morphological and biochemical characterization of four surface regions. *Devel. Biol.*, 76:286-304.

Rockstein, M. (1974) The insect and external environment. in *The Physiology of Insecta* – Vol. II., Academic Press, New York.

Rongsen, L. and Zhunei, S. (1993) Host specificity of *Bacillus thuringiensis* (Delta) endotoxin proteolysed by proteases of larval gut juice. *Acta Entomologia Sinica*, 36:362-271.

Roychoudhury, N.; Paul, D. C. and Subba Rao, G. (1991) Growth, fecundity and hatchability of eggs of *Bombyx mori* in relation to rearing space. *Entomon*, 16:203-207.

Salt, R. W. (1961) Principles of insect cold hardiness. Ann. Rev. Ent., 6:55-74.

Samson, M. V. (2000) Cocoon production and silkworm protection. *National Conference on Strategies for Sericulture Research & Development*, 16-18 Nov., CSR&TI, Mysore, India. pp.38-48.

Samson, M. V.; Baig, M.; Sapru, M. L. and Narasimhanna, M. N. (1986) Efficacy of certain fungicides and disinfectants for the control of white muscardine disease in mulberry silkworms. *Indian J. Seric.*, 2:78-83.

Samson, M. V.; Santha, P. C.; Singh, R. N. and Sasidharan, T. O. (1999a) A new microsporidian infecting *Bombyx mori* L. *Indian Silk* 37:10-12.

Samson, M. V.; Santha, P. C.; Singh, R. N. and Sasidharan, T. O. (1999b) Microsporidian spore isolated from *Pieris* sp. *Indian Silk* 38:5-8

Sander, K.; Guteit, H. O. and Jackle, H. (1985) Insect embryogenesis: Morphology, Physiology, genetical and Molecular aspects. In *Comparative Insect Physiology, Biochemistry and Pharmacology*, Kerkut, G. A. and Gilbert, L. I.(eds.), Vol. I, pp. 321-385, Pergamon Press, Oxford.

Sang, J. H. (1956) Hybrid vigour and animal production. *Animal Breeding Abstracts* 24:1-6.

Sarkar, A.; Jalaja, S. K. and Datta, R. K. (1999) Potentiality of Victory-1 under irrigated conditions of South India. *Indian Silk*, 38:5-8.

Sarkar, Dilip De (1998) *The silkworm Biology, Genetics and Breeding.* Vikas Publishing House, Pvt. Ltd., New Delhi, pp. 338.

Sasidharan, T. O.; Singh, R. N.; Samson, M. V.; Manjula, A.; Santha, P. C. and Chandrashekharaiah (1994) Spore replication rate of *Nosema bombycis* (Microsporidia: Nosematidae) in the silkworm, *Bombyx mori* L. in relation to pupal development and age of moths. *Insect Sci. Applic.*, 15:427-431.

Satenahalli, S. B.; Govindan, R.; Goud, J. V. and Magdum, S. B. (1989) Genetic parameters and correlation coefficient analysis in silkworm, *Bombyx mori. Mysore J. Agric. Sci.*, 24:491-495.

Sato, R. and Watanabe, H. (1980) Purification of mature microsporidian spores by isodensity equilibrium centrifugation. *J. Seric. Sci. Japan*, 49:512-516.

Sato, R. and Watanabe, H. (1986) Pathways of oral infection with four microsporideae in the silkworm, *Bombyx mori* L. *J. Seric. Sci. Japan*, 55:10-26.

Sato, R.; Masahiko, K.; Watanabe, H. and Fujiwara, T. (1982) Serological discrimination of several kinds of microsporidian spores isolated from the silkworm, *Bombyx mori* L., by an indirect fluorescent antibody technique. *J. Invertebr. Pathol.* 40:260-265.

Saxena, K. D. and Rawatt, R. R. (1968) Bionomics of *Drosicha mangiferae* (Green) on citrus including new record of its three natural enemies. *Madras Agric. J.*, 55:309-313.

Seki, H. (1986) Effects of physiochemical treatments on a silkworm densonucleosis virus of the silkworm, *Bombyx mori. Appl. Ent. Zool,* 21:515-518. .

Sekharappa, B. M.; Gururaj, C. S. and Muniraju, E. (1991) Shoot feeding technology for late age silkworm rearing. *Indian Silk,* 30:37-42.

Sengupta, K.; Datta, R. K. and Biswas, S. N. (1973) Effect of multiple crossing on the type of progeny recovered in silkworm, *Bombyx mori* L. *Indian J. Seric.*, 12:31-38.

Sengupta, K.; Kumar, P.; Baig, M. and Govindaiah (1990) *Handbook of diseases and pests of silkworm and mulberry.* UNESCAP, Bangkok, Thailand.

Sengupta, K.; Yusuf, M. R. and Grover, S. P. (1974) Hybrid vigor and genetic analysis of quantitative traits in silkworm. *Indian J. Genetics,* SABRAO, 34:249-256.

Shaheen, A.; Trag, A. R.; Nabi, G. and Ahmad, F. (1992) Correlation between female pupal weight and fecundity in bivoltine silkworm, *Bombyx mori* L *Entomon,* 17:109-111.

Shamachary and Jolly M. S. (1985) Observations on the pattern of driage in three silkworm breeds of *Bombyx mori* (L). *Indian J. Seric.*, 24:83-84.

Shamachary; Samson, M. V. and Krishnaswami, S. (1980) Some useful correlation studies of silkworm and its products such as pupa, shell and egg weight. *Indian J. Seric.*, 19:4-8.

Shapiro, B. M.; Schackmann, R. W. and Gabel C. A (1981) Molecular approaches to the study of fertilization. *Annu. Rev. Biochem.* 50:815-843.

Sharma, A. K. (1992) Economic characters of mulberry silkworm (*Bombyx mori*) in relation to the rearing methods. *Biol. Mem.*, 18:19-22.

Shenyuan, P.; Liguo, G.; Lixia, L; Xiaohui, T.; Simei, H. and Ming, T. (1998) An approach to the method of automatic sex discrimination by single cocoon scaling. *Acta Sericologica Sinica,* 24:91-94.

Sheridan, A. K. (1980) A new explanation for egg production heterosis in crosses between white Leghorns and Australorps. *British Poultry Science,* 21:85-88.

Shi, L. and Jin, P. (1997) Study on the differential diagnosis of *Nosema bombycis* of the silkworm, *Bombyx mori* by monoclonal antibody-sensitized latex. *Sericologia* 37:1-6.

Shimizu, S. and Arakawa, A. (1986) Latex agglutination test for the detection of cytoplasmic polyhedrosis virus and the densonucleosis virus of the silkworm, *Bombyx mori. J. Seric. Sci. Japan,* 55:153-157.

Shimizu, S.; Ohba, M.; Kanda, K. and Aizawa, K. (1983) Latex agglutination test for the detection of the flacherie virus of the silkworm, *Bombyx mori*. *J. Invertebr. Pathol.* 42:151-155.

Shimizu, S.; Tauchi, S. and Arakawa, A. (1991) Protein A-coated latex linked antisera test for the detection of densonucleosis virus of the silkworm, *Bombyx mori*. *J. Invertebr. Pathol.*, 57: 124-125.

Shivakumar, G. R.; Himantharaj, M. T.; Rajan, R. K.; Magadum, S. B. and Datta, R. K. (1994) Effect of transportation of bivoltine seed cocoons on melting and egg production. *Indian Silk*, 33:23-24.

Singh, G. P. and Kumar, V. (1995) Correlation of larval and cocoon weight with fecundity in silkworm, *Bombyx mori* L. *Ann. Entomol.*, 13:15-17.

Singh, G. P.; Mathur, V. B.; Kamble, C. K. and Datta, R. K. (1994) Cold storage of bivoltine female silkworm moths. *Indian Silk*, 33:25-26.

Singh, G. P.; Mathur, V. B.; Vineet Kumar; Kamble, C. K. and Datta, R. K. (1994) Refrigeration of virgin female moths of silkworm, *Bombyx mori* L. (Lepidoptera: Bombycidae) and its impact on fecundity, viability and hatchability. *Uttar Pradesh J. Zool.*, 14:133-136.

Singh, G. P.; Vineet Kumar; Mathur, V. B. and Kamble, C. K. (1995) Synergestic action of acid treatment and surface sterilization. *Indian Silk*, 34:25-25.

Singh, K. and Shukla, G. S. (1992) Ready reckoner for hydrochloric acid treatment of silkworm eggs of weak diapause character. *Sericologia*, 32:51-56.

Singh, R. and Saratchandra, B. (1994) Importance of heritability in silkworm breeding. *Indian silk*, 33:21-23.

Singh, R. and Singh, J. (1984) New record of *Aspergillus candidus* Link, a potential entomogenous fungus in *Indarbela* spp. *Sci. & Cult.*, 48:282-283.

Singh, R. N., Singh, T. and Yadav, P. R. (1993) Suitability of sticky trap in control of uzifly, *Blepharipa zebina*. *Recent Adv Uzifly Res.* eds. G. P. Channa Basavana, G. Veeranna and S. B. Dandin. pp. 253 -256.

Singh, T. (2001a) Studies on the silk productivity in some three-way crosses of the silkworm, *Bombyx mori* L. *Bull. Ind. Acad. Seri.*, 5:75-77.

Singh, T. (2001b) Influence of rearing space on economic traits in the silkworm, *Bombyx mori* L. *Bull. Ind. Acad. Seri.*, 5:111-113.

Singh, T. (2001c) Studies on the evaluation of some three-way cross hybrids of silkworm, *Bombyx mori* L. *Intl. J. Indust. Entomol.* 3:153-155.

Singh, T. (1998a) Behavioural aspects of oviposition in silkworm *Bombyx mori*. *Indian J. Seric.*, 37:101-108.

Singh, T. (1998b) Gamut of sex separation in mulberry silkworm. *Asian Text. J.*, 7:69-71.

Singh, T. (1997) Gamut of selection in the silkworm *Bombyx mori*. *Asian Text. J.*, 6; 68-75.

Singh, T. (1997) Factors affecting cocoon. *Indian Textile Journal*, 108:52-55

Singh, T. (1994) Correlation between pupal weight and fecundity in *Bombyx mori* (L). *Annl. Ent.* 12:5-7.

Singh, T., Chandrashekharaiah and Samson, M. V. (1994) Selection strategies in relation to correlation and heritability in the silkworm, *Bombyx mori* (L). *Bull. Seric. Res.*, 5:37- 41.

Singh, T., Chandrashekharaiah and Samson, M. V. (1998) Correlation and heritability analysis in the silkworm *Bombyx mori*. *Sericologia*, 38:1-13.

Singh, T., Das, M. Senapati and Subba Rao, G. (1992) Heterosis effect on productive qualities in new hybrids of bivoltine silkworm *Bombyx mori* (L.). *Asian J. Zool. Sciences*, 1:11-14.

Singh, T. and Jayaswal, K. P. (1993) Evaluation of some multivoltine races of silkworm (*Bombyx mori*). *J. Adv. Zool.*, 14:100-102.

Singh, T., Jayaswal, K. P. and Subba Rao, G. (1992) Correlation studies between some breeding parameters of silkworm, *Bombyx mori* (L). *J. Zool. Res.*, 5:47-50.

Singh, T. and Mathur, S.K. (1989) The dancing of male silk moths to the perfume to female moth. *Indian Silk*, 28:17-18.

Singh, T. and Rao, G. S. (1994) Studies on evaluation of hybrids by breeding index in *Bombyx mori* (L). *Entomon*, 19:169-170.

Singh, T.; Rao, V.; Jingade, A. H. and Samson, M. V. (2002) Structure and development of silkworm (*Bombyx mori*) eggs. *Sericologia* 43:323-334.

Singh, T. and Samson, M. V. (1999) Embryonic diapause and metabolic changes during embryogenesis in mulberry silkworm, *Bombyx mori* L. *J. Seric.*, 7:1-11.

Singh, T. and Saratchandra, B. (2002) Biochemical changes during embryonic diapause in mulberry silkworm, *Bombyx mori* L. (Lepidoptera:Bombycidae). *Intl. J. Indust. Entomol.* (Korea), 5: 1-12.

Singh, T. and Saratchandra, B. (2003) Microsporidian disease of the silkworm, *Bombyx mori* L. (Lepidoptera:Bombycidae). *Intl. J. Indust. Entomol.* (Korea), 6:1-9.

Singh, T.; Saratchandra, B. and Geetha N. Murthy (2002) An analysis of heterosis in the silkworm, *Bombyx mori* L. *Intl. J. Indust. Entomol.* (Korea) 5:23-32.

Singh, T. and Singh, K. (1992) Physiological influence of retained leaves on developmental growth phases of mulberry (*Morus* sp). *Indian Silk*, 31:21 -22.

Singh, T. and Singh, K. (1993) Heritability and correlations between some economic characters in *Bombyx mori* (L). *Sci. & Cult.*, 59: 51-52.

Singh, T., Singh, K. and Das, Mamoni (1992) Astounding effect of correlated parameters in silk industry. *Indian Text. J.*, 102: 26-30.

Singh, T., Sinhadeo, S. N. and Das, M. (1990) Heterosis in silk productivity as a breeding index in *Bombyx mori* L. *Silkworm Inf. Bull.*, 3:1-3.

Singh, T. and Subba Rao, G. (1993) A multiple traits Evaluation Index to screen useful silkworm (*Bombyx mori*) hybrid genotypes. *Giornale Italiano Di Entomologia*, 6:379-384.

Singh, T. and Subba Rao, G. (1994a) Studies on the evaluation of hybrids by breeding index in *Bombyx mori* (L). *Entomon*, 19: 169-170.

Singh, T. and Subba Rao, G. (1994b) Evaluation of some multivoltine races of silkworm (*Bombyx mori*) under tropical region. *J. Appl. Zool. Res.* 5:19-25

Singh, T. and Subba Rao, G. (1994c) Heterosis in silk productivity in some hybrids of *Bombyx mori* (L). *Indian J. Seric.*, 33:82-83.

Singh, T. and Subba Rao, G. (1996) Heterosis effect on economic traits in new hybrids of the silkworm *Bombyx mori* (L). *Canye Kexue* (Science of Sericulture-China), 22:42-46.

Singh, T.; Subba Rao, G. and Senapati M. Das (1994) Studies on heterotic expression in silk productivity in some hybrids of *Bombyx mori*. *Bull. Seric. Res.*, 5:81-83.

Singh, T. and Tripathi, P. M. (1995) Studies on mating duration and its effect on fecundity and fertility in mulberry silkworm moth *Bombyx mori*. (Lepidoptera: Bombycidae). *Bioved*, 6:15-18

Singh, R. N.; Yadav, P. R. and Singh, T. (1992) Containing the pebrine problem in sericulture. *Indian Silk*, 30:43-44.

Sironmani, A. (1997) Detection of *Nosema bombycis* infection in the silkworm, *Bombyx mori* by Western blot analysis. *Sericologia*, 39:209-216.

Sithanantham, S. (1970) A preliminary study on the occurrence of *Aspergillus tamarii* Kita as a pathogen on the Sesabania stem borer, *Azygophleps scalahs* (Zeuzeridae: Lepidoptera). *Madras Agric. J.*, 57:437-438.

Somme, L. (1982) Super cooling and winter survival in terrestrial arthropods. *Comp. Biochem. Physiol.* 73(A):519-543.

Sonobe, H.; Maotaini, K. and Nakajima H. (1986) Studies on embryonic diapause in the PND mutant of the silkworm, *Bombyx mori*. Genetic control of embryogenesis. *J. Insect Physiol.*, 32:215-220.

Sonobe, H.; Matsumoto, A.; Fukuzaki, Y. and Fujiwara, S. (1979) Carbohydrate metabolism and restricted oxygen supply in the eggs of the silkworm, *Bombyx mori*: Genetic control of embryogenesis. *J. Insect Physiol.*, 32:215-220.

Srikanta, H. K. (1986) Studies on the cross infectivity and viability of *Nosema bombycis* (Microsporidia: Nosematidae). M. Sc. Thesis, UAS Bangalore, India, pp. 106.

Srinivasan, S. and Rao D. Y. S. (1987) New reports of parasites of groundnut leaf webber, *Aproerema* Deventer (Lepidoptera: Pyralidae). *Entomon*, 5:2198-221.

Subba Rao, G. and Sahai, V. (1990) Combining ability and heterosis studies in bivoltine strains of silkworm, *Bombyx mori* L. *Uttar Pradesh J. Zool.*, 9:150-164.

Subramanayam, K. and Murthy, N. C. V. (1987) Effect of rest on the efficiency of male moth in relation to fecundity and hatching behaviour of silkworm eggs. *Sericologia*, 27:677-680.

Suzuki, K.; Fujita, M. and Miya, K. (1983) Changes in super cooling of silkworm eggs. *J. Seric. Sci. Japan*, 52:185-190.

Suzuki, K.; Hosaka, M. and Miya, K. (1984) The amino acid pool of *Bombyx mori* eggs during diapause. *Insect Biochem.* 14:557-561.

Suzuki, K. and Miya, K. (1975) Studies on the carbohydrate metabolism in diapause eggs of the silkworm, *Bombyx mori* with special reference to phosphofructokinase activity. *J. Seric. Sci. Japan*, 44:88-97.

Suzuki, K.;. Tsuda, S. and Miya, K. (1978) Occurrence of non-diapause eggs by injection of odenosine-5'-monophosphate into *Bombyx mori* pupae. *Appl. Ent. Zool.* 13:48-50.

Takami, T. (1946) Experimental studies on the embryo formation in *Bombyx mori*. V. Presumptive mesodermal and neural regions of the eggs. *Seibutu*, 1:208-211.

Takami, T. (1969) *'A General Textbook of the Silkworm Eggs'*. Zenkoku Sanshu Kyokai, Tokyo, Japan.

Takami, T. (1972) In vitro: Development of insect embryos. In *Invertebrate Tissue Culture*, ed. Vago, C., Vol. II., pp. 137-159, Academic Press, New York.

Takami, T. and Kitazawa T. (1960) External observation of embryonic development in the silkworm. *Sanshi, Shikenjo, Hokoku, Sericult. Exp. Stn.Tech.Bull.*, 75:1-31.

Takami, T.; Totani K.; Sugiyama H.; Kitazawa T. and Kanada T. (1966) Embryonic growth of the silkworm, *Bombyx mori* (L) at the early post-diapause stage with special reference to the connection between the growth and nuclear division. *Bull. Sericult. Exp. Stn.*, 20:57-69.

Takeda, S. (1977 a) Stage dependency of diapause egg production by corpora cardiaca and corpora allata complex of the silkworm, *Bombyx mori* (Lepidoptera: Bombycidae). *Appl. Entomol. Zool.*, 12:80-82.

Takeda, S. (1977 b) Induction of egg diapause in *Bombyx mori* by some cephalo-thoracic organs of the *Periplanata americana*. *J. Insect Physiol.*, 23:813-816.

Takesue, S.; Keino, H. and Onitake, K. (1980) Blastoderm formation in the silkworm eggs (*Bombyx mori* L). *J. Embryol. Exp. Morphol.*, 60:117-124.

Tallis, G.M. (1962) A selection index for optimum *genotype. Biometrics*, 18:20.

Talukdar, F.A.; Hossain, M.; Shahjahan, M.; Rahman, A.K.M.M. and Khan, A.B. (1991) Effect of larval population densities of silkworm on larval and cocoon characteristics. *Bangaladesh J. Agric. Sci.*, 18:15-18.

Talukdar, J. N. (1980) Prevalence of transovarian infection of microsporidian parasite infecting muga silkworm, *Antheraea assamensis. J. Invertebr. Pathol.* 36:273-275.

Tanaka, Y. (1964) *'Sericology'* Published by Central Silk Board, India, pp. 67.

Tatsuke, K. (1971) Pebrine disease in silkworms. *A Technical Report*, Overseas Technical Cooperation Agency, Tokyo, Japan.

Tazima, Y. (1964) *'The Genetics of the Silkworm.'* Logos Press, London.

Tazima, Y. (1951) Separation of male and female silkworm in egg stage becomes possible. *Silk Digest*, Tokyo, 61.

Tazima, Y. (1978) *'Silkworm Egg'*, Published by Central Silk Board, Bangalore, India, pp. 1-49.

Thangavelu, K. (1997) Silkworm breeding in India-An overview. *Indian Silk*, 36:5-13.

Thiagrajan, V.; Bhargava, S. K.; Rameshbabu, M. and Nagaraj, B. (1993) Differences in seasonal performance of twenty-six strains of silkworm, *Bombyx mori* (Bombycidae). *J. Lep. Soc.* (California), 47:331-337.

Telfer W.H. and Smith D.S. (1970) Aspects of egg formation. *Symp. R. Ent. Soc. Lond.*, 5:117- 134.

Toyama, K. (1906) Breeding method of silkworms. *Sangyo-Shimpo*, 158:283-286.

Tsuchiya, S. and Kurashima, H. (1956) Study on the heritability of the measurable characters in *Bombyx mori*. I. Heritability in the weight of cocoon shell. *J. Seric. Sci. Japan*, 6:167-168.

Tsukamoto, M. (1963) The log dosage-probit mortality curves in genetic researches of insect resistance to insecticides. *Bol tyre-Kayaku*, 28:91-98.

Tyrell, D. J.; Bulla, Jr. L. A.; Andrews, Jr. R. E.; Kramer, K. J.; Davidson, L. I. and Nordin, P. (1981) Comparative biochemistry of entomocidal parasporal crystals of selected *Bacillus thuringiensis* strains. *J. Bacteriol.*, 145:1052-1062.

Udupa, S. M. and Gowda, B. L. V. (1988) Heterotic expression in silk productivity of different crosses of silkworm, *Bombyx mori. Sericologia*, 28:395-400.

Utsumi, S.; Akai, A. and Nomura, S. (1987) Anti-streptococcal activity of digestive juice in various strains of the silkworm larva, *Bombyx mori. J. Seric. Sci. Japan*, 56:109-115.

Utsumi, S. and Azumai, Y. (1988) Population density and development of antibiotic resistance of *Streptococcus faecalis*. J. Seric. Sci. Japan, 57:8-16.

Utsumi, S and Koidzumi, M. (1988) Analysis of the in-vitro activity of the anti Streptococcus protein contained in the digestive juice of silkworm larvae, *Bombyx mori. J. Seric. Sci. Japan*, 57:171-178.

Utsumi, S.; Okada, T. and Yano, H. (1990) ELISA of anti-Enterococcus (Streptococcus) protein (ASP) in digestive juice of silkworm larvae, *Bombyx mori. J. Seric Sci. Japan*, 59:87-91.

Veeranna, G. and Nirmala, M. R. (1997) Multiple parasitoid release to minimize the uzifly population/infestation in the field. *Annual Report* (1996-97), KSSRDI, Bangalore, P. 104.

Veluswamy, R.; Janaki, I. P.; Palaniswamy, A. and Jaganathan, T. (1973) Pathogenecity of *Aspergillus flavus* on rice skipper *Pepopidas mathias* (Lepidoptera: Hesperiidae). *Madras Agric. J.*, 60:575.

Vemananda Reddy, G.; Biram Saheb, N. M. and Ramanjaneyulu, Y. V. (1992) Re-use of non-oviposited moths in commercial seed production centres for increased egg production. *Indian silk*, 31:40-42.

Venkatareddy, S.; Singh, B. D.; Baig, M.; Sengupta, K.; Giridhar, R. and Singhal, B. K. (1990) Efficacy of asiphor as a disinfectant against incidence of diseases of silkworm, *Bombyx mori. Indian J. Seric.*, 29:147-148.

Verma, M. and Chauhan, T. P. S. (1996) Effect of long-term preservation of eggs on hatching and rearing performance of some polyvoltine silkworm races, *Bombyx mori* L. in Northern India. *Sericologia*, 36:249-253.

Vogel S. and Bretz W. L. (1972) Interfacial organisms: passive ventilation in the velocity gradients near surfaces. *Science*, 175:210-211.

Vossbrink, C. B.; Maddox, J. V.; Friedman, S.; Debrunner-Vossbrink, B. A. and Woese, C. R. (1987) Ribosomal RNA sequence suggests Microsporidians are extremely ancient eukariotes. *Nature*, 326:411-414.

Wang-San-Ming (1988) *Silkworm egg production*. FAO, Agricultural Services Bulletin, Rome.

Wang, Y. X.; Ma, J. Y.; Pan, H. H.; Zou, F. Z. and Mou, Z. H. (1988) Epidermiological study of a densonucleosis virus in *Bombyx mori*. *Canye Kexue*, 14:25-29.

Watanable, K. (1924) Studies on the voltinism in the silkworm. *Bull. Seric. Expt. Stn.*, 6:441-455.

Watanabe, H. (1960) Temperature effects on the heterosis of starvation resistance in the silkworm, *Bombyx mori*. *J. Seric. Sci. Japan*, 29:59-62.

Watanabe, H. (1961) Studies on the differences in the variability of larval body and cocoon weights between single cross and three-way cross or double cross hybrids in the silkworm, *Bombyx mori*. *J. Seric. Sci. Japan*, 30:463-467.

Watanabe, H. (1981) Characteristics of Densonucleosis in the silkworm, *Bombyx mori*. *J.A.R.Q.*, 15:133-136.

Watanabe, H.; Kawase, S.; Shimizu, T. and Seki, H. (1986) Differences in sercological characteristics of densonucleosis viruses in the silkworm, *Bombyx mori* *J. Seric. Sci. Japan*. 55:75.

Wechsung, E. and Houvenaghel, A. (1976) A possible role of prostaglandins in the regulation of ovum transport and oviposition in the domestic hen. *Prostaglandins*, 12:559-608.

Wilde-De J. and Loof-De A. (1973) Reproduction -In '*The Physiology of Insects*', ed. Rockstein, M., pp. 11-95, Academic press, New York.

Wright, S. (1921) Systems of mating. V. General considerations. *Genetics*, 6:167-168.

Yadav, P. R.; Singh, T. and Singh, R. N. (1993) Silk and silk producing arthropods. *Indian Rev. Life Sciences*, 13:149-156.

Yaginuma, T. and Yamashita O. (1977) Changes in glycogen, sorbitol and glycerol content during diapause of the silkworm eggs. *J. Seric. Sci. Japan.*, 46:5-10.

Yaginuma, T. and Yamashita, O. (1979) NAD-dependent sorbitol dehydrogenase activity in relation to the termination of diapause in eggs of *Bombyx mori*. *Insect Biochem.*, 9:547-553.

Yaginuma, T. and Yamashita, O. (1978) Polyol metabolism related to diapause in *Bombyx mori* eggs, different behaviour of sorbitol from glycerol during diapause and post diapause. *J. Insect Physiol.*, 24:347-354.

Yaginuma, T.; Kobayashi, M. and Yamashita, O. (1990 a) Distinct effects of different low temperatures on the induction of NAD-sorbitol dehydrogenase activity in diapause eggs of the silkworm, *Bombyx mori*. *J. Comp. Physiol.*, 8:160-277.

Yaginuma T.; Kobayashi, M. and Yamashita, O. (1990 b) Effects of low temperatures on NAD-sorbitol dehydrogenase activity and morphogenesis in non-diapause eggs of the silkworm, *Bombyx mori*. *Comp. Biochem. Physiol.*, 97 B:495-506.

Yamashita, O. (1984) Control of embryogenesis and diapause in the silkworm, *Bombyx mori*: Roles of diapause hormones and egg specific proteins. *Adv. Invert. Rep.*, 3:251-258.

Yamashita, O. and Hasegawa, K. (1985) Embryonic Diapause—In *Comprehensive Insect Physiology, Biochemistry and Pharmacology*, Kerkut, G. A. and Gilbert, L. I. (eds.), Vol. I., pp. 407-434, Pergamon Press, Oxford.

Yamashita, O. and Irie, K. (1980) Larval hatching from vitellogenin-deficient eggs developed in male hosts of the silkworm. *Nature*, 283:385-386.

Yamashita, O.; Suzuki, K. and Hasegawa, K. (1975) Glycogen phosphoryiase activity in relation to diapause initiation in *Bombyx mori* eggs. *Insect Biochem.*, 5:707-718.

Yamashita, O. and Yaginuma, T. (1991) Silkworm eggs at low temperatures: Implications for sericulture. In '*Insects at Low Temperature*', Lee, R. E. and Denlinger, D. L. (eds.), pp. 424-445, Chapman and Hall, New York.

Yamashita, O.; Yaginuma, T. and Hasegawa, K. (1981) Hormonal and metabolic control of egg diapause of the silkworm, *Bombyx mori* (Lepidoptera: Bombycidae). *Ent. Gen.*, 7:195-211.

Yamayoka, K.; Hashino, M. and Hirao, T. (1971) Role of sensory hairs on the anal papillae in oviposition behaviour of *Bombyx mori*. *J. Insect Physiol.*, 17:871-879.

Yamayoka, K. and Hirao, T. (1973) Releasing signals of oviposition behaviour in *Bombyx mori*. *J. Insect Physiol.*, 19:2215-2223.

Yamayoka, K. and Hirao, T. (1981) Mechanisms of ovipositional behaviour in *Bombyx mori*: time gating and accumulation of the internal factor. *Intl. J. Invertebr. Reprod.*, 4:169-180.

Yan, L. L. (1983) the estimates of heritability of pupal weight, cocoon weight and number of eggs laid in the silkworm (*Bombyx mori*) and its genetic correlation between these characters and path coefficient analysis. *J. Seric. Sci.* China, 9:149-155.

Yokoyama, T. (1957) On the application of heterosis in Japanese sericulture. *Proc. Intl. Genet. Symp. Suppl.* Vol. *Cytologia*, 527-531.

Yokoyama, T. (1963) 'Sericulture'-*Annu. Rev. Entomol.*, 8:287-306.

Yokoyama, T. (1973) The history of sericulture science in relation to industry. In: *History of Entomology*, Ed., Smith, R. E., Miller, I. E. and Smith, C. N., pp. 267-284.

Yokoyama, T. (1979) Silkworm selection and hybridization, working papers, The Rockefeller Foundation. Genetics in relation to insect management, pp. 71-83.

Yokoyama, T. and Sugai, E. (1987) Effect of hot water treatment on early development of eggs of the silkworm. *J. Seric. Sci. Japan*, 56:441-442.

Yokoyama, T.; Sugai, E. and Oshiki, T. (1987) Effect of acid treatment on early development of eggs of the silkworm. *J. Seric. Sci. Japan*, 56:369-373.

Yoshitake, N. (1954) Biochemical studies on the voltinism in Lepidoptera. III. On the change of the voltinism due to the injection of a few inorganic salts and other chemical substances. *J. Seric. Sci. Japan*, 23:349-356.

Yu, S. J.; Chen, J. S. and Hsieh, F. K. (1993) Studies on preservation of eggs of the multivoltine silkworm, *Bombyx mori* L. *Zhongva Kunchong.*, 13:141-149.

Yu, S. J.; Hsieh, F. K.; Hou, F. R. and Chu, H. T. (1991) Effect of acid treatment on the hatchability of *Bombyx mori* eggs at different embryonic stages. *Chinese J. Entomol.*, 11:13-18.

Zhu, J.; Indrasith, L. S. and Yamashita, O. (1986) Characterization of vitellin, egg-specific protein and 30-kDa proteins from *Bombyx mori* eggs and fates during oogenesis and embryogenesis. *Biochem. Biophy. Acta*, 882:427-436.

Ziegler, R.; Ashida, M.; Fallen, A. M.; Wimer, L. T.; Wyatt, S. S. and Wyatt, G. R. (1979) Regulation of glycogen phosphorylase in fat body of Cecropia silk moth pupae. *J. Comp. Physiol.*, 149:321-332.

INDEX

Q

R